REASON AND REVELATION IN HEGEL

Reason and Revelation in Hegel

Metaphysical Dimensions of the Absolute

JEFFREY REID

UNIVERSITY OF TORONTO PRESS
Toronto Buffalo London

Toronto Buffalo London
utorontopress.com
Printed in Canada

ISBN 978-1-4875-6364-6 (cloth)
ISBN 978-1-4875-6366-0 (EPUB)
ISBN 978-1-4875-6365-3 (PDF)

Library and Archives Canada Cataloguing in Publication

Title: Reason and revelation in Hegel : metaphysical dimensions of the absolute / Jeffrey Reid.
Names: Reid, Jeffrey, author
Description: Includes bibliographical references and index.
Identifiers: Canadiana (print) 20250157993 | Canadiana (ebook) 20250158035 | ISBN 9781487563646 (cloth) ISBN 9781487563653 (PDF) | ISBN 9781487563660 (EPUB)
Subjects: LCSH: Hegel, Georg Wilhelm Friedrich, 1770-1831—Criticism and interpretation. | LCSH: Reason. | LCSH: Revelation. | LCSH: Absolute, The.
Classification: LCC B2948 .R458 2025 | DDC 193—dc23

Cover design: Kristjan Buckingham
Cover image: IgorZh/Shutterstock.com

We wish to acknowledge the land on which the University of Toronto Press operates. This land is the traditional territory of the Wendat, the Anishnaabeg, the Haudenosaunee, the Métis, and the Mississaugas of the Credit First Nation.

This book has been published with the help of a grant from the Federation for the Humanities and Social Sciences, through the Awards to Scholarly Publications Program, using funds provided by the Social Sciences and Humanities Research Council of Canada.

University of Toronto Press acknowledges the financial support of the Government of Canada, the Canada Council for the Arts, and the Ontario Arts Council, an agency of the Government of Ontario, for its publishing activities.

Canada Council for the Arts | Conseil des Arts du Canada

Funded by the Government of Canada | Financé par le gouvernement du Canada

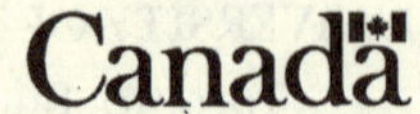

To my loved ones.

Contents

Acknowledgments

I wish to thank the anonymous readers who have taken the time to read and help me with their critical comments. Elements of my research for the present monograph have been applied, in different contexts: *Symposium,* 21, 1 (2017); *Journal of Speculative Philosophy* 31, 4 (2017); *The Owl of Minerva* 45, 1–2 (2013/14); in *Hegel Bulletin* 40, 2 (Aug. 2019); in *Karl Leonhard Reinhold and the Enlightenment,* ed. DiGiovanni (New York: Springer, 2010); *Clio* 48, 1 (2020); in *Hegel: Key Concepts,* ed. Michael Baur (London: Routledge, 2015); *The Owl of Minerva* 53, 1–2 (2022); *Journal of Philosophical Research* 19 (2024).

REASON AND REVELATION IN HEGEL

Introduction

My Hegel is French. When I began learning about him and reading him, at the Université de Paris IV-Sorbonne, where I carried out the entirety of my university studies, most of my philosophy professors found ways of referring to Hegel, even when teaching Plato, Aristotle, or Spinoza. The German Idealist that they professed, I later discovered, had been thoroughly informed by the twin pillars of Hegelian wisdom: Jean Hyppolite and Alexandre Kojève, along with a dash or *soupçon* of Jean Wahl. Since Paris IV was hardly a hotbed of Marxist thought and activism, Hyppolite's reading was predominant. Thus, far from coming to Hegel from an analytic or a neo-Kantian background, I discovered the thinker through a tradition that fully recognized his project in terms of its metaphysical and existential heritage. The idea of "heritage" is necessarily historical, and the way that I was initiated to Hegel and to philosophy in general was through philosophical history, which, I learned, was tantamount to philosophy itself. The French, historical orientation of my studies also informed in me the conviction that philosophy was fundamentally metaphysical, that is, unabashedly concerned with the soul, the world (aka freedom) and God as its privileged objects.

In order to understand Hegel, it was therefore necessary to know something about Descartes, Leibniz, Spinoza, Kant, Jacobi, Mendelssohn, and Fichte. Some knowledge of Heraclitus, Plato, Aristotle, Proclus, Aquinas and, yes, Schelling would certainly do no harm, nor would a passing acquaintance with the fundamental doctrines of Lutheran Christianity. Thus, the metaphysical dimensions of Hegel's thought appeared to me as essential to it, even having philosophical repercussions on the twentieth century atheistic, existentialist, critical theory appropriations of Hegel's thought, for example, through a tacit recognition of Cartesian selfhood or the dialectical nature of thought itself. Indeed, even the rebellious Young Hegelians (e.g., Feuerbach, Marx), who earnestly disavow their master's metaphysical heritage, are often obliged to fall back on notions of reality (for example, "humanity," "materiality," "existence," and "negation") that are fully conceptual, ideal and, thus, in a broad Hegelian sense, metaphysical. Briefly, an apprenticeship in Hegel at l'Université de Paris-IV, at the time when I was there, meant comprehending him in the tradition of Western metaphysical thought, in which I was happy to be initiated by excellent professors in the history of philosophy.

While I could not, and still cannot, claim more than a working knowledge of many of the thinkers mentioned above, I came away from my Parisian studies with the feeling that, when cut off from its metaphysical roots, Hegel's philosophy is senseless, joyless, and vitiated. It is perhaps no accident that my own doctoral supervisor, the incomparable and fondly remembered Jean-François Marquet, initiated his own doctoral research (on Schelling) under the supervision of Jean Hyppolite (before completing it, after Hyppolite's death, under Paul Ricoeur). After decades of reading Hegel and his many commentators, I cannot help returning to the *Genèse et structure de la Phénoménologie de l'esprit de Hegel* with a feeling of coming home.

The present book allows me to fully avow and indulge my metaphysical penchant in Hegel. This has not always been easy. Returning to North America, and learning to write scholarly articles in English, for English-language journals, it became apparent to me that my approach was often viewed by peers discovering Hegel from the analytic, Anglo-Saxon tradition, as too ... metaphysical! The success that I have nonetheless enjoyed, over the years, publishing in the English-speaking world, has sometimes been at the expense of restraining, attenuating, and even dissimulating my penchant for and grounding in French historico-metaphysical interpretations. Certainly, my abiding interest in the linguistic elements in Hegel's thought has allowed me to fly under the neo-Kantian radar, even while my onto-grammatical approach to his logos does acknowledge and explore metaphysical aspects of his absolute idealism. Some of the chapters in this book are reconfigured versions of earlier published articles, but where I now permit myself to give full voice to the metaphysical dimensions that I have always been interested in discovering in Hegel, all of which acknowledge the idea (the Idea) of the Absolute and its agency.

When students ask me about the nature of Hegel's idealism, I present its fundamental archē as "the agency of thought," the fact that thinking cannot be reduced to material neurological activity, data processing, calculating, analyzing and so on, but that thought posits itself or "comes out of our heads," as I put it, and into the world, where thought has performative purchase. Thinking is, for Hegel, the idealist equivalent of what work represents for the materialist Marx.

In presenting Hegel in these terms, where thought is accorded performative, ontological agency, I am acknowledging the fundamentally metaphysical nature of his philosophy. Indeed, if we take the three abovementioned objects of metaphysical thought to be God, the self, and the world, then we immediately see how the agency of thought means that Hegel's idealism is fundamentally metaphysical: The self, to be a self, must posit itself into natural otherness, liberating nature from its heteronomous externality, instilling freedom into the world, according to the human narrative that Hegel calls "*Geist*." The holistic, organic closure of this otherwise never-ending approximation of the True, the Good, and the Beautiful is only afforded by the notion of the Idea, an absolute instance that may be represented as the Platonic idea of the Good or, more recently, as God. However, according to the absolute idealism that Hegel espouses, the Idea (the Good, God) is more than the ultimate object of human striving. For following the recognizably Neoplatonic articulation of Hegel's systematic thought, it is the Idea that "unbuckles itself" or "lets itself go" (*sich entlasst*), in an ongoing act of absolute agency. In other words, both human and Ideal agencies are essentially thought that posits itself. The crucial difference is that the Idea not only posits itself *into* natural otherness but posits itself *as* natural otherness itself. As such, the Idea occurs as the revealed Other against which human reason endlessly strives, in its infinite progress of self-knowing self-liberation. One sees how the idea of thought's ontological agency, as a fact that is also an act, as Fichte expressed it (*eine Täthandlung*), leads seamlessly into the metaphysical realm!

In the last, dense paragraph, I presented the underlying theme of this book: Hegel's metaphysics of reason and revelation. This is the subject of the first chapter, "Reason, Revelation, and the Limits of Worldly Actuality." There, I present the idea that all of Hegel's major works (the *Phenomenology, the Science of Logic and the Encyclopaedia of Philosophical Sciences*) can be read as presenting the twin agencies of human reason and absolute revelation. Left on its own, reason can do no better than an infinite approximation of what it is after, the True, the Good, the Beautiful, an objective content that is only afforded through absolute agency, in the (human) forms of art, religion, and philosophy. In narrative terms, we can say that the absolute dimension ensures the systematic closure which Hegelian philosophy claims to embody. This is how we should understand Hegel's lapidary pronouncement in the introduction to the *Phenomenology*: "the Absolute alone is true and the truth alone is absolute." However, this claim is itself only *true* if we comprehend systematic

Science as involving the reciprocal complicity between absolute and human agencies.

The endless strivings of human reason ensure the organic and living openness of the Hegelian system, providing the reflective content without which the Absolute would be an empty intuition. The ongoing development of such human-informed content takes place in the realm of what Hegel refers to as actuality (*Wirklichkeit*). Consequently, it is wrong to expect too much of worldly actuality (cf. Emil Fackenheim) when left on its own. Actuality is simply incapable of attaining what it seeks: truth that is only attained in and through those activities where human and absolute agencies know themselves in each other as interactive: in the forms of Absolute Spirit (art, religion and philosophy). Hegelian Science is this wisdom, carried out in the syllogistic form of the *Encyclopaedia of Philosophical Sciences.*

The idea of human, reasoning agency only becomes obviously metaphysical when it takes on the world-historical features of Spirit (*Geist*) and thereby presupposes the massive ontological reality of Spirit's object: Truth, the unification of subject and substance, mind and matter, thought and nature. The realization of such a conception of Truth would not be possible without assigning agency to what Hegel refers to as "*das Absolute.*" The second chapter, "Absolute Selfhood and the Otherness of Nature," presents the idea of absolute agency through an investigation of the *Science of Logic (Greater Logic).* Indeed, the overall mission of the *Logic* is thoroughly metaphysical, in traditional Aristotelian terms: the determination of Being as Being.

In the Objective Logic section of Hegel's work, Being is determined by human thought to its highest degree of reality, which is presented as *Wirklichkeit* (actuality). Given the limits of this category, which I deal with in chapter 1, the second and final part of the *Logic,* the Subjective Logic, may be read as presenting the other half of the story: the subjective agency of determined Being, through its different, increasingly vital forms. The final expression of Being's vitality is its "unbuckling," its "*sich frei entlassen*" as nature, which of course is the "subject" (in both senses of the term) of the next book in Hegel's systematic project, the *Philosophy of Nature.* The "unbuckling" of absolute Being into nature takes the form of a "*sich entschliessen,*" a decision, which can more adequately be translated as a "de-syllogizing" (*Schluss* = syllogism).

In order for such a reading to be possible, we must acknowledge the syllogistic structure of the *Logic* itself, and this means grasping the passage from "Judgment" (*Urteil*) to "Syllogism," in the "Subjective Logic" section, as a move wherein the judgment's copula (the verb "to be") is ontologically realized or fulfilled (*erfüllt*) in the syllogism's middle moment of particularity (between Universality and Singularity). The unbuckling of fully determined Being, qua nature, is the release of the syllogism's fulfilled moment of particularity, its content. I apologize to the reader for the apparently cavalier opacity of these assertions, and hope that their elliptical nature is read as an invitation to visit the demonstrations that I attempt within the book itself!

If nature is taken as the fruit of absolute agency, why would it not constitute a sufficient form of revelation? Why is Hegel's philosophy not simply one that involves the immediate contemplation of nature in all its forms, as themselves immediately revelatory of their "divine" source? Why is Hegel not, for example, Schelling? The answer is that nature, in Hegel, remains fundamentally informed with radical alterity, informed by the fact that it presents itself, first and foremost as the *otherness* of the Idea. Nature, in its immediate incarnation is thus scandalously heteronomous. The freedom inchoate within it, the fact that it is the result of a "*frei entlassen*," must be brought out, discovered, determined through the human thoughtful activity of reason that Hegel refers to as "Spirit." Spirit overcomes the otherness of nature, negates it and brings forth its pre-determined meaning and inherent freedom, which is only witnessed by "us" through nature's evanescence, through the life and death of its forms, through its vanishing.

The fact that nature does not remain simply Other, recalcitrant to the activity of reason but is instead invitingly "for us" (*für uns*) is the subject of the third chapter, "Comets, Moons, and the Voices of Nature." There, I present Hegel's portrayal of the solar system, in the *Philosophy of Nature*, as the adequate model for dialectical movement throughout that work. However, investigating what might be referred to as "cometary negativity" within the Hegelian solar system, introduces us, readers of Hegel, to an often ignored fourth moment of his dialectic, one through which we discover how static forms of particularity subvert themselves in a vanishing that is *mediately* meaningful. Following Hegel's reasoning, the unruly, subversive behaviour of comets reveals the vital, functioning movement of the solar system, in the same way that, for example, the study of mental pathologies reveals the essential life of the healthy mind or how crime and punishment reveal the actual, performative truth of a state's system of right. Briefly, if the Absolute reveals itself in nature, it is because natural phenomena are finite and transitory; their meaning is revealed upon their dispersal.

In the first three above-summarized chapters, I present Hegel's Absolute in its revelatory agency, with the closing chapter on cometary negativity and the "for-us" providing the transition to the second theme of the book: human reason, and its never-ending, infinite striving for absolute Truth, which, as we have seen in the first section, is only comprehensible in terms of an agency that constantly overreaches and yet underlies human actuality qua Spirit. The fourth chapter, "History and the Absolute Now" distinguishes the agency of human reason from that of absolute revelation through a discussion of temporality: the historical pursuit of human knowing over against the eternal punctuality of revelation. The question is, ultimately, "Why does the Absolute not simply pour itself out in one instant?" Why is there a historical dimension to time when the whole idea of the Absolute and its truth implies an eternal instant where the necessary fullness of such Truth is, and always has been, fully accomplished (*vollkommene*)? In chapter 4, I address this temporal distinction, between the human-historical and the Absolute-eternal through an examination of Karl Löwith's presentation of Hegel as a philosopher who embodies the essential contradiction undermining Western culture. Falling under the sway of Aristotle's view of time as an eternal "Now," Hegel's thought appears incapable of meeting the historical challenges of either the present or the future, as witnessed in the Young Hegelians' critical responses to him. The chapter shows that the contradiction between the two notions of temporality necessarily arises when the essential significance of the Hegelian *Perfekt* tense is not acknowledged, a tense where the eternal "Now" is conceived as *having been*, and thus informed by its own historical temporality. Briefly, the absolute Idea, as the reconciling complicity of the reciprocal agencies of reason and revelation, must take place in the temporality of the present perfect tense. Further, the theatre where such systematic (Scientific) knowledge is played out and performed is the state university, as Hegel conceives it.

Chapter 5, "Knowledge of God and the Perils of Insight," continues a discussion of the second theme of the book: how reason is involved in the apprehension of the Absolute's revelatory agency. Indeed, if revelation, in its punctual, ever-present and thus eternal disclosure is meant to be known, then is not religious faith, as an immediate form of absolute knowledge, the most adequate human form of such apprehension? The question is particularly pertinent in light of the late eighteenth century German debate known as the *Pantheismusstreit* (Pantheism Quarrel), which pitted Jacobi, and his embrace of Christian faith as a form of intellectual intuition, against Mendelssohn and his apology of dogmatic, precritical metaphysical reason. The chapter addresses this dilemma through Hegel's apparently idiosyncratic use of the term "*Einsicht*" (insight) in the *Phenomenology of Spirit*, showing how, for Hegel, *both* faith/intuition and dogmatic metaphysics are forms of immediate knowing. As such, each requires mediation through its apparently opposed Other in order to arrive at the speculative form of knowing that is required for systematic Science. The unmediated opposition between intuition qua faith and dogmatic reasoning is symptomatic of Kantian *Verstand* (understanding), under whose culture Hegel ascribes his own contemporary epoch. The dangers of allowing the dichotomy between faith and reason to go unreconciled is demonstrated through the *Phenomenological* outcome portrayed in Hegel's evocation of Revolutionary Terror, which follows his discussion of "Insight and the Enlightenment." Less bloody but fundamentally inimical to Science and the world in which it takes place, the German elenchus imagined by Hegel at the end of the *Phenomenology*'s "Morality" chapter, is a culture of ironic individualism and vanity.

Reason, broadly understood as the human, historically informed, cognitive enterprise, whose goal is ultimately to grasp the truth of what is revealed, is again the theme of chapter 6, "Overcoming Understanding: The Language of Representation," however, now from the point of view of philosophical language or logos. Specifically, the linguistic form of judgment (*Urteil*) is discussed as operative within the vast province of what Hegel generally refers to as "*Vorstellung*." Recall that in the first chapters of this book, *Urteil* was discussed, within the context of the *Logics*, as a feature of the Absolute's self-positing revelation, and thus as thoroughly ontological. The absolute dimension of judgment is cashed out in the onto-grammatical move from "judgment" to "syllogism," where the copula is ful-filled, becoming the essential moment of particularity between the Universal and the Singular. Nonetheless, judgment is, of course, also the grammatical form immediately associated with human reason and knowledge. As Kant established, to know is to make knowledge claims that espouse the judgment form whereby a subject is associated with a predicate through the copula. Such claims, as Kant also maintained, are not immediately ontological, and indeed, Hegel recognizes that the basic judgments of human knowledge (e.g., "iron is a metal") do indeed fall within the precinct of the Kantian understanding. As such, they form the language of representation. Chapter 6 shows how the Hegel's reading of Karl Reinhold demonstrates that the judgment form of the common understanding carries within itself the onto-grammatical resources for its speculative vocation in Science.

Carrying out such a demonstration means taking the grammatical form of the proposition (*Satz*) as the iteration of human consciousness itself, a move that allows the form of judgment to be apprehended as enacting the movement of self-identical free thought into difference. In doing so, *Urteil* surpasses its grounding in the human understanding and realizes the speculative nature of its copula. Consequently, the judgment form of human reason and its language of representation is not alien from but rather integral to syllogistic Science. Such an integration is only possible, however, on the condition that Science recognize the inherently speculative nature of its own linguistic content, a recognition that involves acknowledging the inherently speculative nature of the representational judgments upon which Science reflects.

The third section, "Speculative Forms of Presence," in true Hegelian fashion, presents the reconciliation of an apparent opposition: of human and absolute agencies, of reason and revelation, through the three expressions that form what Hegel refers to as Absolute Spirit: art, religion, and philosophy. Chapter 7, "The Death of God and the Beautiful Finitude of Art," presents Hegel's aesthetics in this light: where the beautiful art object is the finite embodiment of both human spirit and absolute revelation. The finitude of art, its ending or rather endings, are essential to its objects, to their meanings and their speculative destination, which is the singular, man-made, and ultimately human incarnation of absolute content. The beautiful art object is the immediate presentation (*Darstellung*) of speculative truth: the singular identity of identity and difference. The most significant iteration of art's essential finitude takes place in what was the culmination of the artistic project: in Christ himself, not in his representation, but in Himself, as the most beautiful, accomplished work of Classical art, where the singular, living human form is presented as entirely adequate to the absolute difference of its divine content. Conceiving Christ as the most beautiful, and most essentially finite work of art helps us apprehend how religion arises as a more mediated, less natural form of Absolute Spirit, where the speculative truth is no longer simply presented (*dargestellt*) but rather represented (*vorgestellt*) in the language of church doctrine.

Chapter 8, "The Hermeneutics of Worship," is thus a continuation of where the discussion of the speculative (human and absolute) nature of art left off, now examining the crucial importance of doctrine in Hegel's philosophy of religion. Religious doctrine is the linguistic form of representation that is more adequate than art to the articulation of speculative truth, to the performative actuality of reason and revelation. In revelatory religion, speculative truth is realized and communally celebrated in shared texts. The linguistic dimension of religion allows us to appreciate how the speculative truth actually takes place in forms and practices of worship. Whereas the penultimate forms of art gave us the architecture of the Ancient world, the death of God has brought forth Spirit in the higher form of doctrinal language. *Darstellung* has given way to *Vorstellung*. The performative reality of doctrine, in communal worship, now fills the empty temples of architectural art, in a human–divine complicity that ensures that doctrinal positivity is always also the instantiation of freedom. Hegel sees the speculative apprehension of doctrine as under threat from a contemporary strain of hermeneutics that he associates with Schleiermacher, and according to which the holistic notion of doctrinal words is sundered into an arbitrary relation between linguistic signs and their alien signification. Given the performative reality of doctrine, the hermeneutic assault on its reality has necessarily worldly and even political ramifications.

Philosophy, as the ultimate form of Absolute Spirit, presents us with the culminating form of "worship," in the communal, performative celebration of the shared texts in the history of philosophy. Only in their historical unfolding, according to the narrative of human reason, are we able to grasp the revelatory content that has always been active within the logos of philosophy. What distinguishes the texts of philosophy from those of church doctrine is the move from representational to speculative language. However, the speculative language of systematic Science does not rewrite the earlier texts of religion and philosophy in its own terms, although this may sometimes appear to be the case. Rather, the goal of Science is to reread the texts that it is presented with and which form its content, and in doing so, to grasp the dogmatic judgments of those forms in their speculative truth. In philosophy, the goal of Science is to grasp the copulas of philosophical judgments according to their onto-grammatical truth, that is, as expressive and performative of the Concept, whose most perfect form is the (onto-grammatical) syllogism. Just as the performative reality of church doctrine *takes place* in forms of revelatory religious worship, the revelatory logos of philosophy, as presented according to the historical narrative of reason, is instantiated within the "temple" of the state university. It is in the ultimate context of the philosophy class, and its historically informed teachings of the philosophical "doctrines" of art, religion, philosophy, as well as those of the state, natural science, the sciences of the mind and metaphysics (qua the *Logics*), that we are able to grasp what philosophy has always been about: knowledge of humanly determined substance that has turned out to be, at the same time, knowledge of subjective freedom.

The final section of the book takes Hegel's metaphysics, as I have presented them in terms of the Absolute, its revelatory agency, and the reciprocal strivings of human reason, and relates those metaphysical lessons to meta-considerations on philosophical systematicity. Chapter 10 takes seriously the popular idea (iterated by Hegel) that the system of philosophical Science is organic. This generally means that the system is made up of inter-related, purposive elements (organs) that ensure the life of Science, which, in turn, confers meaning and life on those elements. The organic trope ensures that the system is not mechanical but, rather, dynamic, lively, and open to new content. As we see in chapter 2, the organic trope implies a certain relation to extra-systematic nature, which becomes alien, natural content upon which the organic system feeds. However, the reassuring organic trope fails to consider an essential element of what constitutes a living organism: excrement. Chapter 10 considers Hegel's detailed examination of animal digestion and excretion, from his *Philosophy of Nature*, and then refers it to the organic system itself. What does Science leave behind?

Chapter 11 applies the revelatory agency of the Absolute and the reciprocal agency of human reason to contemporary Big Bang cosmology. The hypothetical singularity that underpins the dominant, generally accepted cosmological theory can be understood as the Absolute, as we find it presented in Hegel's *Logics*, where initially indeterminate Being is demonstrated to have had, within itself, every reason to be, and so *is*. Just as the Big Bang singularity pours itself out and inflates into nature, the *Logics* demonstrate the Absolute as coming to disclose itself (*sich entschliessen*), as letting itself go into the determinate form of Being that becomes the content of the *Philosophy of Nature*. Nature is what human reason then operates upon, as Spirit whose final form is again absolute. Taking the anthropic principle as a corollary feature of Big Bang theory allows us to understand how the expanding universe is "for us," that is, for reasoning beings for whom the universal "substance" reveals itself as it is. Both the Big Crunch and the Big Chill cosmological scenarios similarly demonstrate the essential finitude of the "for us," how the complicit agencies of absolute revelation and any sort of life-based reason are necessarily temporal and indeed temporary. Hegel's grammatical ontology of the present perfect (*das Perfekt*), of the "having been" as constitutive of what is, allows us to grasp that even given the finite temporal nature of the universe's self-revelation, self-consciousness will always *have been* an essential feature of the universe's trajectory.

Relating Hegel's philosophy of the Absolute to contemporary Big Bang cosmology allows us to see how metaphysics should not be disparaged as abstract, unjustified, and pointless reflections on the un-real but how they fully engage with contemporary *physics*. Specifically, just as Hegel's metaphysics begin and end with philosophical reflections on the Absolute, the physics of Big Bang cosmology begins and ends with the singularity. Drawing from this *rapprochement*, we may comprehend how the closing cosmological singularity must carry within itself the *Perfekt* moment of reason. Further, since singularities have no predicates by which they might be distinguished, the closing singularity is indistinguishable from the absolute beginning, which thus carries within itself its own reason to be, and so *is*. Replaying what we discovered in

Hegelian Science, the history of the Big Bang universe is informative of the eternal, always singular "Now."

Finally, chapter 12 addresses the question of meaning through a consideration of music in Hegel. Meaningful musical tones arise from the vibratory oscillation between selfhood's presiding unity and its temporal ideality or self-positing. Indeterminate meaningfulness arises in music's absolute *Grundton,* pure vibratory sound that forms a kind of background radiation upon which human reason may then configure forms of determinate meaning, in music and then in words and thoughts. The temporal vanishing that underlies sound generally and tones specifically is a pre-linguistic expression of meaning and its ambiguous oscillation between the Absolute and the human. In music, as a form of *schöne Kunst,* the Absolute reveals itself to us, ensuring the very possibility of meaning, without ever determining exactly what that meaning is. Music is a fundamental form of hermeneutical openness. When it moves us, that is what we feel: revelatory meaningfulness opening onto symphonies of ambiguous meaning, one of which is the subject of the present book: Hegel's system of Science.

PART ONE

Absolute Agency and Revelation

1
Reason and Revelation: The Limits of Worldly Actuality

Commentators of Hegel's *Phenomenology of Spirit* often seem dismayed when they come to chapter 7 on religion. Why, having finally reached the neat satisfaction of moral community at the end of chapter 6, where the triumphant reconciling "Yea" expresses the shared freedom prefigured hundreds of pages earlier in the self-conscious "I that is We," are we now plunged into the dogmatic obscurantism of religion? Why not just get on with the more frankly philosophical problem of understanding Absolute Knowing in chapter 8?

Solutions to such disappointment are various but may nonetheless be grouped together under several defined approaches. Hegel can be seen as the proto-Feuerbachian "precursor of atheistic humanism,"[1] (the approach that Emil Fackenheim, in his landmark work, *The Religious Dimension of Hegel's Philosophy*, defines as typical of the Hegelian Left).[2] In this context, Hegel's extensive lectures on religion, some twenty years after the *Phenomenology*, at the University of Berlin, must be explained away as politically expedient, circumstantial, or as not really about religion. Conveniently, the lack of any textual evidence for Hegel's ascribed atheism becomes itself evidence for such atheism, that is, the "proof" of supposed self-censorship in the face of political-theological repression.

A gentler version of the same humanistic, anthropological approach consists of emphasizing the communal dimension at play in religion. Thus, as H.S. Harris writes, "God becomes recognizable as the spirit of the actual community in which we live and move,"[3] or as John Russon puts it, religion is "the rituals of mutual recognition in which a community says 'so that's who we are.'"[4]

Another approach to the religion problem consists in identifying it as "a defective form of philosophy," as Tom Rockmore writes. In this light, we may take the *Phenomenology*'s chapter seven as the place where "Hegel criticizes religion for its reliance on representation that falls short of conceptual thought."[5] This view is comforting in that it accords a place for religion within the state, where representation and picture-thinking (as *Vorstellung* is sometimes translated) are adequate for the benighted citizenry incapable of speculative thinking. Religious thought again becomes a form of anthropological knowledge for the Scientific community, which can now take religion as the object of study because systematic philosophy may recognize itself in this *past* form.[6] This "progressive" approach allows Hegel scholars to acknowledge the existence of religion in Hegel's thought, while relegating it to the status of error, that is, an incomplete yet systematically necessary step in the path to the Truth, as found in the Absolute Knowing of Science. The final approach to the religion problem, of course, is simply to ignore the *Phenomenology*'s chapter 7 altogether, to leave it out.[7]

Tom Rockmore perhaps best summarizes the general state of affairs when he writes, "One of the great, enduring mysteries of Hegel scholarship is the role of religion in his mature theory, including the *Phenomenology*."[8] Rockmore's diagnosis is particularly apt given what might be referred to as the current Anglo-American dominance in Hegel studies, when Rockmore further remarks that the "connection between religion and philosophy ... never existed in the United States and was weaker in England than in continental Europe [and] has been appreciably weakened everywhere else in the philosophical world," with the possible exception of France.[9]

Indeed, what Rockmore shows us is that the dismay and unease some commentators feel when arriving at chapter 7, on religion, in the *Phenomenology of Spirit* is the result of the disappearance, in our own time, of any pre-existing bond between religion and philosophy. This is significant because the explicit goal of Hegel's philosophy of religion is to strengthen and reinforce this very bond, which he already considers to be at risk. He clearly summarizes this project at the end of his own lecture notes manuscript to the *Lectures on the Philosophy of Religion*: "Instead of allowing reason and religion to contradict themselves, we must resolve the discord in the manner appropriate to us – namely, reconciliation in the form of philosophy.... These lectures have attempted to offer guidance to this end. Religion must take refuge in philosophy."[10] The last sentence expresses the urgency Hegel perceives in his project, an urgency already anticipated in the writings of other authors from the late German Enlightenment, where the radical separation between faith and reason is felt as politically dangerous, particularly for the free pursuit of philosophical enquiry.[11]

Our contemporary incapacity to conceive of the link between religion and philosophy or between faith and reason is symptomatic of a condition that Hegel himself viewed as a clear, contemporary malaise when he was pronouncing his courses on religion, in Berlin, and which he makes explicit in his preface to H.F.W. Hinrichs's work on religion.[12] The pernicious theology of feeling that Hegel associates with Schleiermacher arises from the unreconciled dichotomy within the understanding (*Verstand*) itself, that is, between inner intuition (aka faith) and calculative reasoning (aka categorical judging).[13] Perhaps our own inability to come to terms with the philosophy-religion dichotomy reveals a post-modern condition that Hegel already foresaw, where we have come to be torn, as Peter Hodgson puts it, between "philosophical agnosticism and religious fundamentalism, the reigning dogmatisms of our time."[14] In his preface to Hinrichs's work, Hegel laments the disjunctive tenor of his own times, in Berlin, in 1820. It is no accident, for Hegel, that the terrorist murder of the Russian diplomat and playwright August von Kotzebue (1819), which gave rise to the subsequent policies of state censorship and repression, was carried out by a fanatical theology student. As Kant had already foreseen, the radical separation between reason and faith could only bring about arbitrary, dangerous fanaticism and reactionary repression.

The problem posed by chapter 7, on religion, in the *Phenomenology of Spirit*, is indicative of a misunderstanding that goes to the very core of how we have tended to comprehend Hegel's systematic philosophy, namely, our reluctance to consider the role of revelation in his idea of Absolute Knowing and, therefore, in his notion of Science. The misunderstanding thus also involves how other key expressions of systematicity in Hegel are understood: "Concept," "Spirit," and "Idea." Throughout all of these terms, Absolute Knowing is present, not just as our knowledge of a distinct, absolute substance or content but also, and above all, as the subjective, agency of the Absolute itself. The Absolute gives itself to be known and makes itself available to us. In religion, such agency takes the representational form of Revelation. However, religion, in Hegel, does not merely reveal *the fact* that the Absolute exists (i.e., the recognition of something infinite beyond us that religion "points to," as John Russon puts it, in the reference above) but the knowable content of *what* the Absolute is. Reciprocally, as a form of human knowledge, Absolute Knowing must recognize itself as participating in the self-knowing agency of the Absolute itself. In other (Hegelian) words, Absolute Knowing is both content (substance) and form (subjectivity), and it is in such a subjectively substantive way that Hegel's expression, "The Absolute alone is true, or the truth alone is absolute," from the introduction to the *Phenomenology of Spirit*,[15] can express anything other than an empty tautology. Without further muddying these already highly speculative waters, allow me to get away with simply stating, at this point, that the content/form of such knowledge is nothing other than freedom. Indeed, the highest expression of freedom is the revelatory agency of the Absolute, which is consequently an essential aspect of knowledge, of Absolute Knowing, and therefore of Hegelian Science.

What the above-mentioned contemporary accounts of religion in Hegel have in common is that they reproduce the error that Hegel himself remarks on in his *Lectures on the Philosophy of Religion*; humanity has come to ignore the self-revelatory agency of God (aka the Idea, the Absolute), and now understands religion exclusively in terms of human experience: "Taken with religious fervor, we tend to speak only of *our* relation to God ... but a one-way relation is not one at all ... God, in his perfect autonomy in-and-for-itself exists *for* the human spirit, communicates Himself to man ... God *is* and gives himself in relation to man."[16]

The Absolute's revelatory agency grounds the possibility of truth itself, to the extent that human knowing, the process that Hegel presents through his concepts of reason and Spirit, must come to know itself as participating in the self-knowledge of the Absolute. Absolute self-knowledge is made possible through revelation, an act that involves humanity in divine self-consciousness, where all that is known, and that which knows, are never *merely* human. Once again, Hegel states this clearly in his *Lectures on the Philosophy of Religion*, in a pronouncement that perhaps best summarizes the thesis of the present chapter, and indeed of the whole book: "[God] has revealed Himself and continues to reveal Himself, and clearly, in this revelation, it is not human reason with all its limits that knows God but, on the contrary, it is the spirit of God in man [that knows God]; in speculative terms, it is the self-consciousness of God that knows itself in human knowledge."[17]

In this chapter, I want to show that reason and revelation are two distinct and yet complicit elements of Science, representing what Hegel refers to, in a Jena aphorism, as the two cycles of the Absolute,[18] an essentially Neoplatonic logic of emanation and return, which explains why Hegel, in his *Lectures on the History of Philosophy*, promotes Neoplatonism and then Jakob Böhme as the last words in Ancient and Modern philosophy. Both currents anticipate the speculative reality of the Hegelian Idea and the philosophical enactment of its emanation (revelation) and return (reason qua spirit), in the circular movement known as the "Concept." Without revelation, reason remains "human, all too human," essentially limited in its scope, an expression of freedom of the will, as we find in Kant and Fichte, that must constantly position itself against nature. Conversely, however, without the activity of reason, from the perspective of human self-realization, revelation remains the expression of authoritarian dogmatism. In other words, on its own, reason can do no better than Kantian (i.e., abstract) moral freedom, endlessly striving within and yet against a recalcitrant world, endlessly progressing towards a never attained supreme Good; and revelation alone is experienced as a form of heteronomous necessity, of "positivity," to use the word of the time. Thus, to take the reconciliation between reason and revelation a step further, on a path that I will return to further on, Hegel's systematic project can be seen as bringing together freedom and necessity, in the organic, universal singularity that is Science, where the Absolute Idea presents itself as true, good and, perhaps above all, beautiful, following Kant's definition of beauty as a singular work conjoining freedom and necessity.[19]

If we accept the dual agency of reason and revelation in Hegel's theory of Absolute Knowledge, then we might well wonder how the content of revelation takes place in the world. Above, I asserted that such content was essentially freedom. If that is the case, then surely the terrain of human reason that Hegel lays out in the *Phenomenology* and in his *Lectures on the Philosophy of History*, where the story of Spirit is explicitly presented as the story of human, moral freedom through the progressive history of states and their constitutions, should immediately be the terrain where we also find the agency of revelation. In other words, human moral and political (in the broadest sense) actuality (*Wirklichkeit*) should enact the immediate coincidence of human reason and divine or absolute revelation. The communal path of human consciousness, the story of what Hegel calls Spirit, should also be where the agency of revelation plays itself out. History should be providential. This is Emil Fackenheim's conclusion, which I am challenging. In doing so, I want to establish the limits of what Hegel calls "actuality," the worldly instantiations of human reason and its aspirations. My challenge has repercussions beyond Fackenheim, namely on those who evaluate Hegel's philosophy against the failings of the real world. I maintain that Hegel readily recognizes such failings in his conception of actuality as resulting from the exclusive agency of human reason, divorced from that of ideal revelation.

Emil Fackenheim, in his book, *The Religious Dimension of Hegel's Thought*, certainly recognizes the essential complicity of revelation in Hegel, which he describes as the "overreaching [i.e., agency] of the Idea" into the world. For Fackenheim, the Idea/God's revelatory agency combines with the reciprocally contrasting "over-reaching" agency of Spirit (human reason) in order to establish what he refers to as the Hegelian middle, which takes place as worldly actuality. "Hegel's lifelong endeavour was to find the Absolute not beyond but present *in* the world," he writes.[20] The human world is thus the meaningful result of the confluence between reason and revelation. In Fackenheim's words, our world is "doubly overreached": "This modern world, then, already is doubly overreached, by a creating, preserving, and redeeming God and by a Spirit which, manifest in man, accepts itself as created, preserved, and redeemed."[21] The worldly truth of this middle is, for Hegel, according to Fackenheim, incarnate in the actuality of the bourgeois Christian world. Since this middle, as actuality, is the locus where the entire system's realization or Truth takes place, and upon which its success is to be judged, the failure of bourgeois Christian actuality, in twentieth-century totalitarian horrors and particularly those of the Holocaust, must therefore also mean the failure of the whole Hegelian enterprise. According to Fackenheim's theodicy of Hegel, the political failure of the actual world refutes the system.[22]

I am recognizing Fackenheim's noted complicity between reason and revelation as integral to Hegelian systematicity. However, whereas he sees the two as working together throughout the system to produce Truth in the form of actuality, I am claiming that the revelatory agency of the Absolute is specifically carried out not in actuality per se but in the "absolute" elements of Hegel's philosophy, in the manifestations of Absolute Spirit: in art, religion, and philosophy, and in the subjective side of Hegel's *Logics*,[23] that is, in the "Logic of the Concept," and perhaps, although I offer the idea only as a hypothesis, in the appearance of organic life and death in the *Philosophy of Nature* [EN]. Conversely, the agency of human reason has its own place in the system, notably in the first six chapters of the *Phenomenology of Spirit*, in the Subjective and Objective Spirit sections of the *Encyclopaedia*'s *Philosophy of Spirit* [ES] and in the first, Objective Logic part of the *Greater Logic* (I have provided a schema, below, that hopefully makes this extensive list of references easier to envision).

Schema: Reason and Revelation in Hegel's Main Works

Phenomenology of Spirit

Chapters 1–6 = Reason: Actuality as Morality
Chapter 7 = Revelation (art/religion)
Chapter 8 = Reason and Revelation as Absolute Knowing = Science

Greater Logic (GL)

Objective Logic (Being and Essence) = Reason ("Actuality" chapter)
Subjective Logic (the Concept) = Revelation as logos (judgment and syllogism)
Absolute Idea = Reason and Revelation = Science (the University)

Philosophy of Spirit (ES)

Subjective and Objective Spirit = Reason (actuality as world political history)
Absolute Spirit (Art and Religion) = Revelation
Absolute Spirit (Philosophy) = Reason and Revelation = Science (the University)

Philosophy of Nature (EN)

Mechanics and Physics = Reason (actuality as chemical process)
Organics (life) = Revelation as purposive, unified organism
Death = Reason and Revelation = Life as "resurrection" in species/ Spirit?

The stuff of revelation is not to be found immediately in human actuality *generally*, and this is again Fackenheim's problem, to the extent that he presents Hegelian "actuality" (*Wirklichkeit*) as the immediate "synthesis" between the divine and the worldly, which he calls the Hegelian middle. Revelation does, of course, embrace the human, through the histories of art, religion, and philosophy, but it does so because absolute agency is, first of all, distinct from that of human reason.

Divorced from the absolute agency of revelation, reason must end in the logic of actuality. This is the same logic that informs the endless strivings of "Morality" and which prevents Hegel, at the end of Objective Spirit (aka the political *Philosophy of Right*) from subscribing to a cosmopolitan political vision of the happy end of history where freedom is fully realized in a global state constitution. Just as there will never be a terrestrial *summum bonum* (supreme good, heaven on earth), there will never be a perfectly harmonious instantiation of the perfect political constitution. Humanity is just too human. Actuality is just too … actual. Of course, that does not prevent Hegel from dealing with the failing features of actuality, qua reason, scientifically (systematically), which he begins doing by examining the category itself, in his *Logics*.

In order to comprehend the ontological failings of actuality, according to Hegel's Science, we must turn, at least briefly, to how the category itself appears in Hegel's *Logics*, where it is presented on its own, as distinct from the agency of the Absolute. The flawed ontological nature of actuality has profound repercussions on how Hegel is read and interpreted, not only for those, like Fackenheim, who see it as the sole theatre of the divine, but for the Hegelians who refuse the divine entirely and are forced to place all their dialectical hopes (and disappointments) in the successes or failures of the actual world.

Clearly stated, the accounts of those who judge the philosopher's contemporary relevance on the basis of whether the "actual" world lives up to or even contradicts the absolute demands of his system should be confronted with Hegel's own recognition of the endless limitations of actuality itself. This is especially pertinent because Hegel is arguably the only important modern philosopher whose thought is continually questioned on the basis of its relation to the "real world," by critics on the Left (e.g., Marx and Engels) or on the Right (e.g., Fackenheim) of the Hegelian spectrum of interpretation.[24] Those on the Right, who accept the agency of the Absolute, the Idea, or God, and acknowledge the systematic pretentions of their philosopher may be disheartened by the horrible excesses of atheistic, materialistic, totalitarian actuality. Conversely, those on the Left, like Frederick Beiser, feel that ironic, atheistic contemporary actuality has rendered null any systematic, absolute pretentions that Hegel might have had.[25] However, in recognizing where actuality *actually* stands in Hegel's thought, we are able to recognize where the true "Hegelian middle" is really to be found: in the expressions of art, religion, and philosophy, where the revelatory agency of the Absolute comes together with the aspirations of human reason. Once again, the endless limitations of actuality are only scientifically appreciated if we recognize the dialectical difference at play between the agencies of reason and revelation.

The difference between the activity of reason and that of revelation (and thus the possibility of their speculative reconciliation) is fundamental to Hegel's *Logics* and explains the often overlooked binary distinction that underlies his *Science of Logic*: the distinction between Objective Logic (the Doctrines of Being and Essence) and Subjective Logic (Doctrine of the Concept). As is the case at the end of the *Phenomenology*'s sixth chapter (with the moral community), the end of the Objective Logic appears to leave us within the comforting embrace of a meaningful reality, which is explicitly presented as *Wirklichkeit* (Actuality). Just as we may ask ourselves, in the *Phenomenology*, why we must leave the communal "being at home in otherness," in the Spirit chapter, and plunge into the apparently unreasonable obscurity of religion, similarly, in the *Logics*, we are reluctant to leave the meaningful reality that we have struggled to attain, in "Actuality," for the apparently abstract forms of judgment and syllogism that we discover in the Doctrine of the Concept. If the binary distinction between Objective and Subjective Logics is just as puzzling to Hegelian Trinitarians as is the break between chapters 6 and 7 in the *Phenomenology* or perhaps the move from Objective Spirit (the state and world history) to Absolute Spirit in the *Encyclopaedia*'s *Philosophy of Spirit*, it is because the *Logics* (both the *Encyclopaedia* and *Greater* versions) present the fundamental distinction between two points of view or rather two different narratives, each with its own protagonist. Actuality represents the limits of the human story, and an opening onto a new perspective.

Briefly, in the *Logics*, *Wirklichkeit* is presented as shot through with bad infinity and endless regression. In causality, for example, the relation between cause and effect produces a "progress *in finitum*,"[26] an infinite, meaningless chain of efficient causation where each becomes the other endlessly. The lack of any first/final cause is precisely what distinguishes his own take on actuality, Hegel acknowledges, from Aristotle's promotion of the same category as actus (EL 142 Add.).[27] The same logic of endless, efficient reflection is played out in the other reciprocal, oscillatory relationships explored in the ontological categories of the "Actuality" section: between substantiality and accident, and again in the modal character that runs through the section, for example, in the continual interplay between conditions, necessity, possibility, and contingency, and more fundamentally, between identity and difference.[28]

The dizzying dance of Actuality's relational and modal ontological categories allows Hegel, in the Additions to the *Encyclopaedia Logic*, to refer repeatedly to instances of human existence that are endlessly recalcitrant to definitive realizations: to "constitutions and laws" (EL 156 Add.), to "systems of taxation" (EL 142 Add.), or to the contingencies of language, "law, art, etc." (EL 145 Add.); "the Sultan and the Pope" (EL 143 Add.) are even mentioned. Hegel's examples are significant in their familiar banality. They are expressions of human reason (laws, taxation, language, *modern* artistic expressions) that we recognize as caught up in the bad infinity of contingent reality, and which characterizes our everyday lives: the meaningful, meaningless actuality of our world.

The Objective Logic (Doctrines of Being and Essence) recounts the path of reason in its thoughtful determinations of objectivity, which, from the initial point of empty Being, become increasingly essential or meaningful. The goal of the *Logics* is the ontological determination of scientifically significant *Being* qua nature, the object of the natural sciences and the theme of the subsequent tome of the *Encyclopaedia*: *The Philosophy of Nature*. However, the path of determinant Being stalls at "Actuality," where being gets caught up in the endless regressions of causality, subject and accident, and modal contingency. The holistic rounding out, the completion of the *Logics*' narrative, that is, the full determining of Being as existing, knowable nature, for Science, is only made possible through the acknowledgment of the agency of the Absolute, an expression of revelation that takes place in the second half of the *Logics*, in the Doctrine of the Concept. Here, the determination of nature takes on its holistic, unified, purposive quality, without which, as

Kant had seen in his *Critique of Judgment*, we cannot do natural science. The holistic, organic aspect of nature cannot be derived from human reason alone but must be "supplied" by the agency of the Absolute qua revelation, where being is determined as One and whole. Only then can we fully grasp the sense of the ending of the *Logics*, where the Idea (God) freely desyllogizes itself (*sich entschliesst*), discloses itself as nature. In a word, in order for nature to constitute a purposive whole, and thus be the object of knowledge in the subsequent *Philosophy of Nature*, it must be presented as the proffered content of the Idea. In the Doctrine of the Concept, Being becomes the revelatory Word or logos of the Idea's posited selfhood, articulated through the ontological grammar of "Judgment" and "Syllogism," the two main sections of the Subjective Logic (Doctrine of the Concept).

Actuality, which closes Objective Logic, is the highest determination of objectivity that human reason, left on its own, is capable of achieving. Actuality is certainly more meaningful than the emptiness of Being with which the *Logics*' narrative begins; actuality is the locus of human political history, human morality, and even the human, all too human reiterations of modern, romantic art, of biblical hermeneutics, and ironic, unsystematic philosophizing. Indeed, if these worldly, contemporary pursuits strike us, still today, as recognizable, it is because they are logically never-ending. The endlessly tragi-comic play of demise, renewal, and demise, in all human pursuits, the nauseating "slaughter bench" that Hegel refers to in the introduction to his *Lectures on the Philosophy of History*, and which we still see around us today, is what justifies the negative theodicy of Hegelian philosophy, shared by commentators on both the Right and the Left of the interpretive spectrum. However, it is simply wrong to unduly promote the category of actuality in Hegel, and then to judge his philosophy with respect to how that category compares to the "real world." For him, actuality itself and the strivings of the human world must always disappoint and scandalize us; the actual world can never live up to the beautiful reconciliations of the human and the divine that are incarnate in art and religion, and realized in philosophical Science. Actuality alone must always fail, and yet "always failing" already implies a constantly renewed effort, an endless striving for something that only revelation can offer, namely the ideas of the good, the true, and the beautiful, that is, the dynamic unity of freedom and necessity that Hegel presents as the Absolute Idea, with which the *Logics* end.

Consequently, my contention regarding the inescapably metaphysical dimension in Hegel is that the Absolute is never meant to be fully realized in worldly actuality per se, but rather must take place within the systematic embrace of Science itself, which is expressed as Absolute

Knowing (in the *Phenomenology*), in the Absolute Idea (in the *Logics*), and in Absolute Spirit (in the *Philosophy of Spirit*). Consequently, far from constituting the essential Hegelian middle, as Fackenheim calls it, actuality is the highest but necessarily flawed iteration of (human) reason. As such, it is essentially limited, endlessly finite, and ontologically incapable, on its own, of embodying Truth in the full Hegelian sense of the word.

Actuality, within the Hegelian oeuvre, always appears in contexts where the Truth is anticipated but never realized: This is how the category of "Actuality" occurs in the final subchapter of Objective Logic, in the *Greater Logic,* just *before* the Logic of the Concept (Subjective Logic), and how it is found in moral striving, at the end of the *Phenomenology*'s chapter 6 (subchapter on "Morality"), just before Religion, and again as the infinite, always unrealized progress of political freedom in state constitutions and world history, at the end of the *Encyclopaedia*'s "Philosophy of Objective Spirit" (or in the *Principles of the Philosophy of Right*), just before we move onto the forms of Absolute Spirit articulated in art, religion, and philosophy. In each case, human reason ends in the never-ending limitations or infinite strivings of actuality. Nonetheless, and it is crucial to note, the fact that human reason *persists* in spite of its failures already attests to an object beyond that of reason itself, to a content that is the proffered, self-posited substance of the Absolute, which is experienced, in the religious terms of faith, as Revelation.

Let us return briefly to the reciprocal and yet distinct agencies of reason and revelation in the *Phenomenology*. We are generally familiar with the account of the progress of reason in this work: from consciousness, through self-consciousness, to Reason itself in chapter 5, and finally in Spirit (chapter 6), we trace the movement of free human selfhood as it comes to know itself in ever-richer, freer, more selfhood-imbued forms of objectivity. From the Enlightenment individual's certainty of finding itself, qua reason, in all of reality (chapter 5), we come to recognize the historical truth of this realization as humanity's self-reflection in world-historical spirit, in chapter 6. But this is where I believe the journey of reason alone meets its limits: in the endless striving postulated by Kantian morality, towards a cosmopolitan community of the *summum bonum* that it can never actually reach. Reason ends in the endless approximations of human, moral actuality.[29]

The story of reason ends, however, where the story of revelation begins, in chapter 7 on Religion. It is only through the narrative "rounding out" provided by revelation that there is anything to morally strive for: the true realization of freedom as fully instantiated in nature, the realized aim of Kant's categorical imperative, anticipated in his idea of purposiveness.

Such narrative closure means that, for Hegel, the true realization of freedom is *not* present in the world of actuality but rather takes place in the "worlds" of absolute spirit: in art, religion, and philosophy.

Over against the story of reason in the *Phenomenology*, recounted in the first six chapters of that work, stands the story of revelation as told in the Religion chapter, and fleshed out in the *Lectures on the Philosophies of Art* and *Religion.* The Absolute (the Idea/God/the Universal) first reveals itself to us as incarnated in individual, natural objects, that is, where this tree, this stream, this rock may be "illuminated" as sacred or godly. The multiplicity of individual objects betrays the impossibility of the Universal fully inhabiting any one of them. Their bad infinity collapses into an empty universality, a kind of acosmic pantheism where anything in nature may indifferently be taken as holy. Next, in the Religion chapter, the sacred is embodied in the quasi-human art forms of man-made Greco-Roman sculpture, in the syllogistic moment of particularity, where each human-like and yet lifeless stone god represents a particular power: the sea, the hunt, wisdom, war, and so on.

Finally, the Absolute comes to inhabit or incarnate the ultimate "art object," the perfect individual form that is both divine and natural, human and godly, dead and alive, and above all, beautiful: the individuality of Christ. Christ himself, that is, the son of God who *is* God, can thus be seen as the last beautiful work of art, the truly universal singular, the perfect union of absolute form and content in finite form. As I will further demonstrate in chapter 7 of this book, the death of Christ marks, for Hegel, the most crucial end of art, the end of the Ancient world, and the beginning of *religion* per se, that is, the modern era and the truth that the Absolute cannot be contained in any single, natural thing, man or man-made being. The individual body of Christ is sundered apart from within, we might say, by its own universality. God is dead, as Hegel puts it, not so much because he is crucified but because his finite body cannot contain the infinite universal.[30] Revelatory (*offenbare,* which has a more active sense than "revealed")[31] religion then presents a new form of revelation, where the Absolute comes to inhabit sacred words in the texts of religious doctrine,[32] an idea that I will discuss in chapter 8 of this book.

The stories of reason and revelation, which I have just outlined, are, of course, interrelated. In the *Phenomenology,* human spirit rises (and the story of reason begins) as the tragic, unhappy quest to re-enact the lost instance of the Absolute (God) in the World. The re-enactment of this happy condition is indeed the goal of reason and actuality. However, for the Absolute to again take place in the world, we must bracket reason as the uniquely human quest to regain the lost, punctual unity of the

Christly individual art object, and look to the spiritual forms where absolute agency is revealed.

"Absolute Knowing," the final, short chapter of the *Phenomenology of Spirit* recognizes the complicity of human spirit (reason) and revelation, the fact that they are both aspects of the Concept, the truth that, as I quoted above, "the self-consciousness of God ... knows itself in human knowledge." Absolute Knowing is not *humanly* possible without the Absolute having given itself to be known through its own activity of self-knowledge. However, as we know from his dialectical logic generally, the Hegelian unity between reason and revelation can only happen if we first acknowledge and celebrate their difference, within the system itself.

The *Phenomenology*'s "Absolute Knowing" chapter prefigures what Hegel refers to as Science, systematic philosophy as expressed in his *Encyclopaedia of Philosophical Sciences* and taught in the modern state university (of which the University of Berlin provided the model). As we know, the *Encyclopaedia* is comprised of the *Logic*, the *Philosophy of Nature* and the *Philosophy of Spirit*, whose final chapter, "Absolute Spirit," presents the revelatory expressions of art, religion, and philosophy. If the Absolute and the human are to be again complicit in the world, it is in those forms of absolute Spirit where human reason and revelation are one. Consequently, if we look at the worldly forms that revelation takes, we notice that they themselves adopt forms that are increasingly human. Referring again to the "Religion" chapter in the *Phenomenology*, we see how the fetishistic religions of nature, where any natural object may be taken as sacred, give way to the human/divine presentations of Greco-Roman gods, sculpted by human artists, and then to the last ancient "art form," the human God himself, where the human and the divine meet in a singular, living (and dying) individual.

Revelatory religion, the second Hegelian form of Absolute Spirit, following art, continues the narrative of human-Absolute complicity. However, there, the cohabitation of the human and the divine goes beyond the singular form of the art object, to embrace the sacred in a form that involves an essential aspect of humanity: the intersubjective, linguistic reality of human community, which now takes place, in Hegel's terms, in the communal worship and consecration of revelatory church doctrine (*Lehre* = teachings, see below, chapter 8). In this shared, free celebration of sacred text, church dogma loses its "dogmatic," positive, imposed aspect. In fact, as is the case with the other expressions of Absolute Spirit (art and philosophy), religious worship brings together human freedom (worship) and revelatory necessity (dogma) in a concrete form that replays, as I mentioned above, the Kantian ideal of the beautiful, which Hegel presents as the cohabitation of the human and the divine.

Indeed, building on the aesthetic reference, we can trace the destiny of the empty temples that Hegel evokes in chapter 7 of the *Phenomenology*, following the shocking affirmation that "God [as Christ] is dead," back to the discussion on architecture as geometrical space inhabited by stone statues of the gods, in the *Lectures on the Philosophy of Art* [LA].[33] It is these empty "temples" that are now, in revelatory religion, filled with human worshippers freely consecrating the given words of doctrine.[34] I believe we can follow the trajectory of the architectural "temple" even further, beyond its religious determination, to where it becomes the highest space of Hegelian "worship," that which takes place in the shared discourse of systematic, philosophical Science, at the state university. The vocation of philosophical Science, as the ultimate form of Absolute Spirit, is not to abandon the earlier content of revelation (art and religion) but to grasp its speculative nature and thus conserve it as *aufgehoben.* This means acknowledging the histories of revelation as philosophically meaningful, precisely the project that Hegel carries out in his copious lectures on the *philosophies* of art and religion.[35]

Consequently, Hegel's philosophy of religion, as the philosophical interpretation of revelation, and ultimately, of church doctrine,[36] brings a new, fully human form to the Absolute's agency, a worldly place (of "worship") where human reason and divine revelation are again at home together, in the communal celebration of Absolute Knowing. The empty temples are "fulfilled" in the state university, the worldly embodiment, the "temple" of Hegelian Science. It is here that the content of both reason (the human history of Spirit, including the imperfect pursuits of history and politics) and revelation (Absolute Spirit: the philosophical histories of art, religion and philosophy) are taught together in their *Encyclopaedic* form. The state university is, for Hegel, where the re-Incarnation truly takes place, as a mediated, singular form that acknowledges the complicit agency of the human and the Absolute. As such, the state university enjoys an ontological status that participates in actuality (as the expression of human freedom) while recognizing the metaphysical source of that freedom in the Idea.

Saying that the university is, for Hegel, the place where reason and revelation are at home (*bei sich*) together in Science requires comprehending their relation in terms of how he presents the process of "knowing" (*Erkennen*) generally: as a process of self-recognition in otherness. Knowing, in this sense, always involves "recognition," a fact obscured by the habitual translation of *Erkennen* as "cognition." For Hegel, to know something is to know oneself in it, and to know oneself (the goal of philosophy) is to also recognize the "otherness" in oneself. In the sphere of Absolute Knowing, reason has come to recognize itself (to know itself) in the *absolute* otherness of the Absolute's own self-recognition/self-revelation. In Science, therefore, *Erkennen* becomes *Wissen*, a category of knowledge akin to wisdom, in the form of *Wissenschaft* (Science). The *process* of knowing (*Erkennen*) as mutual recognition is what Hegel recounts in the *Phenomenology*, where the narratives of reason are rounded out by the stories of revelation that are recounted in religion.

Worldly actuality can only posit the unity of freedom and necessity as a *summum bonum* and constantly strive toward it without ever attaining it. What is missing is the subjective agency of the Idea/God. The binary division we find in the *Science of Logic*, between Objective and Subjective Logics, clearly establishes the distinction between the human and the divine, a distinction necessary in order for their reconciliation to take place in philosophical Science. For Hegel, the state university is the reincarnated beautiful individuality where human reason (the Faculties of Law and Medicine) and divine Revelation (the Faculty of Theology) are truly reconciled in a universal singularity (the Faculty of Philosophy). It is an existing state institution where human knowledge is freely carried out along with the realisation that "what is to be known," the revealed content of knowledge, is necessarily much more than human.

Many of today's jaded professors, together with business people, journalists, politicians, disenchanted students, and their parents, would certainly find such a promotion of the public (state) university bewildering, perhaps especially in the United States where private universities thrive. It is indeed difficult for us, today, to imagine the ontological status that the founders of the University of Berlin, all philosophers (Fichte, Humbolt, Schleiermacher and, later, Hegel), invested in that pioneering state institution, and how its mission necessarily involved coming to terms with the *Aufklärung*'s fundamental conflict between faith and knowledge, exemplified in the *Pantheismusstreit* between Jacobi and Mendelssohn, and which Kant had already unsuccessfully attempted to resolve at the university level in his essay on the "Conflict of the Faculties." Of course, as a state institution, the university is de facto political, and *actual* to the extent that it is in the world. However, I believe it is fair to say that, for Hegel, the actuality of the state university is truly, "[the actuality] of the Idea itself and not [the] ordinary actuality of what is simply present" (EL 142 Add., where Hegel refers to Aristotle).

The difficulty that we have in recognizing the absolute ontological status of the state university perhaps lies, once again, with us. Because we no longer ascribe agency to the Idea (to God, to the Absolute), we remain stuck at the "end of chapter 6," caught up in the endless endings of human actuality, where the university project is nothing special and certainly not the unique realization of logos, the discursive reality where both revelation and reason find themselves to be at home (*bei sich*).

Have we responded to the qualms referred to at the beginning of this chapter, regarding the religious dimension of Hegel's thought? Perhaps, it might be objected that in seeking to recognize it, I have, in fact, denied it, transforming it into metaphysics. Indeed, if Science allows us to understand revelation as the agency of the Absolute or the self-consciousness of the Idea, do we really need religion? May we not now jump straight to the *Phenomenology*'s final chapter, on Absolute Knowing, the very move that I have been arguing against through my discussion of revelation and the forms of absolute Spirit? Of course, while such an omission has always been possible, I hope to have shown, in this early chapter, that it would be deeply unfaithful to Hegel's thought. To know the truth of the Absolute is to recognize its agency and this is only possible if we not only recognize *that* the Absolute exists but *how* it has given itself to be known in the artistic and then religious forms of revelation.[37] This knowledge takes place in those increasingly human forms of the sacred, celebrated in communal forms of religious worship and, finally, in the university study of philosophy. It is in these absolute forms of worldly reality that the truth as self-knowledge is carried out, in the form of a wisdom that makes knowledge itself possible.

2

Absolute Selfhood and the Otherness of Nature

On one level, this second chapter deals with an important question in Hegel studies: Within the holistic articulation of his system (aka *Wissenschaft* [Science]), how do the *Logics* relate to the *Philosophy of Nature*?[1] While non-Hegelians may find this problem to be of rarified interest, its examination engages a fundamental metaphysical, epistemological, and generally philosophical question: Just how "other" is nature in relation to our thinking of it? On one hand, if nature stands against thought in absolute difference, then we could neither know it nor recognize ourselves in it. Nature would, thus, become a matter of indifference both to our knowledge and to our ethical acting in and upon it. Conversely, if we deny natural otherness and difference, then new epistemological and ethical challenges arise: How can we know the universe as something distinct from ourselves? Why should we care to know something if it is does not represent an *object* for our thought? Crucially, denying the otherness of nature sinks us into natural determinacy and heteronomy, removes the spacing necessary for our consciousness, and the possibility of ethical action. The Hegelian answer to the dilemma is typically conciliatory. In nature, thought encounters something that is both strange and recognizable, alien and yet inviting and knowable. Above all, nature presents itself to us as the meaningful theatre for the possibility of free thinking and acting. As we will see, this is only possible because nature has been "let go" by the Idea/God, as fully determined Being.

Hegel's *Logics* tell the story of how Being is progressively determined by thought, to a point where, as fully determined, it appears to us as worldly nature, open to the possibilities of human agency. Through thinking determination, abstract, indifferent Being is liberated from its absolute otherness, becoming what we know as nature, invested with incipient, inchoate freedom, which is the grounding condition required for thought to be able to recognize itself in nature. The structures of the logical determinations invested into Being in order that it may become *nature* are essentially grammatical. As well, understanding the *Logics* as the progressive determination of Being into nature means taking Hegel's notoriously abstract logic as "first philosophy," that is, as general or ontological metaphysics.[2]

Commentators of the *Logics* can be roughly divided into those who take the works' metaphysical dimensions seriously and those who try to avoid them. Both are faced with difficulties. On one hand, metaphysical readers of the *Logics*, like Charles Taylor, are faced with variations of the problem addressed in this chapter: how the apparently abstract forms of thought that Hegel presents may relate to reality without implying that the entire cosmos operates according to a pre-ordained dialectical program, an idea that, as Taylor himself writes, "may sound mad … to most philosophers."[3] On the other hand, non-metaphysical readers of the *Logics* tend to read them as divorced from any onto-theological considerations, that is, as works of what we generally understand as "logic": self-referential demonstrations of thought thinking itself, removed from any external foundations or presuppositions (Stephen Houlgate, John Burbidge, William Maker, Richard Dien Winfield and legions of others).[4] This approach appears justifiable when the *Encyclopaedia Logic* and the *Greater Logic* can be considered as expressing such idealist programs as, to use Hegel's own words, "the Idea in the abstract element of thinking."[5]

Of course, the non-metaphysical approaches encounter their own challenges. How can the process of thought that Hegel describes "begin" if it has nothing presupposed to think about? How can the veracity of the *Logics*' transitions be guaranteed without reference to anything else? More fundamentally, if we take seriously Hegel's systematic aspirations, what is the relation between the non-metaphysical reading of the *Logics* and the other *realphilosophische* elements of the system: Nature and worldly Spirit? The most popular response to these fundamental questions is to confine one's investigations to discrete elements within the *Logics* themselves.[6]

I would like to propose an onto-grammatical reading of Hegel's *Logics* that fully recognizes their metaphysical mission without engendering either the "madness" that Charles Taylor mentions above (the claim that reality runs along pre-set logical lines) or the contrary idea that the *Logics* have nothing to do with reality at all. Rather, Hegel's logical works tell us how thought determines Being and, in doing so, invests it with grammatical structures that *make sense.* Indeterminate Being is nugatory, silent. Fully determined, Being presents itself as intelligible, knowable and, most importantly, as scientifically pronounceable.[7] This is how the otherness of nature takes its philosophical place within Hegel's idealistic system of science.

The fundamental grammatical form of systematic philosophy, of Hegelian *Wissenschaft,* is the predicative proposition (*Satz*) called judgment (*Urteil*),[8] to use the logical terminology of the day. It is within this form that determinate Being arises. That is why the *Greater Logic* introduces *un*determined Being as initially *nothing,* in a written phrase that is *not* a proposition nor judgment, in a phrase that has no copula, no conjugated verb "to be" between grammatical subject and predicate: "Being, pure Being, without any further determination," Hegel begins. Such unpredicated Being, he then continues, can be "nothing more nor less than nothingness."[9] Being appears first as totally undetermined and therefore as nothing, since there is no copula that is there to determine its existence qua something; consequently, pure Being is not anything (for us) at all.[10]

The reliance on judgment as the privileged form of ontology is understandable and even necessary if we refer back to what I take as Hegel's fundamental intuition: the real agency of thought itself. Thought posits itself; it is essentially a *Setzen* (positing) into Being and consequently must first present itself as a *Satz* (proposition). This idea of the ontological self-positing proposition is certainly derived from Fichte's much debated and discussed fundamental principle of all science, *Ich bin Ich,* a paradigmatic form of judgment which Hegel's early friend Hölderlin, in his crucial text "*Urteil und Sein,*" helps Hegel understand as the original sharing out of identity into difference.[11] As I will show, it is through the interplay between identity and difference that Hegel sees meaningful Being, as grounded nature, arise within the judgment's copula.

In the *Logics,* Being comes to be determined as something significant through the copula, the verb "to be," which relates subject to predicate in the logical form of the determinant, predicative judgment. Such existing determination is fully expressed in neither the subject nor the predicate but rather in the "is" of the copula, telling us that what is determined has some degree of concrete, existing *Being.* The destiny of the judgment form is the "fulfilment" of the copula and the passage to a more concrete form of linguistic determination, realized in Hegel's conception of the syllogism. This is why, in EL 180, at the end of the chapter on judgment, we find the move to the syllogism expressed as the *Erfüllung* of the copula, a term that can be translated as either fulfilment (the choice of Harris, Geraets, and Suchting) or as actual filling.[12] In fact, the ambiguity of *Erfüllung* allows it to refer both to the fulfillment or destiny of the copula and its actual filling, where the verb "to be" comes to really mean what it says through the realized determination of Being. With this filling, the judgment form actually moves beyond itself to its "truth," in Hegelian parlance, and becomes the syllogism, "the form of what is truly rational" (EL 181), what Hegel refers to as the realized Concept, which I will further explain below. It is in this sense that the judgment form *alone* "does not lend itself to expressing what is concrete" (EL 31 R).[13] In more conventional terms, we might say that Hegel's move from judgment to syllogism reminds us that systematic philosophy must involve predicative statements logically folded into the greater organic structure of argument that he calls the Concept (*Begriff*), a structure that retrospectively confers meaning on the constitutive predicative statements.[14]

The fact that in the copula we are dealing with *real* filling and not only purposive fulfilment is clear when we consider Hegel's use of the term "empty" to describe the unfulfilled (i.e., unfilled) copula in EL 180 and when we consider the corresponding moment in the GL, where Hegel describes the "*erfüllte*" copula as "*inhaltsvolle*," or contentful. The copula is consequently no longer "abstract," a synonym here for empty, formal, and devoid of differentiated existence, but now relatively concrete. What first appeared, in judgment, as an empty verb linking subject to predicate, now really *is*, as the existing, unifying movement between thought and Being, which is again what Hegel calls the Concept. Thus, "the Concept is the filling of the empty 'is' of the copula," as we find in EL 180.[15]

With the passage from the proposition's grammatical "is" to *is* as an actual positing (determining) of Being, we move from the logical to the ontological. In so doing, the Concept now anticipates its truest form, that of the syllogism, which is the ultimate form of "Subjective Logic," the last half of both the *Encyclopaedia* and *Greater Logics*, which I will return to below. For now, it is important to note this crucial aspect of the scientific (systematic) syllogism: the move from the logical to the ontological takes place because the filled copula becomes the moment of particularity, the existing and essential middle term between the universal (general) and the singular. It is here, in particularity, where things take on specific qualities and cease being either empty generalities or abstract singularities. For example, in order for someone really to *be* someone, they might take on such particular qualities as "transgendered," "Canadian," "father," "academic," "middle-aged," colonized, and so on. To really *be*, one must be more determined than either the generalized "all people" or the singular individual "John Doe." One must *be* within the particularized middle.

Whether the thinking, determining syllogism moves from the singular through the particular to the universal or in the other direction, the moment of particularity is an expression of "external reality," of essential existence (EL181), of things that have become what they are. Another way to put this is that the moment of particularity, in the Hegelian syllogism (aka the Concept), is where differentiation takes place within a systematic whole. As we will see, it is this feature of difference within whole identity that characterizes essentially meaningful existence, that is, Being that is knowable *for us.* In terms of Hegelian Science, which is what we are discussing here, it is only through its incorporation of particularity that the syllogism comes to embody "*everything* that is rational" (emphasis added, EL 181). Science cannot grasp, and has only a *passing* interest in, undetermined (un-thought) Being.

In the syllogism, the judgment form comes to realize itself as "the genuine particularity of the Concept" (EL 166). The question is, how does particularity actually come into the copula? How does the abstract verb "is" come to actually mean what it says and express knowable Being as its content? How does the logical actually become the ontological?[16] The answer is that it does so as ground (*Grund*), namely, as reason in the sense of "having sufficient reason" to be or what the French call *raison d'être.* As Hegel writes in the GL: In the syllogism, "[t]he determined and filled [or fulfilled] copula, which before was formed by the abstract *is* ... has subsequently been further constituted as the ground [*Grund*] in general, [and] is now present for us [*vorhanden*]."[17] To put this another way, we can say that particularity is an ontological determination where Being has been given *reason to be* and is thus presented as knowable to reason, – worthy of human knowing as outlined in Hegel's *Encyclopaedia of Philosophical Sciences.*

Consequently, to see how particular Being actually arises in the *Logics* (and how Being becomes knowable) through the filling of the copula, I find it helpful to look at the middle "Doctrine of Essence" section of the *Logics,* where Hegel examines determinate Being as having the grounds to be. As is the case (formally) in Aristotle, in Hegel the particular, middle term of the syllogism is where essence (quiddity, meaning) is introduced, precisely because it is in this context where things take on the specific determinations that cause them to actually *be* something, to exist. In Hegel, such scientifically meaningful existence arises (EL115–122) through the interplay of identity and difference, where things exist *because* they are both what they are and what they are not. This apparently abstract statement can perhaps be shown with the following example. It might initially appear that I am a male (my identity) simply because I am not a female (my difference). However, Hegel's dialectic of identity and difference seeks to demonstrate that my difference is also constitutive of who I am, that is, of my existing identity. My "not being a woman" actually means incorporating differentiating womanhood into my determinate existence. This is demonstrably the case, Hegel could argue: as an individual existence, my "reason to be" is grounded or has been brought about through the very real (copulative?) interplay between man and woman.[18]

It is through a discussion of ground (*Grund*) that we see how, for Hegel, that which goes beyond pure, undifferentiated identity has reason to be. Significantly, by considering ground as the determinant element of Being, we see how its discussion opens onto anthropological perspectives. What has reason or essential grounds *to be* shows itself to be knowable *for us* as reason-seeking human agents.[19] I believe this is what Hegel means by the variously translated term *Sache*: "issue," "matter," and the like, all terms relating to knowable existence as grounded, as having reason to be and, hence, as humanly meaningful.[20]

Knowable existence as grounded Being comes into the copula "is" through the interplay between identity and difference. It is therefore not surprising that Hegel's discussion of "Essence as Ground of Existence" (in the "Doctrine of Essence") refers to the predicative form of the proposition (*Satz*), the same form that we began with in the discussion of judgment and the copula. In the context of ground, however, what is now stressed is the copula's role in expressing both identity and difference, where "a proposition [*Satz*] promises a distinction between subject and predicate as well as identity" (EL 115).[21]

Briefly put, what Hegel demonstrates is that judgments of identity (A is A) implicitly involve difference, otherwise, we would simply state "A".[22] After that, we are shown how, conversely, judgments of *difference* actually involve a median identity, as expressed in the principle of non-identity's excluded third. In order to get difference, we must involve identity, which we do in excluding it. As Hegel puts this idea in EL119, "Even the mere plus and minus of a number (have) zero for their third term."[23] Finally, the dialectical interplay between identity and difference brings forth the determinate ground of existing Being – Being that is essential or knowable for us. Such grounds present themselves for us in the language of predication.

The truth of the matter is that identity is always self-*differencing* and difference is always *self*-differencing or the differencing of an identity. The identity of identity and difference, that is, the movement from identity to difference and "back" to identity, is the Hegelian Concept, the real, self-mediating identity of thought, through which Being presents itself *to us* as grounded or having reason to be and hence, as knowable nature. In the *Logics*, the "knowability" of nature involves the determinate forms of the transcendental (Kantian) categories but which have now been "deduced" or determined into *Being* itself. In other words, nature can now be known according to the (grammatical) categories of quality, quantity, modality, and relation, more or less the same categories that Aristotle had taken to be there *immediately* in nature itself.

Concretely, we understand that finite things, which, for Hegel, are the things of "nature," carry within themselves the contradiction of being both what they are and what they are not; they are both self-identical and self-differencing. This inner contradiction is what determines things as coming into existence, changing and finally ceasing to exist, as Heraclitus perceived. The inherent contradiction that determines the real, grounded existence of things also implies their relation to other things. Indeed, to exist is to *be* something, which means being *finitely* and hence being in the sway of other finite things that are something else; such engaging "elseness" is thus an essential part of what things *actually* are,[24] and, as such, opens them up to us as possible objects of knowledge. The essential finitude of things is what presents them to us as meaningful, gives our minds purchase in coming to know them, for example, through their causal relations to other things.

We could follow the trace of knowable Being through higher or more determinate levels of reality in the first "Objective" half of the *Logics*, beyond the being of finite, singular things, through the logical moments of *Erscheinung* (phenomenon)[25] and *Wirklichkeit* (actuality), but that is not necessary in order to demonstrate my point, which has been to show that Hegel's logic, as an expression of his metaphysics, does not dwell in abstract thought but is rather the science of the determinate grounding of Being. For us, as scientists, as knowing agents in the *Encyclopaedic* narrative, existing Being arises in the copula of the judgment form, and is further instantiated in the middle, particular moment of the syllogism, that is, in the *realized* structure of what Hegel calls the Concept. Judgments and syllogisms are thus the two fundamental elements of scientific grammar.

I have so far shown how determinate Being becomes the natural object of scientific reflection, through its grounding and its reason-to-be. However, surely our scientific interest in nature involves something more, something that Kant's Third Critique (of Judgment!) had postulated as purposiveness (*Zweckmässigkeit*), a coherent unicity of reasonableness where nature presents itself to us as a coherent whole, rather than as a bad infinity of random events and objects. It is this necessarily holistic aspect of nature that is presented in the final, "Subjective" half of the *Logics*. It is here that the agency of the Absolute reveals itself in nature.

Because "Subjective Logic" (aka the "Doctrine of the Concept") deals with the grammatical forms of thought (judgment and syllogism) as conceptually *ful-filled*, its perspective provides a necessary wholeness to the account of grounded Being, one that is essential to its determination as nature. Without this narrative rounding out – the syllogistic perfecting (*Vollkommen*) that is recounted in "Subjective Logic" – determinate Being can only arrive at the endless reiterations of finite actuality (*Wirklichkeit*), the level of Being found at the conclusion of the first ("Objective Logic") half of the *Logics*, and whose limits I discussed above, in chapter 1. Remaining at the level of actuality, our knowledge of *nature* would never be coherent because its coherency would never be presupposed and would thus endlessly escape the sole agency of our reasoning activity. In other words, in order to arrive at the full presentation of nature as determinate, knowable Being, the fulfilled copula must be comprehended within the *absolute* judgment (*Urteil*) operated by the Subjective side of the *Logics*.

Quite simply, nature must give itself to be known, must reveal itself as purposive or meaningful in order for human reason to make sense of it. The last half of the *Logics* is "subjective" because what was objectively determined Being now takes on a subjective, self-positing life of its own. The conjoined Truth of objective logic (i.e., the determination of nature through human reason) and subjective logic (i.e., the absolute agency through which nature is given) is expressed as the self-differentiating identity which Hegel refers to, at the end of the *Logics*, as the absolute Idea.[26] Referring back to the judgment form, we discover that the copula is fully determined to be *as nature* through the reciprocal action of subject and predicate, where what was natural, determined objectivity in the first half of the *Logics* has now taken on absolute subjective agency. It is the comprehensive perspective of the absolute Idea that confers on the copula its fully realized fulfillment of identity and difference, where its being has its own reason to be. While the "Subjective Logic" follows the "Objective Logic" in the GL's narrative, it should nonetheless be seen as presupposed, just as actuality will never, by itself, attain a wholeness that is not prefigured at the outset.

Within the systematic context provided by the "Subjective Logic" (of the Concept), the natural object of scientific knowledge appears enfolded in the middle moment of grounded particularity, which I associated above with the syllogistically fulfilled copula. Hence, the object of scientific thought that is invoked here is explicitly determined as intelligible in terms of the science of nature: mechanics, chemistry (physics), and organics. These general objects of scientific enquiry will reappear as the three main sections of Hegel's subsequent book in the *Encyclopaedic* narrative, the *Philosophy of Nature*. Within "Subjective Logic," the holistic, teleological determination of what Hegel calls "the Object" prefigures the ultimate scientific purpose (reason to be) of Being: the human participation in the thinking agency of the absolute Idea itself or, in more "secular" terms, the possibility of comprehending human science within the encompassing narrative of nature knowing itself.[27]

For my ontological-grammatical reading of Hegel's *Logics* to be philosophically believable, it must involve an elenchus, a point where the grammatically fulfilled and grounded determination of Being actually does present itself as nature, a point where the conceptual destiny of the syllogism's particular middle term reveals the truth of the copula, its realized essence or meaning. This is indeed what I take to be happening in the final moments of the *Logics*, where the fully accomplished, perfect (*vollkommen*) syllogism, qua the absolute Idea, lets itself out, freely releasing itself ("*sich frei aus sich zu entlassen*"),[28] and thus reveals itself to us *as nature* (EL 244).

At the end of the *Logics*, this action is described as flowing from a "*sich entschliessen*," which is generally translated as a resolving or "deciding" on the part of the Idea, a meaning that allowed Schelling to make fun of Hegel for entertaining such an absurd notion: the absolute Idea (God) reflectively and arbitrarily deciding to become nature. However, I believe that we have to see this "*sich entschliessen*" differently, that is, as a "disclosure," an opening up, or better still, a "de-syllogizing" (*schliessen* = to conclude, to close or to syllogize) where the fully determined, perfect syllogism (the Idea) reveals itself in its realized truth. Thus, at the end of the *Logics*, we might best translate the key passage in the following way: the Idea "de-syllogizes itself, freely releasing out of itself the moment of its particularity ... as *nature*" (EL 244). The moment of particularity is the moment of knowable Being, fully determined and revelatory in the form of (knowable) nature. It has every reason to be, and so ... is.[29]

The destiny of the copula, through its interplay of systematic identity and absolute difference, grounded in the particular middle term of the syllogism, is de-syllogised (disclosed) and revealed *for us*. Nature is that significant otherness that can be known and expressed through the grammatical structures of thought. Consequently, the *Logics* respond to our most fundamental epistemological questions: How is it possible that our thought may correspond to nature, that we may know nature, and that we may articulate it systematically? The answer: Because nature, as determinate Being, has been invested with the grammar of reason-to-be and purposive coherency; it is therefore scientifically meaningful.[30] As reasoning beings, we find nature intelligible and recognizable. Such recognition cannot leave us indifferent and detached but instead engages us in the endless striving of theoretical and ethical actuality. This reasoning agency is only possible because the object of our activity has revealed itself to be full of life and meaning.

Hegel's *Phenomenology of Spirit*, the work he describes as the "ladder" to the *Logics*, has shown us how knowledge of otherness always involves self-recognition in and through that Other, a mutually liberating experience where self-identity is mediated through difference. Similarly, knowing the otherness of nature means recognizing in it our own selfhood, our reason and finally, our freedom from natural heteronomy. Reciprocally, such knowledge implies conceiving nature as organically lively and thus freed from its objective determinateness, a move presented in the "Subjective Logic" and then carried out in the *Philosophy of Nature*. The concept of natural science as a reciprocally liberating self-recognition in otherness is made possible through the *Logics*' metaphysical grammar[31] and the idea that nature has something to reveal.

3
Comets, Moons, and the Voices of Nature

In the last chapter, we read how, according to the metaphysical narrative of "first philosophy," the progressive determination of Being, through the "Objective Logic" side of *Logics,* brings about a state of affairs where what was objectivity now takes on a subjective life of its own. The section on "Mechanism, Chemism, and Organism," in the subjective "Logic of the Concept." anticipates and grounds the outcome of the *Logics* in the subsequent book of the *Encyclopaedic* system: the *Philosophy of Nature* [EN followed by the *Encyclopaedia* section number]. The question in the present chapter is how something as *physical* as nature can prove open to a meta-physical reading. How is the ideal agency of thought phenomenologically observable in nature itself? In order to explore this question, I will examine Hegel's presentation of the solar system, in his *Philosophy of Nature.*

The dialectical interplay between the earth, the sun, comets, and moons is pivotal to how that enigmatic work should be read, representing a helpful heuristic device that Hegel offers us in order that we may come to grips with the natural side of his philosophy. As he pronounced to his own students: "We shall pursue the solar, planetary, lunar, and cometary [*kometarisch*] natures through all further stages of Nature," whose philosophy is "nothing but the progressive transformation of these four [moments]" (EN 270 Add.). Readers of Hegel might find surprising his reference here to four dialectical moments rather than to the more familiar Trinitarian model that he is usually associated with. Similarly, the inclusion of comets in a standard presentation of the solar system may strike us as odd. In fact, it is such cometary "oddness" that is significant. Examining comets as they appear in the *Philosophy of Nature,* I want to show how they represent the dialectical energy whereby the free agency of the Absolute reveals itself in nature. It is this agency that allows nature to present itself meaningfully for us (*für uns*), allowing our reason to recognize itself in nature's ambiguous otherness.

As we have seen in the first two chapters, I have promoted the notion of absolute, revelatory agency in Hegel's philosophical Science. In chapter 2, we saw how nature arises from the reciprocal agencies of human thought (reason) determining Being as its predicated object, and that object, as the holistic cosmos, taking on subjective agency and "speaking back" to human thought, which can then be seen as its predicate. Science is the speculative reality, taking place in the fulfilled copula of the grand syllogism, wherein the onto-grammatical subject *is* substance; and substance *is* subject. This speculative sentence (*Satz*), as Hegel refers to it in the preface to the *Phenomenology of Spirit*, implies that nature, as fully determinate Being, speaks to us, reveals itself to us.[1] Hegel's topography of the solar system allows us to see how this is meant to happen: how nature is *for us*, that is, how we (as thinking, sense-making beings) may find it meaningful.

Within today's frighteningly chaotic universe of the Big Bang, exponential expansion, black holes, and exploding stars, our solar system still strikes us as reassuringly stable. It is generally seen as comprised of three types of celestial bodies: planets (including earth), moons, and the sun, all locked into thoroughly legislated orbital movements. Against this orderly system, comets, when they do present themselves, appear as celestial intruders, blazing in from somewhere *outside*. Although comets may orbit the sun, their paths are so elliptical that their appearance often remains unpredictable, almost miraculous. New ones suddenly come to light; old ones sometimes disappear, perhaps, but never with certainty, forever. The scientific inclusion of comets in the orbital necessity of the solar system therefore seems to require justification, something Hegel himself acknowledged to his students: "It might seem strange to want to fit comets into this system, but what exists must necessarily be embraced by the Concept" (EN 270 Add.).[2] The question of how such an idiosyncratic astronomical feature is incorporated into the logic of the Concept is what interests me here. As we will see, in the *Philosophy of Nature*, the cometary event is grasped in terms of the evanescent, somewhat ghostly dialectical moment of the for-another, which occurs within the better known Hegelian waltz-step of the in-itself, the for-itself, and the in-and-for-itself. Examining Hegel's comets consequently sheds light on the revelatory action of the for-another (for-us), through the fluidifying action that thought carries out on the recalcitrant "lunar" oppositions inherent in the better known moment of for-itself, its partner in particularity within the Concept's realized, syllogistic form.

Associating the cometary moment with the dialectical expression of the for-another fundamentally determines how the *Philosophy of Nature* should be read, not only because it allows us to concentrate on an often ignored feature of the Concept (the for-another) but, above all, because, as I will show, the dynamic encounter of for-another with the for-itself is what allows essence, the truth of what things mean, to first shine forth or manifest themselves. To the extent that we may understand such essential shining-forth as the presentation of meaning, we might further surmise that, within the context of Hegel's *Philosophy of Nature,* it is when the extraordinary (cometary) confronts and confounds the predictable (lunar) that nature reveals itself *to us* and indeed *for us*. Further still, if we take natural meaning or essence as flowing from the predicative agency of the absolute subject qua substance, then it is in cometary events that we may bear witness to nature's verb.

Using the *Philosophy of Nature* as a way to gain access to the dialectical content of the *Logics* may seem a topsy-turvy way to proceed. Indeed, it is often the *Logics* that provide us with the hermeneutical tools used to explore the "petrified intelligence" of nature.[3] Although lately Hegel's *Philosophy of Nature* has undergone a positive re-evaluation, its "science" still often strikes us as strange or unlikely, and thus hardly deserving of providing a key to the logical realm of thought thinking itself. In fact, one might argue that the entire history of Western philosophy is based on the idea that it is thought that explains nature and not the contrary.

Whether or not the sometimes puzzling figurations in Hegel's *Philosophy of Nature* strike us today as scientifically likely does not matter to my argument, nor does the fundamental question regarding the ontological "otherness of nature" within the system.[4] If we take Hegel's systematic project at its word and recognize the *Philosophy of Nature* as an integral part of that system, then there is no reason why we cannot begin and even remain in its figurations, particularly if our goal is to examine a feature of dialectical movement itself. This is because, in its philosophy, nature is presented to us neither immediately nor empirically but rather as Being already *having been* thought.[5] Since thought is dialectical, as we discover in the *Logics,* so must be its articulations within the *Philosophy of Nature.* Nonetheless, in their natural settings, the dialectical articulations maintain something of their bright, colourful hues, rather than appearing in the tones of "grey on grey" that we witness in the figures of spirit. Thus, rather than simply being phenomena that are only brought to light in order to be explained, the figures of nature may actually do the explaining; like pre-Socratic *archai,* they are natural elements that also act as fundamental principles.

In the lengthy "Addition" to *Encyclopaedia* section 270, Hegel provides a reading of the solar system that is based on the dialectical architecture of the syllogism, which, as he writes in the *Encyclopaedia Logic,* is generally understood as "the form of what is rational" (EN 181). However, far from constituting a purely formal entity, the Hegelian syllogism is meant to actually embody "posited [i.e., determined] reality." In its fully carried out expression, it is consequently "*everything* that is rational" and "the essential ground of everything true" (EN 181). As is the case with the classic form of logic, which Hegel disparages as formal, the speculative syllogism nonetheless incorporates three terms: the universal, the particular, and the singular. Although in Hegel the syllogism may move from singular cases to generalized universality, the predominant form of systematic thought moves from a universal moment to one of reconciling Singularity (the one that is all). In that case, it is the middle *particular* term that provides the "external reality," the existence and, in the limited sense that we discovered in chapter 1, the "actuality" (EN 181) of the whole.[6] In more familiar dialectical terms, the universal moment corresponds to the Hegelian Concept as immediately *in-itself*; the particular moment is usually presented as the externalized, mediating *for-itself*, and the moment towards which the whole Concept tends is the *in-and-for-itself*, where thought, having experienced otherness, is reconciled, we might say, in a singular, concluding narrative.[7] Thus, the syllogism "is nothing but the posited ... real Concept" (EN 181 R). Hegel's presentation of comets and moons shows how particularity, within the syllogistic whole,[8] actually involves two separate sub-moments and how these are complicit in the presentation of essence.

In the *Philosophy of Nature*, the sun is presented as the in-itself or the first, universal moment of the solar system. The sun is its own centre of gravity and rotates around itself. The earth, on the other hand, is the syllogistically reconciled in-and-for-itself of the solar system; it is the totalized or universal singular that expresses systemic oneness. This does not imply actual geo-centrism. It means that as an actual and rational *system*, the solar system "comes home" (is *bei sich*) *for us*. It is meaningful for us as earth-bound scientists. Significantly, however, Hegel remarks that if there were only the sun and the earth, they would only exist in abstract difference, making it *in*different which one is seen to revolve around the other (EN 270 Add.). In order for the solar system to exist as such, to *be* a system and not just an abstraction, there must be *particular* bodies between the universal (sun) and singular (earth). The particular bodies are moons and comets. Syllogistically, the actual existence of the solar system qua system depends on the real differentiation of content that particularity introduces into the relative indifference between the universal and the singular.[9]

Moons and comets exist in the particularity of dynamic difference and opposition. Their particular natures destine them to be "dependent bodies." As opposed to the free individual celestial bodies of earth (planets) and sun, Hegel's moons and comets do not have their centres of gravity in themselves. This means that rather than rotating on their own axes (as do the sun and the earth) comets and moons revolve around other bodies – around planets (for moons) and around the sun (for comets).[10] The *Philosophy of Nature*'s presentation of the solar system shows us that the two elements within the mediating moment of particularity, the lunar and the cometary, are not mutually indifferent. Rather, their Hegelian celestial embodiment shows them to be essentially "Bodies of Opposition," as they are presented several paragraphs later, in EN 279.

Hegel presents the lunar element as falling under the logical category of the for-itself; conversely, the opposing cometary aspect falls under the category of the for-another. Thus, by further examining the characteristics of the two particular bodies and understanding how the cometary element is negatively opposed to the lunar, we can see how one logical category is related to the other. The conceptual significance of the solar system and its oppositional moments of particularity are reinforced in the EN 270 Add. where, as I quoted above, Hegel affirms that the *Philosophy of Nature* in its entirety is "nothing but the progressive transformation of […] the solar, planetary, lunar, and cometary (*kometarisch*) natures through all the further stages of Nature." My exploration of the two inter-related moments of particularity, the for-itself and the for-another, through their lunar and cometary natures, is thus of determining significance to reading the *Philosophy of Nature.* Further, the logical underpinning of the astronomical articulation means that the planetary characteristics may be extended beyond nature and into the domains of reasoning human endeavour that Hegel refers to as *Geist.* However, for now, let us remain in the realm of astronomy.

The Hegelian moon, as a "material being-for-itself," is characterized by its rigidity, its dryness, and its hard, crystalline nature, inflexible and recalcitrant to change. Hence, it has neither atmosphere nor transformative meteorological activity on its surface. In EN 279 Add., Hegel elaborates: As a waterless crystal, the moon expresses a self-relating identity that remains "shut up within" itself in its rigid for-itselfness or selfishness. To put this another way, we might say that as being-for-itself, the moon is defined in purely exclusive terms, that is, as simply not being anything else. It represents pure hardened difference devoid of any process, which always implies otherness or self-othering. As a hard individuality, lunar reality is grounded in the exclusivity of the geometrical point, the constituting element of the crystal and generally of all that is brittle and dry. The moon's opacity and darkness are expressed in the fact that its "other" face is always turned away.[11]

The comet, contrarily, is pure "otherness [*Anderssein*]," a "body of dissolution" that is the "opposite to the body of rigidity" (EN 279 R). Comets are gaseous, luminous, and fluid, devoid of any real centre. They give off light, whereas the moon simply reflects. Comets are fleeting, evanescent, and transparent, existing in elliptical and ultimately unpredictable movement. Their elliptical orbits reflect the dynamic opposition of attraction and repulsion (to the sun and the other stars). Comets exist "in a sphere of aberration or the effort to get away" (EN 270 Add.); their existence is a "whirl," where they are "always on the point of dispersing and scattering themselves to infinity or into the void of space." While the moon is "rigidly controlled" by the earth, comets express an "intended freedom." They revolve around the sun, which is fitting, given their own luminous nature, and yet, in spite of their solar thralldom, they "push out into the future." Notwithstanding such eccentricity, however, the comet "remains a necessary moment of the whole" and thus, its insipient freedom or, we might say, its oppositional negativity remains expressed within the conceptual and real solar system.[12]

The solar system therefore involves the in-itself (the sun), the for-itself (moons) and the in-and-for-itself (the earth). The syllogistic integrity of the system means that the different figures within it are comprehended in the final earthly figure, a reconciliation of difference that would not be possible without the fleeting, dissolving moment of cometary particularity and its fluidifying overcoming of the dry recalcitrance, the hard, fixated opposition and opacity of the lunar for-itself. Briefly, it is the *kometarisch* moment that ensures the lively, holistic movement that Hegel refers to as the Concept.

The spontaneous luminosity of the comet can also be understood, in the terms of Hegel's logic of essence, as an *Erscheinen*, a phenomenal shining forth that is for-another essentially. Indeed, whereas the lunar moment expresses opaque, inner reflection and purely recalcitrant difference (in-difference),[13] the comet manifests the dynamic nature of opposition, the fact that any abstract opposition is, in reality, the matter for further reflection outward, beyond lunar self-reflection. Whereas the moon's reflective glow is merely an illusory *Schein* and not the manifestation of its essential side, which remains dark and hidden, the comet expresses the dynamic nature of opposition, a reflection upon inner reflection that brings about the shining forth of essence, a phenomenal *Erscheinen* that actually *is* for-another.[14] Indeed, the comet is the bright, outwardly manifest reflection of the essential interplay of difference between the various entities of the solar system, what would otherwise express hard identities based on exclusive differences, as expressed by the dry opacity of the moon. The relation between cometary action and the logical moment of the for-another is made clearer in the following examples also drawn from the *Philosophy of Nature.*

In direct relation to the dialectic at play in the essential shining forth of light, the for-another is also instrumental in the production of colour, which arises, according to Hegel, through the interplay between light and darkness. The production of colour is best observed within the hard, brittle surfaces of the crystal, Hegel's interpretation of what Newton saw with his prism. Just as in geometry (and mechanics), where the line is reproduced ad infinitum to form a surface, the magnetic "line" that is drawn between north and south poles is further determined or reproduced to form the constituent planes of the crystal. To put it another way, the bi-polar opposition of the magnet is expressed in the hard surfaces of the crystal (EN 315 Add) where we may recognize the angular fixity of the lunar surface discussed above.

The punctual nature of the crystal, its status as a brittle body of geometrical points, lines, and surfaces, betrays its dry, static for-itself nature, just as, reciprocally, the moon was described above as "crystalline." Similarly, the crystal first appears as the expression of immediate, self-related difference. Each individual crystal is distinct simply because it is exclusively "not another." While no two crystals are identical, their difference is purely formal, like that of geometric points or numerical digits, an abstract difference that ultimately collapses into indifference. In all such cases, what is missing is any real qualitative, particularized distinction.

However, if we look and reflect again, as Hegel invites us to do, upon the apparently indifferent medium of the crystal, we witness something new and deeper: the inner reflection between the bright and dark facets within. In fact, what we witness here, in the contradictory interplay between these contrasting elements, is the truth of the hard difference (indifference) that first appeared (as *Schein*) in the crystal for-itself but which can now be seen to radiate out (*Erscheinen*) as colour. The dissolution of hard, crystalline difference through further reflection has brought about the essential, phenomenal shining forth of the dynamic opposition between light and dark, now as colourful light. The flash of colour that we observe in the crystal is the manifestation of its fleeting, evanescent cometary moment, an expression of painterly chiaroscuro shining forth for-another, for us.[15]

The conceptual nature of these moments means that we may discover other expressions of the dissolvent for-another by searching within articulations of particularity throughout the *Philosophy of Nature.* Such moments always involve the dynamic reflection of difference, and usually precede recapitulating, unifying moments of relative concreteness or speculative truth in-and-for-itself. In all these cases, we observe the operation of negativity as the negation of a self-externality (a purely exclusive self-identity: something is what it is because it is *not* something else), and the dissolution of the recalcitrant for-itself, of its hard difference (indifference), through the contradictory reflection for-another. While in the above instances the cometary aspect of the for-another is expressed as light, this can obviously not always be the case throughout the entire *Philosophy of Nature.* The last case that I will discuss presents the for-another phenomenon of cometary action in terms of sound.

In the "Physics of Particular Individuality" (EN 290–303), Hegel introduces specific gravity as the uniform inner essence of individual material bodies, which immediately differentiates bodies through their particular inner cohesiveness. A body has the specific gravity that it does because its inner cohesiveness is specific to it and not to other bodies. Consequently, specific gravity first appears as typically for-itself, as a particular form of inner hardness that is recalcitrant to otherness, allowing a body to constitute its individuality by not being anything else. However, upon further reflection, we realize that inner cohesiveness is actually only measured or determined (thought of) in its relation to outer pressure or violence. Cohesiveness is, in fact, only meaningful to the extent that a material body's inner hardness makes itself "for-another" by submitting to pressure while at the same time maintaining its own integrity. In this way, we see how the truth of cohesiveness is not hardness but elasticity, the measured ability to "bounce back," thereby reflecting an oscillatory movement that is both inner and outer.

The relation to otherness, the phenomenal shining forth of essence, is expressed here in the elasticity of the cohesive body, not as light but rather as sound stemming from the vibrations brought about through receiving and reacting to otherness, as an oscillation between inner and outer that is reflected externally.[16] Such oscillation is the negation of the recalcitrant immediate difference set up as the self-centred specific gravities of individual objects. The being-for-another, the outward dimension of inner elasticity, of objects' essential cohesiveness, is manifest as sound. In Hegel's evocative terms, sound is the "freedom of the object from heavy matter that at the same time is in heavy matter." It is the "plaint of the ideal in the midst of violence," voiced by an object that is subjected to violence. Here, "the ideal" should be taken as that which is distinct from purely material reality; it may thus be associated with Hegelian notions of selfhood and the expressed freedom of thought (*das Denken*). Sound, we might say, is the manifestation of that object's inchoate "subjectivity," its essence or its truth *for us* (Enc. 300Z). We will explore the ideal dimension of sound later, in our discussion of music and meaning, in chapter 12.

Sound reflects outwardly the inner essence of a body in a way that is akin to light and colour, and to the nature of the comet. Sound, like the comet's movement, is oscillatory and free while remaining determined by material otherness, just as a musical instrument produces sound because it is strummed, struck, or bowed, and colour is tied to the crystalline opposition between light and dark. Again, like the comet and like colour, sound can only tend toward freedom while remaining in the sway of the material. In the same way that the comet's light partakes of the sun's ideality without actually being it, colour and sound are only "the plaint" of the ideal embodied in matter.

Here are some conclusions that we may draw from our brief review of the *particular* figures within the *Philosophy of Nature.*

1) There are not one but rather two moments of particularity within the Hegelian syllogism (the realized Concept): the for-itself and the for-another; together they mediate between moments of universality (in-itself) and singularity (in-and-for-itself). Hegelian dialectic, therefore, involves four, rather than three distinct moments.[17]
2) The for-another's fluidification of the hard, exclusive nature of the for-itself is an essential feature of dialectical movement, presupposed by the systematic in-and-for-itself, the reconciled identity of identity and difference. Putting the system into movement, the *kometarisch* may be seen as the *life* of the system.
3) Hegel explicitly remarks that the solar, terrestrial, lunar, and cometary moments occur throughout the *Philosophy of Nature,* determining its progress. The interplay between the cometary and lunar elements of particularity should therefore be seen as fundamental to our reading of that work.
4) Further, since these astronomical elements are inscribed in the logical moments of the for-itself and the for-another, we may fruitfully seek the interplay between the lunar and the cometary throughout the Hegelian system, not only in the *Logics* themselves but in the sciences of *Geist* (Spirit's *Phenomenology* and its *Philosophy*).
5) The action of the for-another is related to the shining forth of essence; that is, the things of nature are only really what they are to the extent that they are not merely for-themselves but meaningful for-another. If we take nature as the absolute substance having become subject (*natura naturans*), then it reveals itself to us through cometary agency.

Indeed, following this last point, if we take Hegel's *Philosophy of Nature* as indeed philosophical, and therefore as having something significant to say about our own relation to nature itself, then the cometary aspect can be seen as the element through which natural otherness becomes meaningful for us.[18] Hegel's comets express the living movement of the substantial cosmos, where it strains against mechanical, orbital obedience. Within crystallized reality, the play of light on dark and luminous surfaces dissolves into the vibrant chiaroscuro of colour. The string tightly wound between two fixed poles responds to the violinist's bow, drawing forth musical notes. If the cometary event calls out to us, it is because in it we hear the plaint of nature's incipient, never absolute, always "intended" freedom. Thus, in knowing nature, we may recognize ourselves.[19]

To the extent that nature (substance) reveals itself to us as essential, that its finite manifestations occur to us as *Erscheinungen*, as meaningful phenomena, which Hegel presents as expressions of inchoate subjectivity, we can recognize the voice of the Absolute in nature itself, as an act of revelation. Of course, as we have seen in the first two chapters, the Absolute's act of revelation is concomitant with the human agency of reason, conceived, in Hegelian terms, as self-knowledge through worldly otherness. In the realm of nature or, more precisely, the realm of natural science, the Absolute reveals itself to us through our scientific reflection. Briefly, when we take nature as the object of our reflective thought, it *reveals* itself to us. There is nothing obvious about this fact, although we commonly assume it to be so. Indeed, why should nature reveal anything to us at all? Why should our thinking reflection assume that it can get to the heart of natural things? Hegel's account of the cometary for-another acknowledges the miraculous aspect of "givenness" through the process of *Nachdenken* that I described above with regard to crystals and specific gravity: when we are attentive, when we look again (reflect), we literally see the light and hear the voice of nature, but only to the extent that nature speaks (back) to us. Only then may we recognize ourselves (our freedom) in its verb.

The repeated references that Hegel makes to comets as expressing or tending towards freedom, within what would otherwise be a clockwork cosmos of mechanistic, lunar determinacy, make it clear that the essence, meaning, or truth that we seek to know in nature is really the expression of freedom, and that our *self*-recognition in natural otherness only takes place because we hear and recognize our own free selfhood in it. Cometary insurgency awakens us to the miraculous freedom shining forth from within nature's weighty material presence, shaking us from our dogmatic complacency. After all, philosophy begins, and ends, in wonder.

Reciprocally, within the systematic narrative of Hegelian *Wissenschaft*, as I have been presenting it, absolute agency qua revelation should also be acknowledged as an activity of absolute *self*-revelation. Accepting the subjective agency of nature, of hearing its voices and witnessing its colours implies that we must also accept its self-consciousness. Indeed, if the essence of Hegelian subjectivity is to seek self-knowledge in otherness through the act of judgment (*Urteil*), then how could we deny such activity to a subjectivity that is absolute? I will return to this cosmological consideration in chapter 11, on the revelatory dimensions of Big Bang theory.

PART TWO

The Temporalities of Reason and Revelation

4
History and the Absolute Now

There is a persistent and profound question that surfaces when we consider absolute agency in terms of revelation, according to the reading of Hegelian Science (system) that I am putting forward. If the Absolute is really *absolute*, then why should its revelation take place over time? In other terms, why would such revelation not be ever-present, eternal, and eternally "now"? If we conceive of the Absolute as Hegel appears to do at the end of the *Encyclopaedia*, in explicitly Aristotelian terms, as a divine, motionless self-contemplation or self-revelation, then why would such a maximal Being bother to make itself historical, measuring itself out in the coffee spoons of earthly, human time, instead of instantaneously taking place in an eternal present or presence?

In fact, through our earlier chapters, we already anticipate the Hegelian answer to these questions: Because Science conceives of absolute revelation as concomitant with human reason, it *must* make itself historical. Simply put, that is how human reason operates: over time, historically, and, we may add, pedagogically. Just as Lessing had conceived the human narrative in terms of an education, unfolding historically over time, Hegel's idea of human self-knowing must progress gradually, incrementally building on acquired knowledge. To investigate the relation between eternity and history, I will look at Karl Löwith's crucial misreading of Hegelian temporality, in his magistral *Von Hegel bis Nietzsche*.[1]

Perhaps we might begin by wondering why Löwith, in his important book, addresses the German idealist first and foremost through a discussion of the notion of time. Indeed, in Hegel, whose philosophy is fundamental to the entire progression of Löwith's book, temporality per se does not constitute a privileged subject matter that is dealt with in a sustained and explicit fashion. The question "why time?" is all the more concerning since Löwith, in order to enter into the matter, refers to three fragmentary and marginal texts, on the outskirts of Hegel's main body of work.

Of course, a thinker like Hegel, who dares philosophize on such a broad range of subjects and who develops systematic philosophies of nature, spirit, and *history*, in its political, aesthetic, religious and indeed philosophical forms, must of course address temporal themes. Further, a nineteenth-century thinker dealing with the fundamental questions of free subjectivity in its multiple relations to substantial objectivity, and who practises philosophy following the Copernican temporal revolution brought about by Kant, should invite us to reflect on the objective engagements of a subjectivity whose essential form must, from that point on, prove temporal. Thus, for Hegel, time articulates itself through forms of consciousness, of temporally informed subjectivity instantiating itself, and thus its time, in the world. The worldly reality of Hegelian time allows Löwith's early mentor, Heidegger, to judge that, in Hegel, time only has meaning in that it passes, in the shadow of figures of worldly, and ultimately vulgar presence that form the historical configurations of *Geist*.

Löwith does refer to Heidegger's analysis of Hegelian time. Indeed, even though the former does not share his teacher's insistence on the *possible*, on the futurity of existential time, he nonetheless shares with Heidegger the conviction that Hegel's conception of time is fundamentally common and erroneous.[2] So, the question remains: Why does Löwith concentrate on Hegelian time when his very notion of temporality is judged to be lacking and deeply problematic? In this chapter, I will explore the fundamental temporal contradiction that Löwith attributes to Hegel's thought, in a way that brings to light the relation between historical, human time and the eternal "Now" that absolute revelation seems to imply. It is the supposed contradiction between these two temporal expressions that informs Löwith's entire project, as carried out in *Von Hegel zu Nietzsche*, and which, according to him, brings about the tragic failure of German philosophical thought in the nineteenth century.

In his analysis of time in Hegel, presented in a few short pages of a quasi-Hegelian density, Löwith begins with the claim that the German idealist is above all inspired by Aristotle, for whom the "Now" expresses the punctual moment that is both instantaneous and eternally present, a Greek vision inspired by the "circling constellations of the heavens and the real ether."[3] Briefly, according to Löwith, Aristotelian time, determining Hegelian temporality, should be comprehended as the instantiation of the contemplative and immobile activity of god.

It is this Greek notion of time as a Truth that is ever-present in the "Now," which brings about "a contradiction, an enigma" when it is placed in relation to the temporal idea, equally found in Hegel, of an "emancipation of Spirit resulting from the advent of Christianity." Consequently, according to Löwith, the Hegelian idea of time as an "eternal present" will always be pulled between "the historical instant" of Christ's actual, worldly birth and the immobile eternity of the First (and final) Cause. In other words, time as the eternal "Now" enters into conflict with the fundamentally historical structure of the Christianity-inspired narrative, according to which the Truth unveils itself in a progressive and salutary movement toward the different forms of the Hegelian Absolute. The Hegelian successors that Löwith discusses, principally Feuerbach, Stirner, Marx, Kierkegaard, Ruge, and Bruno Bauer, should then be seen to incarnate more or less radical expressions of this same contradiction, between two apparently opposed notions of time. On Löwith's reading, these thinkers are consequently condemned to a fundamentally futile self-contradiction, cashed out in the aporia of Nietzschean philosophy.

The fully actual stakes involved in the path leading from the Young Hegelians to Nietzsche implies, according to Löwith, that their failure is ultimately that of the Western world itself, whose Christian history and culture has always been in contradiction with its essentially Greek foundation. Thus, Nietzsche represents and indeed embodies the aporetic character of the Western project itself. As Löwith writes in his chapter titled "Nietzsche, Philosopher of Our Age and Eternity," "The question is whether, beyond Nietzsche, there is any practicable path at all."[4]

To support his fundamental notion of Hegelian time as an eternal present, a notion central to the argument of his book, Löwith refers to a passage from the Jena *Logic*, the unpublished sketch of what will later become the mature works that are the *Science of Logic* and its *Encyclopaedic* cousin, aka the *Greater* and *Lesser Logics*.[5] As well, Löwith refers to EN 259 Add. (W9: 55) and finally, to a sentence fragment that is supposed to be found in the preface to the *Principles of the Philosophy of Right* but which I have not been able to locate. Curiously, the well-known passage from the same preface, and which Löwith does not cite, is precisely the one where the true sense of Hegelian time is to be found, there where philosophy "paints its grey on grey," at dusk, when the famous owl of Minerva takes flight (W7: 28). For, as I will show in this chapter, the flight of Hegelian scientific wisdom implies a historical movement toward an actually present moment where the eternal Truth has indeed come to light, albeit in the form of Science (systematic *Wissenschaft*).

Although the "entelechial" sense of Hegelian philosophy is essential to Löwith's argument and even forms the title of a chapter in the book *From Hegel to Nietzsche*, the historical movement that Löwith finds in Hegel is one that can only culminate in a fundamentally mundane inevitability, that is, in the "present" merely conceived as the current bourgeois, Christian *actuality*. The problem, according to Löwith, is that such an actuality can never attain to the eternal "Now" that is nonetheless imagined by Hegel and which is prefigured by the temporality of Greek cosmology. Briefly, Löwith's argument is based on an apparent contradiction that he finds, in Hegel, between his notions of time and history.

Besides the distinctly marginal nature of the texts presented by Löwith in support of his "eternal" notion of time in Hegel, the fact that he refers to the most nontemporal dimension of the Hegelian system, that is, to his logic, is already problematic. Indeed, within the economy of the Hegelian system, the mature *Logics* are always presented downstream from historico-introductive articulations, the best known of which is the *Phenomenology of Spirit.* Here, in this emblematic ladder-like work, historical time comes to be explicitly expiated, finished off toward the end of the book, in the "Absolute Knowing" chapter, in an eruption of pure nontemporal thought, which will ground the entire *Encyclopaedic* endeavour that follows and which begins, in fact, with its own *Logic.*[6] Time only reappears, and initially in an entirely abstract and indeterminate manner, at the beginning of the *Philosophy of Nature*, the second book of the *Encyclopaedia.* In that systematic articulation of Hegelian Science, time that is fully determinate and meaningful does not return until the last book, namely in the *Philosophy of Spirit.* It is in this ultimate context that the spiritually *human* expressions are actualized in an appropriately historical form, that is, articulated in the retrospective narratives of the development of individuals, states, art, religion, and philosophy itself. In other words, discussions of temporality in Hegel must involve us in a reflection on the human aspects of what he refers to as Spirit, either in its *Phenomenology* or in its *Philosophy*, the *final* book of the *Encyclopaedia of Philosophical Sciences*, the first of which is the nontemporal *Logic.*

In distinguishing worldly historicity from temporal essence, as Löwith does when he presents Hegelian temporality in the mode of the eternal "Now," the latter must be divorced from any historical character. Briefly, the (eternal) Truth is cut off from its own story. Further, the comprehension of Hegelian time essentially according to its "Logical," that is, nontemporal expression, leads Löwith to affirm a contradictory break between the temporal dimension per se and the idea of a historico-political progress, which was so dear to the Young Hegelian legacy. This tendentious reading, which separates the historical dimension from the Truth, leads Löwith to ignore what is perhaps the best known and most determinant pronouncement that Hegel makes on time, which I referred to briefly above, namely where, in the last pages of the *Phenomenology*'s chapter on "Absolute Knowing," time is defined as "the Concept that is there ," that is, as the activity of thought (the Concept) that exists in the historical movement of Spirit (W3: 584, 591).[7] Significantly, this reference is found immediately prior to the prelogical culmination of historical time in the ecstatic instant that Hegel describes poetically with the famous image, borrowed from Schiller, of the overflowing chalice (W3: 591). Here, in the last moment of the *Phenomenology*, thought has finally freed itself from its *past* forms (errors). It is now free to make itself *Logic*, the first moment of *Encyclopaedic* Science, the systematic setting where the culmination of human historical time (in art, religion, and philosophy) is now presented, in the "Absolute Spirit" chapter, as fully revelatory of the Absolute's complicit self-knowing.

In the recognition of absolute agency, in Absolute Sprit, time does appear as an eternal self-reflection, and Hegel does acknowledge Aristotle's unmoved mover in the lengthy quote from the *Metaphysics* with which the *Encyclopaedia* ends. Such an outcome shows that it is indeed the historical destiny of the *Phenomenological* Concept that leads us to grasp the eternal "Now" for what it truly is, namely the retrospective comprehension that is instantaneously recapitulative of its own past course, now necessary and "rational," according to the implicit sense of the *Logic*, where human reason partakes in and of absolute revelation. It is this implicit sense that is rediscovered, fully demonstrated in the culminating singularity of the Idea (cf. Aristotle's god), at the end of the *Encyclopaedia*'s "Absolute Spirit" section.

To the extent that the eternal "Now" is first expressed in the nontemporal context of Hegelian *Logic*, it should nonetheless be apprehended as the culminating result of the *Phenomenological* path that pours itself out in a moment of recapitulative achievement. Such a moment, far from being empty and abstract, thus carries within itself the remembrance, or indeed the *spirits* of past human experience. In other words, the eternal Hegelian moment, embodied in the *Logics* and recaptured at the end of Absolute Spirit, is neither conjugated in the past nor in the present but rather in the grammatical time of the *Perfekt*, where the content of the present is expressed through the auxiliary verb "to have," which affirms the whole past experience as *having been* acquired and thus possessed by and constitutive of the present.[8] In Hegelian terms, the comprehension of the Truth of the eternal "Now" is therefore an *Erinnerung*, an internalized remembrance of its past historical course. It is this experiential content, told through the epic journey of the Concept, that guarantees the tenor of the terminal, recapitulative "Now," which is now anything but empty. Contrarily, the vacuity of the purely punctual and abstract "now" can be found at the departure points of Hegel's great works, in initial positions that are always stamped with natural immediacy. This is the case, for example, in the *Phenomenology*, in the chapter on Sense-certainty, where we learn that any attempt to conceive the immediate singularity of sense experience according to its punctual sensuous reality dissolves into the indifferent "now" of empty universality. The same is the case in the *Encyclopaedia*'s *Philosophy of Subjective Spirit* (section 448 Add.) where Hegel describes the pure mental apprehension of time (and space) as providing only "extremely impoverished, superficial determinations." In other words, the immediate and momentary feeling of the present "now" has no other tenor than the vanishing vacuity of immediately sensuous experience.[9]

Time's association with the movement of the Concept grasped retrospectively as the *Erinnerung* of its past course clearly shows that Hegelian history must not be understood as a dialectically predetermined progression towards a future that is "to come." Such a model would, indeed, espouse the logic of the Christian narrative, according to which history is said to either end in the Germanic, bourgeois, Protestant state or (and this is Löwith's view) tragically, in the infinite and ever-failed approximation of its absolute purpose, where, taking the last sentence of Löwith's book, "the Christian pilgrimage" is a perpetually "homeless land where it has never been at home."[10]

On the other hand, the logic of the Concept in its temporal unfolding shows that Hegelian history leads to a "Now" understood as a self-knowing (*gnothi seauton*) where the selfhood of humanity (what Hegel calls Spirit) recognizes itself in the history of its own course, apprehended as essentially *past*. It is precisely this self-recognition in the world as *having become* that Hegel calls "Reason" in the historical context. Consequently, when Hegel, in the *Phenomenology of Spirit*, defines reason as "the certainty that consciousness has of being all reality" (W3: 179), then that reality should there be conceived as historical, that is, as a phenomenon articulated according to the time of the *Perfekt* grammatical tense. The famous formulas according to which Hegelian history is supposed to be, above all, an affair of reason should not be understood in the sense where the movement of history is predetermined by an implicit dialectical rationality but rather according to the idea where human consciousness is brought to the certainty of being able to recognize itself in its own past. It is precisely this aspect of self-recognition in historical otherness that will pose a problem for the Young Hegelians discussed by Löwith (Feuerbach, Ruge, Stirner, Marx, Kierkegaard, and Bauer). In refusing to recognize themselves in Hegelian history, they also refuse, by that very fact, the *reason* in that history and the tenor of the present world which is its essential result.

Such a humanistic reading of Hegelian historical temporality, where the "Now" appears as the recapitulative moment of a human experiential epic, already encourages us to see the punctual moment that Löwith attributes to Hegelian temporality as something other than an instantaneous grasp of emptiness. Nonetheless, we might well wonder how such a rich tenor, developed over the course of human historicity, can espouse the eternal aspect that Löwith discovers in the Greco-Hegelian "Now." The answer to this question, whose apparent insolubility leads Löwith to observe a fundamental contradiction (between the historical and the eternal, between the Christian and Greek temporal narratives), can be found in the "absolute" qualification that Hegel attributes to the completion of the human epic of self-knowing, and which I have been presenting in the previous chapters.

Indeed, in Hegel, at the level of Spirit, that is, of humanity as a world-historical phenomenon, self-knowledge as the retrospective grasp of Spirit's own past course is realized in a moment of ecstasy that invites us to interpret this journey in light of something that stretches infinitely beyond us, but yet in which we do participate. If the expression "absolute knowing," the title of the *Phenomenology*'s final chapter, remains ambiguous enough to lend itself to a whole palette of interpretations, sometimes contradictory, the one that I want to, above all, put aside, and which makes Hegel into a Feuerbach before his time, is the reading where the qualifier "absolute" is applied solely to the historical activity of humanity, understood simply as a species. Contrarily, the "absolute" dimension, as I have demonstrated in the previous chapters, implies the recognition that human self-knowing partakes in and of the movement of self-contemplation that is essential to the life of the Absolute itself, the movement evoked, as I explained above, in the long quote from Aristotle's *Metaphysics*, which closes the *Encyclopaedia of Philosophical Sciences.*

It is indeed in this ultimate context, at the end of the *Encyclopaedia* chapter on "Absolute Spirit," that both the human and divine activity are qualified (by both Hegel and Aristotle) as "eternal." In other words, our self-knowledge, at the level of Absolute Spirit, is conjugated with divine self-revelation. As Hegel expresses it in his *Lectures on Religion,* which we will look closer at in chapter 8, humanity is the historical actor in the self-conscious activity of God or the *Idea,* to use the speculative or Neoplatonic term favoured by Hegel. Returning to the *Phenomenology of Spirit,* we thus see why the chapter on religion replays the *history* of Spirit but from the point of view of divine revelatory agency and immediately precedes the last chapter on "Absolute Knowing," where the self-knowing activities of the human and the divine are harmonized in a beautiful, eternal unity between reason and faith. This ultimate reconciliation was the highest object of the main currents of German post-*Aufklärung* thought, an outcome which Lessing, Kant, and Schiller had already postulated. Within this absolute unity, conceived by Hegel's philosophy, the relation between history and the historically informed eternal "Now" (understood as Revelation), proves itself to be entirely complementary and hence noncontradictory.

For Hegel, Absolute Knowing, as I just presented it – as the conjugation of human and divine agencies of self-knowing – should not be comprehended as a kind of golden fleece that the reader of the *Phenomenology of Spirit* should strive to grasp and which would only present itself in the last station of the long and twisted trail the book recounts. For according to the logic of the Concept, which espouses a circular or spiral epistemology, the realized result must already be found there, at the departure point but only in an immediate or intuited form. Put differently, the absolute "Now" that appears at the end of *Phenomenology*, depicted in the image of the foaming chalice, must already be there at the outset but as an empty moment, namely as an instantaneous intuition of the Singular universal, of the *hen kai pan* (the One and the All) that the Hegelian narrative tasks itself to fulfill. Such a preliminary, as yet totally indeterminate and thus ambiguous intuition is indeed to be found first in the preface of the *Phenomenology*, where the famous expression of the "night where all cows are black" (W3: 22), evokes Schelling's notion of intellectual intuition, and then, as I mentioned earlier, in the chapter on Sense-certainty, where the punctual and instantaneous "now" of sensible intuition dissolves into the experience of an unfulfilled *universality* without content.

In order to fully comprehend the critical (in both the momentous and polemical sense of the term) character of the *Phenomenology of Spirit*, it is necessary to grasp the fact that intellectual intuition, whose universal immediacy so strongly interpellated Hegel's speculative thought, constitutes a massive datum of scientific actuality at the beginning of the Germanic nineteenth century, a fact equally evidenced in the philosophical reflections of his friends Schelling and Hölderlin (also present in the intuitional forms of knowledge in Jacobi, Schleiermacher, and Novalis). The demands of the time, felt by Hegel and to which he so thoroughly and systematically responds, consist in *carrying out* the intellectual intuition of the eternal "Now" and finding in it the tenor that will save it from a purely sensuous and empty fate. It is this rich tenor that Hegel subsequently develops according to the three syllogistic moments of the Concept: the Universal, the Particular, and the Singular (the Whole) of the system of Science articulated in the *Encyclopaedia of Philosophical Sciences*, the system actualized and practiced in the university teaching of that work. However, before taking on such an *Encyclopaedic* performance, the task that Hegel gives himself is to *demonstrate* that the intellectual intuition which is acknowledged in the German philosophical scene around 1800, in spite of its Kantian proscription, already carries within itself all the richness of its own *Phenomenological* history, that is to say, the content of human self-knowing in complicity with divine Revelation. Consequently, in Hegel, the systematic complicity between the *Phenomenology of Spirit* and the *Encyclopaedia* guarantees that the two temporal dimensions, namely the eternal "Now" and history, become manifest as actually and objectively united.

The temporal reconciliation operated by Hegelian thought implies two fundamental conditions, and it is precisely these conditions that are problematic for the post-Hegelian philosophers presented by Löwith: first, the sense of historical movement must be apprehended in an essentially retrospective fashion; second, this movement toward Absolute Knowing must be comprehended in terms of a self-revelation that is both human and divine. The Young Hegelian legacy very clearly refuses both the idea of a divine complicity involved in human self-revelation and the essentially retrospective view of historical time; for such a past-directed view must necessarily result in the idea of a present that is fully informed with an absolute character and thus standing against any temporal logic directed toward fulfillment in the future.

Both of these aspects of refusal are clearly presented in the chapter of Löwith's book entitled "The Reversal of the Hegelian Philosophy by the Young Hegelians," where the author discusses their legacy in three moments: Feuerbach and Ruge; Bauer and Stirner; Marx and Kierkegaard. These three moments form an oppositional progression that ends, with the last pair, in the critical destruction of the "bourgeois-Christian world,"[11] that is to say, their own contemporary world. Each of these rebellious successors proves to be "hungry for the future [...], out of step with the world as it is [...], with the wild idea that their first job is to set right a world that has gone off the rails."[12] However, condemned as they are to adopt forms of dialectical historical progression devoid of any "absolute" culmination, and whose anticipated culmination and purpose must therefore espouse the vague forms of an endlessly *future* golden age, the Young Hegelian current of thought is condemned to finish tragically, as Löwith very clearly observes, in the post-human vision of Nietzsche. Consequently, the post-Hegelian failure can be comprehended in terms of a contradiction between historical and eternal notions of temporality but only on the condition that we are aware of how the disciples knowingly refuse the reconciliation proposed by the master.

In his analysis of Hegelian thought, Löwith appears fully aware of the recapitulative character involved in the idealist's take on history, as is clear from the chapter on "The Eschatological Meaning of Hegel's Consummation of the History of the World and the Spirit," where one reads: "The history of the Concept [*des Begriffs*] comes to an end with

Hegel; in recollection, he understands all history … as the fulfillment of ages."[13] However, it is also clear that, because it is the result of a unilaterally human progress, the spiritual presence that is manifest in such a recapitulation can never meet the demands of an eternal Aristotelian "Now," to which it must endlessly strive. The "enigma" that Löwith encounters in Hegelian temporality is thus the result of an unhappy contradiction between the Greek notion of time and the entelechical character of the Christian narrative. Indeed, "the ultimate basis of Hegel's eschatological system lies in his absolute evaluation of Christianity."[14] Löwith's error, to call it such, lies is the failure to understand that Hegel's project was precisely to overcome and reconcile the opposition between these two temporal notions, in the idea of a "Now" that is both eternally absolute and worldly human or historical. In Hegel, this absolute reconciliation is presented (and made present), following the *Phenomenological* apprenticeship, in his *Encyclopaedia of Philosophical Sciences.* This work represents the actual realization of the original intuition of the eternal "Now," expressed at the time as an intellectual intuition but now deploying itself syllogistically out of the first universal moment, that is, the *Logic.*

To the extent that the *Encyclopaedia*'s vocation was thoroughly pedagogical (academic), it is helpful to recognize the performative actuality of the Hegelian system within the state university, taken as a place where a self-knowing that is both human and divine comes to recognize itself in and through its history. More precisely, as a teaching manual, which systematically incorporates a philosophical reflection on every aspect of university-level knowledge, the *Encyclopaedia*'s vocation was to form a discourse whose true presence would be embodied in the recently founded (1810) University of Berlin.[15] It is not by accident that Hegel perceived in the three main faculties (theology, medicine, law) the reflection of the three books of his systematic philosophical teaching manual, namely the *Logic*, the *Philosophy of Nature* and the *Philosophy of Spirit.*[16] Judged according to such a perspective, the different academic failures or rejections experienced by the Young Hegelians, which are discussed by Löwith, become completely coherent with their refusal to recognize the reconciliation of the two apparently opposed notions of time as actualized in the Hegelian university project, a fact obscured in Löwith, who tends to reduce the academic failures of the Young Hegelians to their personal lack of the intellectual capacities necessary to solve the temporal enigma that was already present in Hegel himself.

The failure of the Young Hegelians is, thus, attributed to the philosophical weaknesses that Löwith finds in Feuerbach, Ruge, Bauer, and Stirner (less in Kierkegaard and Marx). Indeed, "their writings are manifestos, programs, and theses, but never anything whole, important in itself. In their hands, their scientific demonstrations became sensational proclamations ... leaving an impression of insipidity."[17] Consequently, lacking the resources to resolve the temporal challenge apparently posed in Hegel, these largely journalistic or *pamphlétaires* thinkers found themselves caught in an insoluble dilemma that they inherited, and which they dealt with by simply abandoning one of the temporal alternatives, namely the notion of the eternal "Now," while conserving the idea of a salutary historicity, one which must necessarily prove aporetic. Löwith does not seem to realize that it is above all the refusal of any Hegelian complicity between the two temporal notions that condemns his successors to failure. For by unilaterally suppressing the absolute dimension of time as an eternal present, the essentially dialectical and progressive project of the Young Hegelians no longer has an endpoint. Briefly, without the moment of the recapitulative "Now," their narratives, like their century, are condemned to iterate stories that have neither meaning nor end.

Hegelian philosophy is essentially informed by and informative of the modern state university; the same is true of its author. Indeed, almost everything we read today under Hegel's name was conceived and written either as a teaching manual or in the form of course notes, his own assembled together with those of his students' notebooks. Moreover, given the epistolary reports that Hegel drafted for the government officials responsible for public education, and his own administrative work in the recently founded University of Berlin, it is apparent that he was solidly involved in the development of university-level pedagogical policy at the national level.[18] The absolute character of Hegel's philosophy – its systematic dimension – cannot possibly remain purely ideal and abstract. It must concretely form and perform the scientific *word* (*logos*) of the university institution, conceived as the *present* space where the past course of self-knowing, both human and divine, has been actualized.

Nonetheless, it would be inaccurate to claim that the Hegelian university is exclusively retrospective, entirely fixed on the great past works of human history. As with Hegelian Science itself, the university is constantly hungry for new content, depending upon the positive (empirical) sciences for new material upon which to reflect.[19] However, it is equally true that in its academic embodiment, Hegelian philosophy always comes after. Its vocation is to reflect again on the acquired products of human spirit; in this way, philosophy does paint its "grey on grey" (W7: 28). That is why, according to Hegel, philosophy takes flight only at the fall of day, in end times, even in those of decadence, where the colours are less vibrant, when the period has lost the lustre of youth too immersed in the immediacy of life. Briefly, it is only when the intoxication of youth gives onto the sober reflections of maturity that philosophy does its work.

According to Hegel, the state university enjoys an ontological status that is informed by the absolute quality of the philosophical system that animates it, conferring upon it its actual meaning. Consequently, distinguishing Hegel from his "Young" successors in terms of time cannot but be reflected in their opposed ways of conceiving the university itself: either along the lines of Hegelian reason, that is, as a present state institution where the Absolute's self-knowing deploys and reveals itself through the knowledge that students may acquire of their past, or, if those students are unable to recognize themselves either in their present time or in the history leading to it, as an outmoded, bourgeois institution. Indeed, in the latter case, the university then only represents a pointless institution of the past, one that transmits knowledge that is no longer meaningful, and worse still, one that advances and supports everything that is false and flawed in the present. Löwith sums up perfectly the Young Hegelian distain for academic philosophy when he writes that for them, "philosophers no longer comprise a separate class; they are what they are in perfectly ordinary relationship to the state: civil-servant teachers of philosophy."[20]

So Löwith may be right in remarking that the terminal nature of Hegelian philosophy is drawn on the faded background of the crumbling Holy German Empire. Indeed, his philosophy ends with the world in which it came into being. Thus, again borrowing from the Hegelian palette, the philosophical poverty of his rebellious successors can be explained in light of the too harsh colours of the new European world – liberal, nationalist, imperialist, Bismarckian – that is, in light of the youthful character of that time and its revolutionary demands. The epoch is simply too busy living and feeling, too full of the future to give itself over, in its search for meaning, to the calm retrospective reflection implied by the university community and its worshipful adherents. It is precisely this hope in youth that Nietzsche argues for in his *Untimely Considerations*, but only on condition that the future generations be formed outside the university institution, which Nietzsche himself had forsaken in favour of atemporal philosophical wanderings.

5
Knowledge of God and the Perils of Insight

In the preceding chapters, I have distinguished the agency of human consciousness and knowing, qua spirit, from that of the Absolute (aka the Idea, God). In doing so, I have associated the former with reason and the latter with revelation, elements that were very much in play and at odds with each other during the late German Enlightenment, a conflict that represented a fundamental challenge for Hegel's conciliatory conceptual thinking. In the last chapter, we saw how reason, as human striving for absolute truth, engages a temporality that is fundamentally historical, where truth is unveiled pedagogically over time as it passes through progressive stages. Revelation, on the other hand, tends to speak in the instant, in the eternal "Now." Hegelian Science brings the two dimensions together in the *Perfekt* tense where the massive truth of the present moment is fulfilled by the content of what has been.

However, in recognizing the ahistorical aspect of the eternal "Now," and taking it as an expression of absolute agency whereby the Idea gives itself to be *known*, then we should be able to recognize a form of actual human knowing that is correspondingly immediate and punctual, one which is distinct from the historical narrative of reason. Such a form of immediate knowing is how Hegel characterizes faith (*Glauben*), that is, as an immediate, massive, and human intuition of the revealed Truth. The Hegelian challenge is that the immediate intuition of faith, experienced in the revelatory "Now" of the Absolute, must be demonstrated as infinitely more fulfilling and fulfilled than the empty "now" of the sensuous intuition that we witness in the Sense-certainty chapter of the *Phenomenology*. The immediate intuition that characterizes religious faith demands the differentiated content that only human reason, in its historical unfolding, can supply. In other words, the immediacy of intellectual intuition must be mediated by what first appears as its other: the human story of knowledge. In this chapter, I will show how the revelatory intuition of the Absolute, as presented in the form of religious faith, comes to overcome its immediacy through its self-recognition in the otherness of reason. Conversely, of course, pure reason, divorced from intuitive wholeness, will discover its own form of immediacy and the reciprocal requirement for it to seek mediation through an Other. Consequently, each form of knowing is required to mediate itself through its other, only then bringing about the holistic form of systematic Science and overcoming the unbearable late-Enlightenment opposition between faith and knowing. The crucial opposition between the two approaches to the Truth takes on different figures in the "Culture" section of the "Spirit" chapter (6) of the *Phenomenology of Spirit*, which I will examine through Hegel's use there of the term "*Einsicht* " (insight).

Among the different binary oppositions presented in that section of the *Phenomenology*, I have always found the subchapter on "Faith and Pure Insight" (W3: 391/M 527)[1] particularly intriguing. While the story that it appears to tell, of the conflict between religious faith and reason, is hardly out of place in the *Lumières* context where it is found, framed by references to Diderot and the French Revolution, Hegel's use of the term *Einsicht* ("insight") itself has always struck me as peculiar. Why does Hegel choose the term here to describe Enlightenment reason? Why not simply use "reason" (*Vernunft*), a term that certainly fits in with the surrounding references to Deism, Encyclopaedism, French utilitarianism, Jacobinism, and so on, and which Hegel does, in fact, refer to occasionally in the subchapter that I am discussing?[2] Why does Hegel favour the term *Einsicht* here, I wondered. What is so specific about this form of mental activity that it finds its way into chapter 6 of the *Phenomenology* and nowhere else, in the same sustained manner, in the entire oeuvre? Indeed, the index to the Suhrkamp *Werke in 20 Bänden* only lists one other occurrence of the term (*Register* 139), in the *Lectures on the Philosophy of Religion*, which I will visit below.

Perhaps, one might suppose, Hegel uses the term in order to describe a specific type of subjective mental activity appropriate to the form of individual human consciousness that arises in the "Culture" chapter. In that case, *Einsicht* could have a precise psychological meaning, definable against the historical backdrop where it appears in the *Phenomenology*. If indeed *Einsicht* were such a feature, then we might possibly find some reference to the term in the "Psychology" section of Hegel's *Philosophy of Subjective Spirit*, in his *Encyclopaedia of Philosophical Sciences*. This is not the case. "Insight" is not presented among the psychological elements of mind (*Geist*) examined in *Subjective Spirit*: we find intelligence, intuition, imagination, *Phantasie*, thinking (*das Denken*), memory, feeling, but no *Einsicht*. With neither a clear psychological definition nor a convincing historical-cultural reference, we are left with the question, why *Einsicht*?

Investigating the provenance of *Einsicht* in the Enlightenment setting where it appears helps better define the specific meaning that Hegel attaches to it in chapter 6 of the *Phenomenology*. Historically contextualizing the term in this way might thus contribute to a clearer understanding of how the "Faith and Pure Insight" section is to be read. My investigations have led me to conclude that Hegel derives his use of *Einsicht* from its use in the German Enlightenment and specifically from its appearance within the *Aufklärung*'s famous *Pantheismusstreit* (Pantheism Quarrel) between Moses Mendelssohn and Friedrich Jacobi, as well as in Kant's article "What Does It Mean to Orient Oneself in Thought." The present chapter supports this conclusion, thus comprehending "insight" in a way that is pertinent to the fundamental metaphysical issue that I am dealing with: questions surrounding the knowledge of the Absolute.

In order to make my argument clear for the reader, I have laid it out in the following steps. First, I will show that the other, rare technical occurrences of *Einsicht* (outside the *Phenomenology*) take place in a religious context, where the knowledge of God is at stake; I will then show how this religious/epistemological issue forms the substance of the epochal *Pantheismusstreit* between Mendelssohn and Jacobi, which Hegel certainly had in mind in the "Insight" chapter. Subsequently, I will discuss how Kant, in a well-known essay of the time, assigns the term *Einsicht* to the foundational intuition underlying Mendelssohn's metaphysical reasoning, in a way that anticipates the rational faith postulated by his own (i.e., Kant's) moral philosophy. This will then lead me to examine the use of *Einsicht* in Jacobi, in his surprisingly celebratory reference to Spinoza's idea of the intellectual love of God, thereby stretching his own (i.e., Jacobi's) definition of faith to mean a foundational metaphysical intuition. These investigations will allow me to show how grasping *Einsicht* as a foundational intuition, in both Mendelssohn and Jacobi, enables Hegel to understand it as a form of immediate knowing common to each of the apparently opposed Enlightenment authors and thus common to both faith and reason. Finally, reference to the *Vorbegriff* (Preconception) of Hegel's *Encyclopaedia Logic* allows us to comprehend how the forms of immediate knowing found in both reason and revelation stand in need of the reciprocal mediation afforded by (Hegelian) Science.

Searching for other significant references to *Einsicht* within the Hegelian oeuvre, besides what is found in the *Phenomenology*, we discover a preliminary instance in the *Lectures on Religion*. Revealingly, the religious context of this first extra-*Phenomenological* reference is consistent with Hegel's statement at the beginning of the "Faith and Pure Insight" section (W3: 392/M 528): "Religion – for it is obviously religion that we are talking about ..." However, significantly, what the reference to *Einsicht* within the *Lectures on the Philosophy of Religion* also shows is that the issue that it is associated with is not predominantly one of reason's liberation from dogmatic, positive religion, as we generally find in the *philosophes* of the French Enlightenment, but rather, the conflicting claims between reason and faith as rival means of knowing God. In the *Lectures on the Philosophy of Religion*, the religious stakes involved with *Einsicht* are clearly those of the *Pantheismusstreit* between Mendelssohn and Jacobi, and their opposing views regarding the absolute pretensions of traditional, pre-Kantian (pre-critical) metaphysics (Mendelssohn's position) in proving God's existence, versus the knowledge claims of religious faith (Jacobi). In polemical terms, Jacobi qualified all metaphysical reasoning as reducible to Spinozism and thus reducible to deterministic, materialistic nihilism, while Mendelssohn implied that Jacobi's reliance on faith was an expression of unreason and thus a nascent form of religious fanaticism (*Schwärmerei*).

In comprehending the Pantheism Quarrel as taking place between two forms of *knowing*, as Hegel points out when he recognizes, in "Faith and Pure Insight," that the activity of thought is a "cardinal factor in the nature of faith, which is usually overlooked" (M 529), we see how the religious issue, where *Einsicht* is evoked in the *Lectures on the Philosophy of Religion*, is fundamentally epistemological. The debate is not first and foremost between *atheistic* reason and religious faith, but rather between the rival approaches of thought in its quest to *know* God as the Truth. It is the shared, absolute object of each approach (pre-critical metaphysics and faith) that makes their rivalry all the more devastating, for religion but also for the ethical and political vocation of philosophy qua systematic Science.

The religious dimension of the term *Einsicht* in the *Phenomenology* is reinforced by its appearance in the *Lectures on the Philosophy of Religion* (LR 56), where the issue at stake is clearly the knowledge of God. In the *Lectures* text, "insight" represents metaphysical reasoning (Descartes, Leibniz, Spinoza, Wolff and, above all, Mendelssohn), as practised before Kant's critique of the synthetical limits of a priori reason came to be generally accepted. However, Hegel's point in the *Lectures on Religion* is not to reiterate Kant's criticism of metaphysics but rather to emphasize the dangers of relying exclusively on *faith* and the absolute agency of divine Revelation in a way that simply casts aside metaphysical reasoning. It is the very exclusivity of the faith-based position that carries the risk of falling into the excesses of religious feeling and fanaticism (*Schwärmerei*): "[I]n this divergent state of affairs, man casts aside the demands of insight and wants to return to naïve religious feeling," remarks Hegel.

Reference to the dilemma posed by the *Pantheismusstreit* throws into relief the danger of allowing the discord between faith and reason (as "insight") to persist, a danger further emphasized in the second reference to *Einsicht* that we find in the *Lectures on the Philosophy of Religion*: "If discord arises between insight and religion, it must be removed by cognition or it will lead to despair and drive out reconciliation. This despair is the consequence of one-sided reconciliation. One rejects one side and holds fast to the other, but no true peace is obtained thereby" (LR 107–8 n. 69). Making the dilemma of the Pantheism Quarrel central to Hegel's presentation of the Enlightenment, in the *Phenomenology*, allows us to see what is, for him, first and foremost at stake in the (German) *Aufklärung*: man's knowing relation to the Absolute, which can only be realized when religious faith is truly reconciled with thinking reason. Only such a reconciliation can save humanity from "despair." The mission of systematic (Hegelian) *Wissenschaft* (Science) is consequently to overcome the exclusive immediacy of the apparently opposed epistemological positions represented in faith and reason, and their knowing relation to the Absolute.[3]

Systematic Science's conciliatory mission is clearly outlined in the other significant occurrence of *Einsicht* in Hegel, which I mentioned above, namely in the "Immediate Knowing" section of the *Vorbegriff* (Preconception) to the *Encyclopaedia Logic*, roughly contemporaneous with the *Lectures on the Philosophy of Religion* (1820s). In the *Vorbegriff*, Hegel presents the dangers that epistemological unilaterality represent for Science and how such dangers cut two ways. The single-minded reliance on the "insight" of metaphysical reasoning is just as pernicious as the exclusivity of faith, not only to Science viewed as a holistic endeavour that acknowledges the reciprocity of human and absolute agency but to the world in which such knowing is meant to take place. I will return to this reference toward the end of the chapter and show how it reinforces an important lesson regarding the ethical and political reach of *Einsicht* in chapter 6 of the *Phenomenology*.

Since Hegel's use of the term *Einsicht*, in the *Phenomenology*, in the *Lectures on the Philosophy of Religion*, and in the *Vorbegriff*, does seem to make clear reference to the type of metaphysical reasoning championed by Mendelssohn over against Jacobi's appeal to faith, we might expect to find the term itself, as a term of art, in Mendelssohn's philosophical writings, particularly in the texts of his actual debate/correspondence with his philosophical adversary.[4] However, this is not the case. Mendelssohn himself does not use the term in any significant way. Where we do find the term associated with Mendelssohn's thought, however, is in an important commentary on the *Pantheismusstreit*: in Kant's short but well-known essay of the time, entitled "What Does It Mean to Orient Oneself in Thinking?" This is where I believe Hegel discovered the term *Einsicht* associated with the reasoning of classical metaphysics, as promoted by Mendelssohn. In other words, it is Kant's use of the term in his "Orienting" essay that allows us to place it in the context of the *Pantheismusstreit* and the late *Aufkärung*, and to understand its crucial role as a form of immediate knowing of the Absolute.

Kant wrote his short essay, which appeared in 1786 in the *Berlinische Monatschrift*, in response to those seeking his arbitration in the *Pantheismusstreit*, a quarrel which, one might say, he had already "resolved" in his first *Critique* (first edition, 1781) with its prefiguring of his conception of rational faith as articulated in his later *Postulatlehre*.[5] Given Kant's stature, but also given the apparently ambiguous compromise that his *Critique* presented between reason and faith, where each is fundamentally justified in moral science, it is not surprising that both Mendelssohn's and Jacobi's camps sought his partisanship in their adversarial struggle. If Jacobi himself expected Kant's position to support his own notion of rational faith (which conflated religious faith with the axiomatic positing of empirical reality), he must have been very disappointed. While Kant's essay does condemn Mendelssohn's overarching use of uncritical, "speculative" reasoning, Kant applauds Jacobi's adversary for his unreserved promotion of reason itself, particularly in the face of contemporary expressions of "fanaticism [*Schwärmerei*]," "genius," and ultimately, "superstition" [*Aberglaube*] ("What It Means To Orient Oneself in Thinking?" [OT]: 17/145),[6] all positions where Jacobi might well have felt himself (unjustly) targeted.[7] Above all, Kant's essay concludes with a poignant plea for reason as the guarantor of freedom of thought against impending (with the death of the Enlightenment emperor Frederick the Great) censorship, and against those (like Jacobi?) who would assail reason's universal human vocation.

Despite Kant's reservations regarding Mendelssohn's over-extension of reason's claims in the area of theoretical knowledge, Kant recognizes shades of his own idea of reason in Mendelssohn's promotion of the universality of sound common sense. Mendelssohn's error, according to Kant, was failing to understand that the fundamental universality of reason cannot be limited to the particular expressions of common sense but is rather to be found in reason's legislative vocation, which must orient it toward the *summum bonum*. In other words, the vocation of reason, for Kant, is ultimately practical (moral) and as such undergirds the possibility of human freedom that the Enlightenment promises.

The problem for Mendelssohn, according to Kant was, therefore, that he "misunderstood" his own idea about reason being oriented by sound common sense, or, as Kant calls it, by "sound human reason" (OT: 13/140). Thus, while Mendelssohn is correct in making reason the final arbiter in all judgments, through the guiding principle of "rational insight [*Einsicht*]" (OT: 13/141), he fails to recognize the moral vocation of such insight. On Kant's reading, Mendelssohn's guiding principle remains one of theoretical reason, which he mistakenly promotes in place of Kant's idea of rational faith, that is, self-legislating (universalizing) moral reason whose vocation lies beyond the theoretical realm. As Kant puts it: "By contrast, rational faith, which rests on a need of reason's use with a practical intent, could be called a postulate of reason – not as if it were an insight which did justice to all the logical demands for certainty ..." (OT: 14/141).

In spite of his criticism of Mendelssohn's metaphysical use of theoretical reason, Kant nonetheless cannot help but salute him for his uncompromising promotion of reason itself, even though this takes the abstract form of rational insight underlying common sense. On the other hand, the danger that Jacobi's faith, qua *Schwärmerei*, represents, according to Kant, is that even if it is directed solely against rational insight in its purely theoretical employment, it cannot help but bring harm to (moral) reason itself. This is because Jacobi does not recognize the Kantian notion of rational faith as expressed in his *Postulatlehre.* Further, Jacobi's position strikes Kant as particularly pernicious since reason is, in its self-legislative vocation, the quintessential expression of human freedom. Injury to reason is consequently an assault on self-legislation, heralding a state of "declared lawlessness in thinking" (OT: 17/145). Indeed, religious fanaticism is "another kind of faith where everyone can do for himself as he likes" (OT: 15/143). Such a state of anarchic lawlessness will necessarily bring down upon itself the heteronomy of political repression and censorship.

While it is not my aim here to explore all the possible links between Kant's OT and chapter 6 of the *Phenomenology*, it is remarkable that the Kant text anticipates Hegel's move from "Faith and Pure Insight" to "the Struggle of Enlightenment with Superstition," and then to the state of lawlessness and repression we see portrayed in the "Absolute Freedom and the Terror" section. Perhaps most remarkably, we might note that the transition, again in chapter 6, from the theoretical issues involved in the *Pantheismusstreit* (i.e., the question of the knowledge of God through reason or through faith) to the ethical concerns in the *Phenomenology*'s "Morality" section, replays Kant's argument about the ultimately moral orientation of Reason itself. My point is that Kant presents *Einsicht* as a kind of axiomatic intuition that is involved in both speculation and common sense (i.e., healthy human reason), which grounds Mendelssohn's promotion of pre-critical, theoretical reason over against the counterclaims of religious faith, as played out in the *Pantheismusstreit.*

As Allan Arkush notes, Kant in his OT essay probably derives his notion of a Mendelssohnian *Einsicht* (in common sense) from the "Allegorical Dream" section in chapter 10 of Mendelssohn's *Morning Hours.*[8] Indeed, a look at that chapter shows that "orientation" is the predominant theme of the Dream itself. Travellers in the Swiss Alps are given two (orienting) guides, one, a rustic simple youth who represents common sense, and the other, a fantastical female "with a deeply introspective look and a visionary physiognomy,"[9] including a wing-like fixture on the back of her head! In the dream, finding the way involves seeking "to orient myself" with reference to these two characters, either by common sense or by "speculation." Significantly, and what must surely have pushed Kant into Mendelssohn's camp, the dream's arbiter, and the true guide, appears in the form of an "elderly matron approaching [...] with measured steps," who identifies herself as "reason" and who shows the travellers how common sense should be used *together* with speculative insight when the latter leads the thinker astray. The allegory teaches us that insight (qua speculation or contemplation) is in fact the wiser of the two guides, but only when it allows "herself" to be nuanced by common sense. On the other hand, common sense on its own is often too stubborn and dull to yield when "she [insight] is in the right" (Mendelssohn, *Morning Hours* 59). Mendelssohn's allegory thus teaches us that a deeper sense of reason is the true guide when its insights are grounded in common sense. We might say that Mendelssohn's allegory shows reason as mediating between common sense and speculation, a claim Kant would certainly be comfortable with, if we take "common sense" for *Verstand* and "speculation" for the regulative function of ideas, although of course Mendelssohn's use of "reason" does not articulate the moral vocation that grounds Kant's idea of "orienting."[10]

If Hegel, in the "Faith and Pure Insight" section, indeed derives the term *Einsicht* from Kant's presentation of Mendelssohn's position over against Jacobian faith, then we may already note that insight is more than the type of pre-critical, metaphysical reasoning normally associated with the Enlightenment. In a way, we might say that what Kant takes away from Mendelssohn's allegorical dream is the trace of his own idea of reason, of a foundational orientation that is deeper than ratiocinating reasoning itself, an orienting which Kant refers to as *Einsicht.* In adopting the term, therefore, Hegel has already taken on its intuitional aspect, one which will thus prove related to the notion that it initially appeared opposed to: Jacobi's faith. For the dialectical lesson that Hegel presents in the *Phenomenology*'s chapter 6, and which is explicated in the EL's *Vorbegriff,* consists in showing how the opposition between faith and insight is an erroneous one to the extent that each pole can be shown to contain its other within itself. Each is thus open to reciprocal mediation. Failure to recognize this fact through the maintaining of each position as strictly opposed to the other (expressed in the next subchapter, "The Struggle of the Enlightenment with Superstition") brings about the unhappy state of affairs presented in "Absolute Freedom and the Terror." If Hegel is right about insight, that its intuitional aspect actually incorporates the supposedly opposed position of its other, then we might expect to find reference to the term in Jacobi's texts from the *Pantheismusstreit*.

In fact, Jacobi does use the term *Einsicht* in his *Pantheismusstreit* writings. Fittingly, he does so in a way that is itself highly ambiguous, through reference to Spinoza. Recall that Spinoza is ostensibly what the whole quarrel was about: whether Jacobi was correct in reporting the great Lessing's "death bed" conversion to Spinozism, and thus to pantheistic atheism, which was how Spinoza's philosophy was generally viewed at the time. Jacobi clearly shares this view, since he frankly states, in his "Concerning the Doctrine of Spinoza," that all metaphysical arguments, when coherently pushed to their conceptual limits, end up determining all of reality as finitude which is fully conditioned by material causation. Such a terminal state of affairs is exemplified, for Jacobi, in Spinoza's completely determined Substance.[11] The issue of Lessing's supposed Spinozism was particularly important to Lessing's closest friend and confidant, Mendelssohn.

What is surprising, however, is that Jacobi, in his own reported response to Mendelssohn, actually seems to recognize in Spinoza himself a kind of *Einsicht* that is very much akin to his own definition of faith, understood as a fundamental intuition guaranteeing the reality of objective finitude and the possibility of our knowing it. Jacobi writes (to Mendelssohn), "You go further than Spinoza; for him insight was above everything (CS: 190)." And further on, "For Spinoza, insight is the best part in all finite natures, for it is the part through which each finite nature reaches beyond its finitude."[12] The ambiguity of such a promotion of insight in Spinoza, where it becomes something akin to intellectual intuition or, indeed, faith as Jacobi himself understands it, is that it clearly flies in the face of Jacobi's ultimate statement of his "positions in the clearest terms." His six lapidary propositions begin with "Spinozism is atheism," and include: "Every avenue of demonstration ends up in fatalism [i.e., materialistic determinism]" (CS: 233–4). However, on another level, Jacobi's promotion of insight in Spinoza is very much in keeping with the rhetorical device that he employs when he writes, rather unctuously, "My dear Mendelssohn, we are all born in faith and must remain in faith ..." (CS: 230). For what Jacobi is claiming here is that faith grounds the possibility of all knowledge, including the empirical. Through the audacious conflation of axiomatic intuition and religious faith, Jacobi seeks to show that since they rely on intuitional insight even such Jewish metaphysicians as Spinoza and Mendelssohn are already living as Christians, whether they recognize it or not. Conversion is therefore not such a big step![13]

Consequently, while in associating *Einsicht* with Spinoza's philosophy it may seem that Jacobi is indeed associating it with atheistic rationalism, in fact, what Jacobi implies by the term is something altogether removed from rationalistic "demonstration." Rather, insight now appears as the universal intuition that underlies the Spinozistic system, as found in the *Ethics*' seminal "Definitions," and again in the ultimate expression of the intellectual love of God, with which that work ends, and which the definitional beginning actually presupposes. Briefly, for Jacobi, all that distinguishes insight from faith is simply the latter's clear recognition of its godly (Christian) source.

By now, I have perhaps confused my reader about where in the Pantheism Quarrel "insight" actually falls. Through Kant's OT essay, we encountered *Einsicht*, in Mendelssohn's *Morning Hours*, as the guiding principle of speculative reason, when working together with common sense; on the other hand, in Jacobi, the term is associated with Spinoza's foundational intuition, in such a way as to resemble Jacobi's own idea of faith! In fact, I am trying to show that this ambiguity is precisely the point that Hegel is making in the "Faith and Pure Insight" section of the *Phenomenology of Spirit*: faith and insight present themselves erroneously as exclusive epistemological positions whereas *in truth*, as Hegel is fond of saying, they enjoy an *essential* degree of reciprocity.[14] This discovery is best understood with reference to the German Enlightenment and its *Pantheismusstreit*.

What Hegel might well have taken away from Jacobi is the idea that faith is to be comprehended as a form of intuitional knowing, the same axiomatic "insight" that Jacobi celebrates in Spinoza (albeit from which the latter's subsequent metaphysical demonstrations distance him). Further, in accepting faith as such insight, Hegel can associate it with the meaning that Kant ascribes to the term in Mendelssohn, where it refers to a guiding principle. In all these cases, expressions of insight can be understood as instances of foundational intuition. Further still, Kant's OT essay allows Hegel to conceive of the reconciliation between faith and knowing as not merely theoretical but as actually carried out through the moral vocation of Reason itself, that is, through the universal insight that orients humanity toward the *summum bonum*. Still following Kant's argument, the unilateral positions expressed in the Pantheism Quarrel are dangerous because their exclusivity is injurious to (practical)

Reason and, consequently, to the actuality of human freedom, a cautionary point that Hegel seems to adopt in the "Struggle of the Enlightenment with Superstition" section and, ultimately, in "Absolute Freedom and the Terror." Against this bloody outcome stands the Kantian elenchus, as sketched in the "Orienting" essay, where the Enlightenment's fundamental opposition is reconciled in moral truth, a position taken on by Hegel in the concluding "Morality" section of the *Phenomenology*'s chapter 6, a chapter whose whole point might be said to show how the German Enlightenment (through Kant) has succeeded where the French version so disastrously failed![15]

Following the narrative arc of the "Culture" section of the *Phenomenology*, in light of our findings regarding the provenance of *Einsicht*, we see how the danger posed by the Enlightenment resides in the inability to resolve the issues at stake in the Pantheism Quarrel, leaving two unreconciled, unilateral, and dogmatically opposed attitudes between reason and religious fanaticism. The exclusivity of these positions leads to the evacuation of essential reality, the ground upon which real freedom must take place, leaving only vacuous Deism with "its empty Absolute Being," on one hand, and material utilitarianism, "the lack of selfhood in the thing that is useful" (W3: 423–4/M 573) on the other. The section on "Absolute Freedom and the Terror" represents the adequate expression of this etiolated reality, one where the world "cannot achieve anything positive, either universal works of language or of reality [...] of laws and general institutions of conscious freedom" (W3: 434–5/M 588), where "the actual destruction of the actual organization of the world" (W3: 436/M 590) has been completed. If the opposition between faith and knowing is to be overcome, this must first happen in the context of actual ethical agency, in the conclusion of chapter 6, where the unilateral oppositions of culture become lively and enlivening differences within the ethical community. Only through such an ethical outcome do we find, "God manifested in the midst of those who know themselves in the form of pure knowledge" (W3: 493/M 671). In other words, the ethical community is the politically embodied reconciliation of faith and knowing or, put differently, between the dual agencies of absolute revelation and human reason, in the domain of religion.

The religious stakes involved in the Pantheism Quarrel show us that the epistemological question of absolute knowing is a moral and political one as well.[16] However, as I have shown earlier, in chapter 1, the moral community that closes the *Phenomenology*'s chapter 6 is a feature of actuality. Consequently, the question of insight, as it appears in the "Spirit" chapter of the *Phenomenology*, refers to the human possibilities of knowing the givenness of absolute revelation. The revelatory agency of the

Absolute itself has yet to be acknowledged and comprehended in the forms of absolute spirit that we discover in *Phenomenology*'s chapter 7, on Religion. Only then is Absolute Knowing (chapter 8) possible, along with its ethical/political embodiment in the state university.

For Hegel, the key to reconciling the opposition between faith and reason lies in the fact that both are forms of immediate knowing called "insight," but whose erroneous exclusivity threatens any real, ethical, and hence political mediation. The same theme is reiterated in the final sections of the *EL*'s *Vorbegriff* (Preliminary Concept), where Hegel deals with forms of immediate knowing in their relation to systematic Science. I would like to turn briefly to this text, which I mentioned at the outset, in order to further support my argument that Hegel derives his notion of *Einsicht* from the *Pantheismusstreit*, involving positions put forward by Jacobi and Mendelssohn, through reference to Kant's OT essay. Reference to the *Encyclopaedia Logic*'s *Vorbegriff* also supports my point that Hegel discovers a reciprocal commonality in the adversarial claims between pure insight and faith, in that *both* are forms of immediate knowing. Such commonality anticipates the vocation of Hegelian Science and its mission of overcoming fixed positions which are one-sided from an epistemological point of view and carry real ethical and political dangers.

The term *Einsicht* reappears in section 74 of the EL's *Vorbegriff* more than two decades after its first significant usage in *Phenomenology*. Appropriately, "insight" is again found in a passage that deals with the religious question of the knowledge of God. The *Vorbegriff* makes the point that such absolute knowledge cannot be arrived at immediately but must instead involve the real content that is supplied throughout the *Encyclopaedia of Philosophical Sciences* and particularly through its *Philosophies of Nature* and *Spirit*. Immediate knowing can only claim *that* God is, whereas true knowledge of God must reveal to us *what* God is. Immediate knowing intends to avoid the particular, finite manifestations of its infinite object, and thus remains a pure form of knowing that can never reach beyond self-reflection. The critique of immediate knowing applies just as well to Cartesian, Leibnizian, Mendelssohnian metaphysics as to Jacobi's espousal of unconditioned faith. As Hegel puts it, "abstract thought (the form of reflective metaphysics) and abstract intuition (the form of immediate knowing) are one and the same" (EL 74). It is this "one and the same" form of immediate, abstract thinking that he refers to, in the *Vorbegriff*, as "diese Einsicht" (EL 74).

I believe that Hegel's point, in the dense and convoluted text of EL 74, is that insight, as immediate knowledge of God (qua the Absolute), is always in contradiction with itself and thus never true or complete in itself; it is this very contradiction that brings about mediation. On one hand, when insight is taken as a priori metaphysical reasoning, as the pure self-reflective *form* of knowing per se, then, precisely as form, it *must* be open to particular, conditioned content in order to be fulfilled. Pure insight, as immediate, a priori knowing, cannot help but determine otherness – finite, particular content; the demonstration of this vocation for the determination of particular otherness is carried out in the *Encyclopaedia Logic* itself.[17] Briefly, insight, as pure reason, cannot help but determine content and thus cannot remain pure.

Equally contradictory is immediate knowing in the form of faith, that is, in the position maintained by Jacobi contra Mendelssohn. Namely, when faith, as the immediate intuition of absolute revelation, claims to divorce itself from metaphysical reasoning, and consequently, from the over-conditioned finitude of Spinozistic materialism, it cannot help but make itself into a similarly metaphysical form of knowing or axiom – an insight whereby it becomes the grounding condition of all that is "finite and untrue" (Jacobi's position).[18] Hegel's point in the *Vorbegriff* is thus that, from a systematic (Scientific) point of view, the two exclusive positions of immediate knowing, anchored in the "either/or" of the understanding, cannot help but mediate one another, thereby surrendering their immediacy. The use of *Einsicht* again shows how each position is, in fact, reciprocally complicit with the other. The problem is that when removed from this dialectical Scientific development, insight's formal purity renders it dangerously arbitrary, leaving itself receptive to any content at all, even content that is "ungodly or immoral" (EL 74). Such an outcome can perhaps be seen as the dying echo of the earlier *Phenomenological* ending in "Absolute Freedom and the Terror." In both cases, the epistemological failure in *knowledge* of the Absolute spills over into the ethical/political domain.[19]

As always in Hegel, the danger here is one of lunar fixation, where the polarity of unilateral positions is not dissolved into the cometary fluidity (see chapter 3) of dialectical movement and Science. This is the danger that *Einsicht* represents when it is *not* taken as the third and final position of the *Vorbegriff* qua immediate knowing, a position both pre-supposed by and anticipatory of Science itself. As immediate knowing, insight can be comprehended as the axiomatic intuition of the Absolute, already anticipating its logical unfolding into actual Scientific knowledge. On the other hand, as a unilateral, recalcitrant expression of the understanding (*Verstand*) (EL 76), insight appears as an "exclusion of mediation," in the dogmatic oppositions of the "either-or" form of thinking (EL 65) paradigmatically expressed in the *Pantheismusstreit.* In the *exclusive* positions of *Einsicht,* we discover the same sort of dilemma as those that underlie all the oppositional dualities of the "Culture" section in chapter 6 of the *Phenomenology*. They are the dilemmas inherent in the culture of *Verstand* (understanding), which Hegel sees as determining his own epoch, and which we will further explore in the next chapter.

In the *Phenomenology*, the Enlightenment's erroneous oppositions are swept away by the overarching negativity of the Terror. In the calmer, logical context of the *Encyclopaedia*, three decades later, such terrible negativity has been re-thought as "the dialectical moment ... essential to affirmative Science" (EL 78), whose cometary work is to dissolve "the abstraction of the understanding." The dialectical, reciprocal mediation of forms of immediate knowing ensures that *Einsicht* becomes insight *of* something, bringing about the "speculative or positively rational" (EL 79) actuality of systematic Science. Above all, reference to the *Vorbegriff* reinforces the ethical and political destiny of *Einsicht*, which we discovered through our investigation into chapter 6 of the *Phenomenology*, and which we now see as the vocation of Hegel's Science itself, and its pedagogical destination, where the immediate expressions of human reason and absolute revelation come to mutual mediation and acknowledgment.

6
Overcoming Understanding: The Language of Representation

In the last chapter, we saw how the use of *Einsicht*, in the *Phenomenology of Spirit*, presented the two apparently opposed forms of immediate knowing that characterized the epochal *Pantheismusstreit*, raising for Hegel (and some of his contemporaries) the pressing demands for a mediated reconciliation of the two positions, in the form of systematic Science. We saw how the binary features of faith and reason could be comprehended as epistemological expressions of intuition over against discursive, Enlightenment-style cognition. Since both these aspects reside in Kant's transcendental topography of the understanding (qua intuition and concepts), the need for reconciliation takes on the form of a struggle to overcome and move beyond the *Verstand*, not only as a feature of cognition but as a moment of what Hegel refers to as *Geist* (spirit). Certainly, Kant himself anticipated the need of the age, to acknowledge the limits of common understanding as an opening onto the plane of Reason. However, his solution, in defining the realm of Reason as that of the ideal could never be satisfying for a philosopher seeking to move beyond *Verstand* as a historical moment of dangerous division and dispute. From the outset, I have been presenting the Hegelian conciliatory project in terms of reason and revelation and their cohabitation in systematic Science.

In this chapter, I want to discuss Hegel's approach to Karl Reinhold as significant in the attempt to overcome the *Verstand* as a moment of human consciousness, determinant of an age where the fundamental opposition between reason and revelation cries out for systematic resolution. Briefly, Hegel's reading of Reinhold brings to light a key aspect of the (Kantian) understanding and its instantiation in spirit: representation (*Vorstellung*). Although the idea that the understanding is ambiguously complicit in the subjective production of objective representations is certainly present in Kant's transcendental aesthetics, Reinhold takes the representational activity of the understanding and makes it the basis for *his* notion of a universal science.

My position is that representation, for Hegel, is above all a form of discourse, and, as such, is the way by which the *Verstand* instantiates itself in the world as a moment of spirit. I will further develop this idea in the next chapter, on Hegel and the end of art, where I will juxtapose the language of representation with that of presentation (*Darstellung*). For now, I want to show how the essential link between the understanding and its performative discourse can be discovered through Hegel's reading of Reinhold as the paradigmatic philosopher of his age, of the *Verstand* and therefore, of representation (*des Vorstellens*). Reference to Reinhold's theory of representation allows Hegel to comprehend *Verstand* not only as an epochal expression of the opposition between reason and revelation, between ratiocination and intuition/faith as binary expressions of immediate knowing but also as a certain form of discourse that performs such binarity, and thus, must be supplanted with a form of discourse proper to systematic Science, one which Hegel refers to as "speculative," whose grammar has realized, achieved, and fulfilled the judgment form (*Urteil*) in the onto-grammatical form of the syllogism, as we saw earlier, in chapter 2.

The discourse of representation is nonetheless a necessary, even essential element of Hegelian Science and its syllogistic fulfillment. Representation bespeaks the discourses of the positive sciences that make up the rational content of *Encyclopaedic* (syllogistic) Science. The language of representation can even "represent" speculative truth intuitively, as is the case in the revelatory language of (Christian) religion. However, it is precisely this ambiguity, the fact that the representational language of the understanding is either that of reason or that of revelation that makes it the privileged discourse of immediate knowing, which is only overcome in the mediated discourse of Science. First, a little background on Hegel's ambiguous appreciation of Reinhold. Then, we will explore an early Hegelian text where Reinhold's theory of representation is related to language. Finally, we will see how the logos of Science moves beyond, while incorporating the binary languages of representation and the culture of the *Verstand*.

In December 1794, while still stuck in Bern, Hegel, in a letter to his friend Schelling, refers disparagingly to the state of philosophy at his old school, the Tübingen seminary, writing: "as long as someone like Reinhold or Fichte doesn't fill the chair, nothing serious will take place there."[1] However, a month later, in January 1795, still in Bern, Hegel admits to knowing the depths of Kant's critical philosophy, "as little as those of Reinhold," further remarking that such speculations seem to have little bearing on the religious and political realms that really interest him.[2] The following month, in February 1795, Schelling writes to Hegel, predicting that, thanks to Reinhold, "we will soon be at the highest peak of philosophy."[3]

Between 1795 and 1801, there is a sea change in Hegel's and Schelling's attitudes toward Reinhold. This is probably because, in the latter year, Reinhold had published a critical review of Schelling's *System des transcendentalen Idealismus* (*System of Transcendental Idealism*), in the *Allgemeine Literatur-Zeitung*, at Jena, and, in his *Beytäge zur leichtern Übersicht des Zustandes der Philosophie beym Anfange des 19. Jahrhunderts* (*Contributions to a Simpler Overview of Philosophy at the Beginning of the 19th Century*), Reinhold had gone on to espouse C.G. Bardili's philosophy of logical realism, in opposition to Schelling's (and Hegel's) philosophy of identity.[4]

Hence, in 1801, in a letter to G.E. Mehmel, philosophy professor at Erlangen and editor of *Erlangenliteraturezeitung*, Hegel lumps Reinhold together with "Bouterwek, Krug etc.," writing that "each of them qualifies his insignificant, arbitrary form of reasoning as original and behaves as if he were truly a philosopher," when, in fact, "these men have absolutely no philosophy."[5] More substantially, in 1801, Hegel takes Reinhold to task in his *Differenz des Fichte'schen und Schelling'schen Systems der Philosophie* (*Differenzschrift*) which is Hegel's main text on Reinhold (W2: 116–38). It is a response to Reinhold's *Contributions to a Simpler Overview.*

In the *Differenzschrift*, Hegel criticizes Reinhold for not distinguishing Schelling's philosophy from Fichte's subjective idealism. Reinhold, claims Hegel, is ignorant of Schelling's new objective philosophy, his *System of Transcendental Idealism*, which includes incipient philosophies of nature and art. It is true that for Reinhold, in his *Contributions to a Simpler Overview*, intellectual intuition, in both Fichte and Schelling, is reduced to being a vacuous and thoroughly subjective intuition of the individual thinker. Surprisingly, Hegel's defence of Schelling against this charge is rather unconvincing, consisting mainly of citing Schelling's affirmations on the objective side of his philosophy, regarding his early philosophy of nature. Perhaps this is because Reinhold's criticism of intellectual intuition prefigures Hegel's own later criticism of immediate, intuitive knowledge, and ultimately of Schelling, in the preface to the *Phenomenology of Spirit*'s reference to the famous cowless night of indifference. Reinhold's critique of intellectual intuition also anticipates Hegel's polemical take on Jacobi and Schleiermacher, whom Hegel describes as the highest "*Potenzirung*" of the former, in *Glauben und Wissen* (*Faith and Knowing*), in 1802 (W2: 287–433),[6] and again 20 years later, when Hegel attacks Schleiermacher in his preface to Hinrichs's *Die Religion im inneren Verhältnisse zur Wissenschaft (Religion, in the Inner Relations to Science)*, which we will return to in chapter 8. In this text, Hegel fully adopts Reinhold's idea that intellectual intuition is ultimately nothing but subjective feeling, applying the critique to Schleiermacher's notion of religion as a feeling of the universe. This allows Hegel to make the notorious remark that if feeling were the foundation of religion, a dog, who strongly feels dependence towards its master, would be the best Christian (W11: 58).

In the *Differenzschrift*, Hegel also describes the tortuous path Reinhold has taken, how he has moved from a Kantian position, to a Fichtean position, to Jacobi, before finally coming to rest with Bardili's logic, a journey that Hegel ironically qualifies as a "metempsychosis." Although Hegel seems to present this trajectory as evidence of dilettantism or philosophical flakiness, one is tempted to see his presentation of Reinhold's series of intellectual revolutions as a caricature of the very path of error that Hegel will later portray, in the *Phenomenology of Spirit*, as the process of truth itself, even to its apotheosis in a type of realistic logic (W2: 116). In any case, in the *Differenzschrift*, Hegel still defends, to a certain extent, Schelling's and his philosophy of identity, where speculative identity takes place in the primal indifference point between subject and object.

Hegel's later references to Reinhold seem to indicate a positive re-evaluation. In the *Greater Logic*, Hegel acknowledges Reinhold for his early speculative thinking on the question of the beginning in Science (W5: 69), a question that goes to the heart of the Hegel's systematic enterprise and to which he returns almost obsessively in the introductions to all his major works. In fact, the problem of finding the system's beginning is just as difficult and pregnant as the better known issue of accepting or refusing its end, which is hardly surprising given that, in Hegel's encyclopaedic science, the beginning is the end and the end is the beginning. Nonetheless, before concluding that, in the *Logic*, Hegel had definitively revised his earlier negative opinion of Reinhold, we should recall that his *Lectures on the History of Philosophy*, from the 1820s, reproduce almost word-for-word the same derogatory expression we find in the 1801 letter to Mehmel, where "Reinhold, Bouterwek, Krug, etc.," are presented as insignificant and unphilosophical (W20: 387).

I now want to turn to the earlier, anonymous Hegelian reference to Reinhold that I mentioned above. This "hidden" reference is found in a text that Johannes Hoffmeister dates from 1794 and gives the title, *Materien zu einer Philosophie des subjektiven Geistes*. The text is pivotal to grasping Hegel's view of the *Verstand* and its central role in the recalcitrant, oppositional relation between faith and knowing that we discovered in the last chapter. Significantly, the text presents the understanding as the faculty of representation and language.[7]

The early textual reference to Reinhold is a hybrid affair, with a problematic philology, which bears mentioning if we are indeed to attribute the writing to Hegel. In the summer of 1789, while at Tübingen, Hegel chose to take a private, elective course given by J.F. Flatt, a professor who is best, although imperfectly, known as the assistant to the dogmatic theology professor Gottlob Christian Storr. Flatt's course was entitled "Empirical Psychology and the Kantian *Critique*." Hegel incorporated the content of the course on psychology from his own class notes into the 1794 manuscript on psychology or subjective spirit. Hoffmeister's remarkable analysis of the central portion of the 1794 manuscript establishes that its content represents a compilation taken from a number of sources: the *Critique of Pure Reason*, but also from secondary literature, such as works by J.F. Abel, C.C.E. Schmid, Johann Schultz and, most significantly, Reinhold.[8] Hegel faithfully took and conserved the class notes that he would later incorporate into his 1794 catalogue of psychological concepts, and even decades later into the *Philosophy of Subjective Spirit* in the *Encyclopaedia*.[9]

While the content of Hegel's 1794 manuscript may contain elements from such Kantians or psychologists as Schmid, Abel, and Schultz, a substantial part of the text is informed by Reinhold's theory of representation, as found in his *Elementarphilosophie*.[10] Flatt, in teaching Kant, was really teaching Reinhold's Kant, apparently emptying the first *Critique* of any ontological or metaphysical discussions, concentrating entirely on the psychological elements from the transcendental aesthetics, those elements dealing with individual human consciousness. Hegel's letter to Schelling (1794) shows that, at this time, he still values Reinhold as an important philosopher, although to what extent he could distinguish Reinhold from Kant and Flatt is debatable. This might explain his 1795 comment to Schelling, that he knows little of Reinhold's theoretical philosophy. Perhaps, having followed Flatt's course, he knew more than he realized.

Reinhold is central to the psychology text on two levels. First, his proposition of consciousness is used to ground epistemologically the very possibility of a speculative science of psychology. Then, more broadly, his theory of representation enables Hegel to grasp the true relationship between faith and knowing, the substance of the pantheism quarrel, that is, to comprehend the underlying discursive complicity between these two forms of immediate knowing.

Reinhold's proposition of consciousness makes the science of psychology possible, for Hegel, by allowing it to get over a classical epistemological hurdle: How can the object of enquiry (the mind) also be the instrument of enquiry? This is the same problem, put differently, that so frustrated Hume – can we know our personal identity? In Kantian terms, as expressed in the 1794 manuscript, how can we know our own minds when "the concept of rational psychology is not based on any (sensuous) experience?" How can we have an empirical experience of the rational soul? The manuscript evokes this epistemological challenge at the outset and responds to it, further on, by faithfully citing Reinhold's proposition [*Satz*] of consciousness: "In consciousness, the representation is, through the subject, distinguished from and related to both the subject and the object – proposition of consciousness" (GW1: 169). The Hegel text immediately cautions against deriving or deducing the particular branches of psychology from the proposition, as Reinhold wanted to do. However, since the power of representation is the general power of the subjective mind, conscious thought allows us to study our psychological representations as distinct from ourselves. In other words, we can now take our mental phenomena as scientific objects since, as conscious beings, we distinguish ourselves from our subjectivity as it relates to objectivity and to itself, in its representations. Within ourselves, we are able to distinguish from ourselves both the representations of subjectivity and those of objectivity. Given the fundamentally linguistic nature of *Vorstellens* that I am arguing, it is important to emphasize that Reinhold's largely forgotten and yet deeply insightful definition of consciousness is presented as a *Satz*, as *a Setzen*, as a proposition that is a self-positing. In other words, Fichte's foundational proposition of the self-positing "I" had a predecessor. Given the onto-grammatical reading of judgment that I have been espousing in Hegel, whose archetypal expression can be found in the Fichtean "*Ich bin Ich*," a proposition whose subject is both grammatical and psychical, Reinhold's earlier contribution is particularly significant. The act of consciousness, qua representation, is fundamentally linguistic.

Of further significance, regarding Hegel, is that the proposition of consciousness introduces the idea of an over-arching scientific subjectivity, a kind of meta-subjectivity capable of observing and reflecting upon the self as it relates to the world. This bidimensionality of subjectivity is essential to Hegel's idea of a phenomenology of consciousness, where the progression or movement of consciousness through its various, predetermined forms is "for us," Hegelian scientists, while, at the same time, taking place "behind the back" of consciousness itself (W3: 80/M 87). And because it is a proposition, the *Satz* of consciousness also introduces the possibility of an over-arching meta-discourse that Hegel refers to as Science (*Wissenschaft*). Already, in the 1794 text, through reference to Reinhold's proposition of consciousness, psychology can take the point of view of a scientific subject that observes its own mental phenomena or facts of consciousness, both subjectively and objectively produced, as (linguistic) representations. This is what the first third of the psychology text does: It deals with *Empfindungsvorstellungen*, the representations arising from outer sensory input, as well as those arising from inner feeling. Both types are representations arising from intuition, in the Kantian sense; they are spontaneously represented images stemming from inner feeling (through the pure form of time) or from the outward directed (space-related) senses.

Representations from the outer senses are empirical. In psychology, we are dealing with the "laws and conditions under which, in the soul, a sensible intuition is brought to consciousness" (GW1: 170) or how we come to be affected by objects through our senses of taste, smell, hearing, sight, touch and still distinguish these sensations from ourselves. On the other hand, the inner sense deals with objects "which we represent to ourselves solely in time" (GW1: 172). These are inner feelings of our deepest soul (*Seele*), of our deepest self. "The fundamental power of the soul is a representing power" and within itself it perceives moods, feelings, dreams, and conditions of *Gemüt* (GW1 172).[11] Here, we discover the deepest "self-feeling," at a pre-conscious level, where we immediately intuit changes within our bodies, a dreamlike experience and the possibility of dreams, sleep-walking and mental derangement through *idées fixes*, as well as the escape from the confines of the inner soul through the outward-directed exercise of habit (GW1 173). In this material, we recognize the building blocks (*Materien*) of Hegel's fully developed anthropology, in the Subjective Spirit section of the 1827 and 1830 editions of the ES, particularly in sections 401 to 409. For example, in the 1827 edition, the title preceding section 403 was, "The Soul that Dreams and Habituates Itself" (Reid 2013).

The 1794 manuscript then deals with cases of *Phantasievorstellungen*, representations arising from conscious memory, but also through fever, drunkenness, dreams, madness, religious or supernatural fanaticism, and visions, as well as in artistic creation. This level of psychological activity refers to the actual production of representations, whether stemming from the unconscious, inner, natural soul or from outer-directed and informed consciousness. Here, once more, we find original elements that can be rediscovered in Hegel's mature science of subjective spirit. Most importantly, concerning the linguistic reading of representation that I am putting forward, Hegel will never abandon the view of *Phantaisie* as the imaginative power productive of representations in language, through the mental investment of linguistic signs in order to produce meaningful words (ES 457–60). While the language of representation is that of the common understanding, and, on a higher mission, is performative in the positive, historically derived sciences that form the content of Science itself, its highest destiny takes place in religion, as a form of Absolute Spirit. Unfortunately, the translation of *Vortellung/ Vorstellen* as "picture-thinking" erases the specifically linguistic determination of representation, in Hegel, allowing it to be confused with that other form of Absolute Spirit: art. As we will see in the subsequent chapter, Hegel's aesthetics distinguishes between artistic presentations (*Darstellungen*) and religious linguistic representations (*Vorstellungen*), a distinction that is often lost in translation.

The speculative, conceptually articulated language of Science, fulfilled by the representational languages of its contents (philosophies of nature, law, mind, art, religion ...), has comprehended representation's form of discourse (judgment [*Urteil*]) syllogistically, where the copula of its judgments is now taken as the mediating, particular moment of the speculative sentence. The speculative discourse of Science does not re-invent the representations that make up its content. Rather, it reads and grasps such language according to its speculative truth. This is the case with religious doctrine; it is also the case with philosophy, where the representational discourses that make up its history are now comprehended in their truth. For example, the quadripartite Neoplatonism of Jakob Böhme, whose writings, for Hegel, *represent* the crowning achievement of modern philosophy, is read by the latter as an early articulation of the syllogism, whose most perfect *(vollkommen)* expression is the Concept.

Following the reference to representations as produced by the faculty of *Phantaisie,* in the 1794 text on psychology, understanding is addressed, true to Kantian form, as "the faculty of concepts." However, the *Verstand* is then given a distinctly Reinholdian flavour, for its concepts are presented as "general representations that grasp within and under themselves other representations" (GW1: 184). Significantly, therefore, Reinhold's theory of representation allows Hegel to grasp the understanding as a faculty that produces and draws upon both outer, empirical content (sensations) and the representations of inner feelings and intuitions. In other words, the understanding operates in the apparently opposed fields of what appeared, in the last chapter, as two facets of immediate knowing. Further and above all, the Reinholdian presentation of the understanding as essentially a judgment faculty allows Hegel to make the important link between judging (*Urteilen*) and representation (*Vorstellung*): language. Indeed, as we have seen, judging is a grammatical operation, one that is productive of propositions (*Sätze*), joining together a psycho-grammatical subject with its predicated object through the copula.

Hegel applies this truth to an area in which he is intensely interested, religion and the relation between faith and rational knowing, between the immediate forms of knowing proper to revelation and reason. He does this in such a way that faith may be conceived in terms of subjective inner feeling (e.g., how Hegel portrays Jacobi in the 1802 essay, "Faith and Knowing"), as opposed to empirically derived conceptual reasoning. By presenting both inner feeling and reflexive empirical knowing as productive of judgments that espouse the language of representation, Hegel is able to grasp them not as irrevocably opposed theologico-philosophical tendencies, as they are presented in the starkest depiction of the pantheism quarrel (between Mendelssohn and Jacobi), but rather as features of the pervading culture of *Verstand* and its performative discourse. Reinhold's theory of representation shows Hegel that the secret to overcoming the division between faith and dogmatic rationalism lies not in choosing a winner but in discovering a form of discourse that goes beyond the representational judgments of the understanding, which is common to both. In the early Hegel days of the manuscript on psychology (1794), the necessarily speculative overcoming of the *Verstand*'s binary oppositions is still expressed in Kantian terms, significantly, as the *Critique of Judgment*. That is why the manuscript closes with final pages that depart from the content of Flatt's course on "Empirical Psychology" and engage in a short discussion of Kant's recently published (1790) third *Critique*.

Hegel sees his own age as taking place under the sign of the understanding. Thanks to Reinhold, Hegel now sees that the *Verstand* is limited to the linguistic activity of representation, which inevitably draws upon outer and inner sources while remaining fixated in their dichotomy and opposition. It is the terminally bipolar aspect of the understanding and its representations that allow Hegel to grasp the pantheism quarrel and understand the Enlightenment. In fact, in Hegelian terms, the pantheism quarrel should be seen as the performative truth or actuality of the Enlightenment. To the extent that this cultural moment promotes the ratiocinating form of *Verstand*, it cannot but express itself in the language of unilaterally opposed, yet mutually dependent representations of rational empiricism and feeling (rational determinism vs. faith and feeling).

The divisive nature of the dichotomy is inimical to the organic vision of systematic science. This is illustrated, in other contexts, by Hegel's use of the term "Barbarei" to describe either the unilateral representations of sentimental faith or those of empirical rationality. The concept of barbarism aptly reflects the insult, and indeed the threat that the fixated dichotomy of the *Verstand* opposes to the Athenian whole of Science. In parenthesis, Hegel seems to derive the idea of unilateral barbarism from Schiller's *Letters on the Esthetic Education of Man,* where *Barbar* and *Wilder* are applied to those who espouse either the Reinhold-derived *Formtrieb* or *Stofftrieb,* at the expense of the reconciling *Spieltrieb.*[12] In the historical context of Hegel's manuscript on subjective spirit, the barbarism of understanding's dichotomy (and the unresolved conflict of the pantheism quarrel) has given rise to the anti-scientific expression of modern skepticism. Significantly, the skepticism of Gottlob Ernst Schultze's *Aenesidemus* stems from a reflection on Reinhold's *Elementarphilosophie,* the source of Hegel's grasp of the understanding as the seat of inner and outer representation and their discursive judgments. In any case, the only way to get beyond the pantheism quarrel and the epochal problem of faith and knowing, without falling into skepticism, is to get beyond fixation in the understanding and its unilateral representations. This is the project first undertaken in the *Phenomenology of Spirit,* whose brilliant solution consists in harnessing the very negativity of skepticism as the cometary agent dissolving the unilateral positions of the *Verstand* and putting them into dialectical movement.

As we saw in the last chapter, Hegel's project of overcoming the opposed positions of representational understanding by incorporating them into a dialectical movement is again presented in a later, post-*Phenomenological* context, that is, in the preliminary concept of the *Encyclopaedia* Logic, where we discovered how both Enlightenment reasoning and intuitive faith were expressions of immediate knowing. In both cases, Hegel's early knowledge of Reinhold's theory of representation has allowed him to comprehend such binary knowledge as that of the understanding and its representational language of judgment. Overcoming the epochal binarity of the late-Enlightenment means finding a new form of knowing and, necessarily, its new form of discourse.

Nonetheless, the discursive reality of representation has a positive role to play within the holistic economy of Science. Crucially, representational language has an essential pedagogical mission within the historical narratives of Reason that make up the content of Science, and which ensure that its fulfilment is both by and for humans. All of Hegel's "philosophies of" are configured historically, and all of them tell the same story: that of human consciousness and freedom. Although Hegelian Science may be ultimately enunciated in the speculative language of the Concept and its syllogistic grammar, without its representational and historical content, its words would be empty and meaningless, bespeaking only the night in which all cows are black.

Finally, from the outset, I have been presenting the vocation of Hegelian Science as the holistic realization of mutual self-recognition between human reason and absolute revelation, where each has come to know itself in and through the other. This is possible not only because they have something essentially in common: freedom, but, as well, because the language of human understanding, qua representation, and that of absolute revelation both espouse the same grammatical form, that of judgment (*Urteil*). In fact, Science does no more than recognize the onto-grammatical commonality of the judgment form, as an essential self-positing shared by the human and the Absolute, in the mediating, fulfilled copula. Ultimately, if reason and revelation are to be complicit in their reciprocal acknowledgment, then they must speak the same language.

PART THREE

Speculative Forms of Absolute Presence

7
The Death of God and the Beautiful Finitude of Art

In the last section, we have been discussing forms of human reason in their historical apprehension of the Absolute. The temporality of absolute revelatory agency, left on its own, one might say, presents itself instantaneously, in an always present and yet eternal "Now." Such revelation is ill suited to the unfolding that Hegel attributes to reason generally, specifically in the world-historical form of spirit. *Geist* is a process of *Bildung*, of culture, in the broad, pedagogical, formative sense of the word. Spirit does not pour itself out in a "pistol shot," as Hegel was fond of saying. Rather, spirit, as the story of human reason, builds slowly and progressively, taking into account and yet progressing beyond its past acquisitions. Nonetheless, as we have seen in Part Two, human cognition is far from impervious to the instantaneous pouring out of absolute revelatory agency, which occurs to human reason in the forms of intellectual intuition, faith, or feeling. Indeed, without such an immediate apprehension, reason would have nothing to strive for.

In the epochal culture of *Verstand*, in which Hegel finds himself, immediate, intuitional forms are presented in opposition to those of dogmatic, metaphysical reasoning. As we discovered in the last chapters, Hegel seeks to overcome this bicameral approach to absolute truth by presenting each as a form of immediate knowing, of *Einsicht*, requiring the reciprocal mediation informative of speculative Science. Such an outcome is possible, because, as we found in the last chapter, the logos of reason shares with that of absolute revelation the grammatical structure of judgment: the predicative act between subject and predicate. In grasping judgment speculatively, as the ontological/psychical positing of the grammatical subject into the predicate and the reciprocal *Anstoss* of the predicate rebounding on the subject, the copula ("to be") between subject and predicate takes on the particularity necessary for syllogistic completion. This outcome is only achieved because philosophy has shown how the language of representation (*Vorstellens*) is more than it took itself for, or rather, is more than it *has taken* itself for, according to the temporality of the *Perfekt* tense, where, as we saw in chapter 5, what occurred as intellectual intuition has become fully informed by the historically derived content that makes it what it is.

In the past section, we discovered this scientific happy ending mainly from the point of view of human reason, in its striving for absolute knowledge. Now, through the three chapters of the present section, we will look at scientific reconciliation principally from the perspective of absolute agency, a view that implies apprehending the logos of revelation linguistically, first as it configures linguistic signs and then meaningful words, and finally, as these elements come to form meaningful sentences that are taken up into the systematic narrative of Science. From the perspective of absolute logos, the first step, the configuration of signs into words, takes place in art. The second moment, whereby the words are enfolded into sentences, is (revelatory) religion. Finally, philosophy presents the process by which the representational language of religion (doctrine) comes to be grasped speculatively. This three-step program is recounted by Hegel, in the *Encyclopaedia*, as the story of Absolute Spirit, an expression that fittingly evokes and unites both the Absolute and the human (Spirit).

In order for us to comprehend the revelatory nature of *beautiful* art, (*schöne Kunst*), and thus, how it participates in the narrative of Absolute Spirit, we must grasp the essential finitude of its objects. Such finitude not only characterizes the limits of art per se, the degree to which its signs are inadequate to the absolute content that invests them but demonstrates how such content requires the more holistic languages of religion, philosophy and, ultimately, Science. Finitude is an essential feature of beautiful art to the extent that its meaning always outstrips its individual forms, leading us (humans) to more adequate expressions. I write "us" because while the beautiful artwork, for Hegel, presents the singular embodiment of absolute agency, it is always "man-made" and for us humans. Thus, from the start, the forms of Absolute Spirit present the complicit agencies of the human and the divine. It is this complicity that is developed, integrated, and further enriched in the subsequent forms of religion, philosophy, and Science.[1]

Contemporary readings of Hegel's philosophy of art concentrate on the anthropological aspect of artistic creation: how art's creative enterprise reflects that which is best in human endeavour. Absolute spirit thus becomes a form where human consciousness slips the bonds of the mundane in order to reach higher realms of spirit. This view is, of course, a reflection of the anthropological destination that we moderns attach to art. With regard to Hegel, it is not wrong; it merely tells half the story. Briefly put, we do not understand art in Hegel if we do see that it is always also a revelation of the Absolute, of the Idea, and, although I hardly dare say it, of the "divine." This is why, in the *Phenomenology of Spirit*, reflections on art appear in chapter 7 on Religion and later near the end of the *Encyclopaedia of Philosophical Sciences* as one of the figures of Absolute Spirit, along with Religion and Philosophy. If we leave aside the revelatory or "absolute" aspect of art (or religion or philosophy) and concentrate solely on its anthropological destination, then we are doing Feuerbachian humanism, not Hegelian (absolute) idealism.

Placing art under the sign of the Absolute's self-revelatory agency is what Hegel does in the opening paragraphs of the *Phenomenology*'s Religion chapter. There, the subject of discussion is no longer spirit per se, that is, the human odyssey of reason that we have observed through the first six chapters of Hegel's book. Now, we are looking at "the spirit of religion," where the Absolute undertakes its own, reciprocal odyssey. This newly presented form of spirit is "again [like human spirit] the movement away from its immediacy towards the attainment of the knowledge of what it is in itself" (W3: 499/M 680), but now from the point of view of the Absolute, that is, from the point of view of the "absolute Being [*Wesen*, also essence]."

It may be difficult to see why, in the *Phenomenology*, art appears under the umbrella of religion. One might object that art as such only appears later in the subchapter entitled "*Kunstreligion*," where religion takes the form of art in the Classical world of sculpture. However, I would argue that art is there, in the Religion chapter, from the outset, in the different natural embodiments that characterize art in the "Natural Religion [*die natürliche Religion*]" section, first, in the shape of "God as Light" (W3: 505/M 685), then in the shapes of "Plant and animal" (W3: 507/M 689) worship. In all these embodiments, the Absolute Being (*Wesen*) takes on forms that are clearly presented *artistically*, perhaps with reference to Egyptian culture. Specifically, "Natural Religion" deals with artistic forms that espouse "the shape of shapelessness" (M 686), where "revelation" (M 685) takes the form of the "all-pervading essential light of sunrise" (M 686); subsequently, in the "Plant and animal" section, we find "a form that is produced by the self," a "self that becomes a thing" (M689). In both these "religious" contexts, Hegel is therefore talking about sacred objects in which the Absolute reveals itself in nonhuman forms. These objects are nonetheless man-made artworks, a truth of which we contemporaries have thankfully become aware.[2] In other words, in "Natural Religion" Hegel is not referring to natural things but to their presentation as fashioned, sacred art objects, for example, in animal sculptures and hieroglyphics.

The third subchapter in "Natural Religion," the "*Werkmeister* [architect/builder]" (W3: 508/M 691) section deals with sacred architecture, for example, pyramids or the stone of Mecca. Here, we are clearly in the Hegelian province of art, as indicated by the fact that, in the later *Lectures*, architecture forms a fundamental element of his aesthetics. Consequently, the "Religion" chapter has already been discussing art, throughout the "Natural Religion" section, before the word "art" is explicitly mentioned in "*Kunstreligion* [Religion as Art]" (W3: 512/M 699).

The fact that Hegel, in the *Phenomenology*, begins chapter 7 on Religion with a discussion of art demonstrates two things: first, from its conceptual beginning in the fashioned presentation of natural objects in "Natural Religion," art will always remain infected with the natural. And the natural, for Hegel, is, above all, characterized by the singularity of its objects, where finite things (of nature) collapse into forms of undifferentiated universality. This fundamental dynamic is already at play in the *Phenomenology*'s first chapter on sense-certainty where the immediate apprehension of finite things dissolves into the indifference of "here" and "now." The objects of art cannot shake their natural embodiment.

Second, the inescapably natural aspect of art, its reliance on singular embodiments, allows us to distinguish it from Revelatory Religion (i.e., Hegel's presentation of religion per se, in the *Phenomenology*)[3] where the sacred is no longer revealed in singular forms but in linguistic forms of shared (in worship) doctrines. In fact, in coming to espouse linguistic forms, such as epic poetry and tragedy, art is already moving on to Revelatory Religion. As I will discuss below, the move to actual religious language is a consequence of art's natural, finite, singularly embodied forms.

In Hegel, the most catastrophic but also the most essential and "revelatory" enactment of art's essential finitude (its end) took place about 2000 years ago, with the destruction of the most perfect work of beautiful art: the singular body of Jesus Christ. I do not mean representations or images of the Son of God but rather the death of God himself, in the Passion and crucifixion of his individual natural, human form, considered as a divine work of art.[4] In the divine singularity of the actual body of Christ, the human and the Absolute find their complete, immediately revelatory aesthetic expression. Thus, the Christ fully realizes Hegel's definition of the beautiful art object: the perfect cohabitation of individual *natural* form and universal content. In this light, the human body of Christ should be seen as the fulfilled, living embodiment of the "beautiful individuality," which Greco-Roman art could only, up until then, present in the stone configurations of divine human shapes. In the living, perfect art object that is the actual body of Christ, the individual human form is fully incarnated with universal content, and thus immediately true, good, beautiful, and *alive.* In other words still, the natural necessity of individual bodily form is fully invested with the highest content of freedom: the life of the infinite Idea itself,[5] forming an instance in *schöne Kunst* that Classical sculpture could only present in its beautiful and yet ultimately lifeless forms. In Hegel, the fact that the *depictions* of Christ herald the beginning of a new, modern chapter of spirit should not occlude the fact that, in the story of art, his crucifixion presents the culminating moment of the Classical world and, indeed, of beautiful art itself. The undeniable beauty of Classical sculpture that Hegel stresses in his *Lectures on Aesthetics* is not contradicted by Christ, but rather, is realized and fulfilled in his terminal, *singular* form.

It may seem that, in the paragraphs above, I have been playing fast and loose with the terms "singularity" (*Einzelheit*) and "individuality" (*Individualität*), and indeed Miller's translation of the passages in the *Phenomenology* that I am discussing encourages such equivocation. However, my use of these terms attempts to reprise the general distinction found in Hegel's usage of them, a distinction that is germinal to our discussion of the art object and its finitude. Hegel generally uses "singular" and its derivatives when he is referring to the singular's dialectical role in the syllogistic logic of the Concept, where the immediate, innumerable singularities of finite natural entities dissolve into generality or universality. Of course, the *Singular* does reappear, finally, in the systematic conclusion of the syllogistic whole (*Schluss*), but then as the *universal* Singular: the one that is all, according to the onto-logic of the Concept, in the movement of thought through the moments of Universal, Particular and Singular. This syllogistically realized Singular is what Hegel presents as Science. On the other hand, singular entities, as fundamentally natural, are always predisposed to vanish into greater conceptual configurations.

Conversely, "*Individualität*" is generally used when the singular resists its conceptual destiny, when individuality refuses its inherently terminal, finite nature and hangs on to its ipseity by investing itself with fixed properties and qualities. This enterprise is meaningful but ultimately futile. In fact, individuality remains essentially finite because the qualities and properties that it uses to determine and maintain itself are themselves universal and predispose it to *general* particularity. This is the paradoxical dynamic that Hegel describes in the "Perception" chapter of the *Phenomenology* (W3: 105/M 130), where perceived individual things attempt to anchor their truth in a profusion of essential properties but under whose particular *generality* individuality itself must fall.

The problem is that the art object is always ambiguously both singular and individual. To the extent that it is the locus where the Absolute reveals itself, the beautiful art object is singular. Its sacred embodiment guarantees the fact that there is nothing else like it. In Kantian terms, it is beautiful according to a reflective judgment that falls under no general rules; the singular art object is its own law. In Hegelian terms, the natural singularity of the beautiful work of art is completely invested with, overwhelmed, and overcome by the universality of the Absolute that it is meant to embody. Its universality overflows its singular form. Thus, as Hegel writes in the "Natural Religion" section, in the art object, "Spirit beholds itself in the form of Being [*Sein*], though not of the non-spiritual being that is filled with the contingent determinations of sensation [i.e., individuality] ... On the contrary, [the artwork] is Being filled with spirit" (M 686). As "filled with Spirit," the singular art object is swept up in its syllogistic destiny, overcome in its finitude and folded into a larger structure of meaning.

On the other hand, as a finite object, the work of beautiful art cannot also help being a beautiful *individuality*. In the Greco-Roman context that Hegel discusses in *Kunstreligion*, *individuality* is a feature of the sculptures of the gods. As such, they are never *entirely* singular but always also *particular*, a generality. A statue of Athena is a beautiful art object whose individuality is sculpted into its form: It represents the particular, general qualities of that goddess: war-like, beautiful, wise, capricious ... And her sculpture presents particular traits that express those qualities and properties that ensure her individuality and make her recognizable in "Athena" statues sculpted throughout the Greek world.

If we take Christ as the *absolute* art object, because it conjoins the human (reason qua Spirit) and the divine (revelation qua Absolute Spirit) in one unique figure, then we must also recognize its ambiguity as both singular and individual. As singular, it is destined to go under, to go to ground (*zu Grund gehen*) as spirit. The absolute universality of its content cannot be contained in such a singular vessel, and indeed Christ's destiny is to die and *become* Spirit. As an *individual*, however, Christ is a human figure, with the particular qualities and properties that make him so, and without which his vanishing would be humanly meaningless. We might say that, as the ultimate (last) art object, as the fully realized beautiful Classical sculpture, he dies as an individual (man) but his singularity ensures his meaningful resurrection as Spirit, within the larger discursive framework of Revelatory Religion.

The textual support for my interpretation of Christ as the ultimate (Classical) art object can be found in (W3: 534–15/M 702–4), that is, *not* in Revelatory Religion but rather toward the end of the introductory paragraphs to "Religion as Art," where Hegel is still presenting Classical Greco-Roman art. It is thus at the culmination of the Classical period that art reaches its fulfilment in the death of (the son of) God. This is what Hegel means when he writes, "In such an epoch, absolute art makes its appearance" (M 702). Absolute art *is* Christ. His finite nature is made clear: "Later on, spirit transcends art in order to gain a higher representation of itself (ibid.)," namely in Revelatory Religion. However, spirit's actualization in religion is only possible because Christ has died. Following a clear reference to the Last Supper and betrayal (M 703), we find that "ethical spirit is resurrected as a shape freed from nature and its own existence" (ibid). In other words, the resurrection of spirit implies that Christ as a beautiful art object is freed from its natural, bodily individuality. It is this individuality "that spirit selects to be the vessel of its sorrow … [and which] suffers [the] violence of the universal" (M3 515/M 704). The *finite* nature of Christ's individuality ensures his singularity and his resurrection qua spirit.

While I acknowledge the idea of taking Christ as the ultimate artform may be shocking to both those who want to attach a strictly human vocation to artistic production and to those who prefer to take their Hegelian Absolute in either more obviously religious or metaphysical terms, I believe that Hegel's phenomenological narrative leads us to this conclusion: the death of (the Son of) God is the most significant ending of art. As such, it is the definitive enactment of art's essential finitude, the destiny and meaning of all its beautiful, individual forms qua singular. The hard lesson is this: No individual form of *schöne Kunst*, no matter how beautiful, is adequate to absolute content. Beauty is always also singular, and as such, must disappear and be enfolded into a structure of greater meaning, first, into the narrative of Revelatory Religion and then into systematic Science. The question that the present chapter leaves us with is whether the syllogistically realized Singularity of Science may itself be qualified as beautiful.

If you are uncomfortable with the religious connotations and prefer your artistic references to be resolutely anthropological, then you are already modern, or in Hegel's view, Romantic, or rather late-romantic and perhaps, ultimately ironical. Romantic art, for Hegel, is the modern human pursuit that endlessly yearns to reproduce what, in fact, can no longer be *artistically* presented: the indwelling of absolute meaning in an essentially finite, human, or human-made form.[6] By extension, ironic art has given up on this pursuit entirely, that is, on the idea of sacred embodiment in individual form. I will return to irony and the endless actuality of art's history below. For now, I want to continue the discussion of the beautiful art object itself and the linguistic fate of its essential finitude.

The death of the Christly art object as the final, singularly beautiful individuality and its outcome in spirit directly imply the second way of conceiving the finitude of art, as syllogistically enfolded into greater structures of meaning. Specifically, beautiful art, which Hegel presents as Classical art culminating in the living/lived Christly artwork, gives way to a new form of the sacred that is no longer artistic but genuinely *religious*. Revealing its conceptual singularity, the individual, all too natural art object has given up the ghost (*Geist*), and that "holy ghost" now becomes the animating spirit of what Hegel refers to as Revelatory Religion (*offenbare* is perhaps better translated as "revealing" or "revelatory"). While Revelatory (Christian) Religion does have its art objects and icons (particularly in Catholicism), they are now to be seen as painfully nostalgic (Romantic) presentations, for example, in the depictions of the Stabat Mater or the crucifixion, of what is missing: the Absolute Being (*Wesen*: essence or meaning) that was once incarnate in the most perfect artwork of the Classical world. The same painful yearning is again expressed in Romantic landscape painting, where the things of nature are no longer presented as sacred in themselves but rather as pointing achingly to a lost essence, to the "beyond," to the now departed spirit of the dead God. Consequently, the objects of modern (Romantic) art are always symbolic of the essence that they can only point to. Endless striving for the "beyond" is a feature of artistic actuality (*Wirklichkeit*), as I will discuss below, whose narrative of infinite progress is only possible because, on Hegel's reading, the last and most perfectly beautiful art form has come and gone.

Before moving on, it is important to stress two points here. Presenting the death of Christ as the paradigmatic expression of art's finitude (i.e., its "end") means comprehending this terminal moment as the end of *schöne Kunst*, and thus, of the possibility of producing art objects that are truly beautiful. Artistic beauty per se, as a human-informed *individual* object invested with universal content, as the perfect cohabitation of spirit (freedom) and nature (necessity), can do no better. All the undeniable beauty realized in the particular stone forms of Classical sculpture is finally achieved in the living/dying Christ. Consequently, we can say that the end of art as the end of *schöne Kunst* (which is what Hegel is concerned with) is the achievement of *das Schöne in der Kunst*. Second, in demonstrating how the *Phenomenology*'s "Religion" chapter clearly moves between distinct discourses on art and religion, I have shown how that work operates the same distinction between these two expressions of Absolute Spirit that we find in later forms, in the *Lectures on Aesthetics* versus those on *Religion*, and in the final section of the *Encyclopaedia*. Consequently, the "Religion" chapter of the *Phenomenology*, which I am concentrating on, provides a crucial, Hegel-penned text on the terminal nature of art.

The essential *content* of Revelatory Religion, that is, the "beyond" that art can henceforth only aspire to, without ever reaching, is now *represented* in narrative form, in the communally celebrated language of worship (*Cultus*). Here, art's missing essence actually *takes place*, not in the individual art object, but in something less natural, more spiritual: in discursive language, which, in Revelatory Religion (specifically, in Protestantism) takes the form of shared church doctrine (*Lehre)*, which I will return to in the next chapter. While the idea that art ends in church doctrine may appear almost blasphemous in our own atheistic, individualistic, and yet deeply Romantic culture, it is true in Hegel, a fact that may perhaps be made more palatable by acknowledging how the move from art to church doctrine takes place in the very human context of language, together with the pedagogical role of doctrine (*Lehre* = teaching). More precisely, the move from the singular art object to Revelatory Religion is a move from *Darstellen* to *Vorstellen* (from presenting to representing), a transition obscured by persistent translations of *Vorstellung* as "picture-thinking" and the lumping of art and religion together as expressions of it over against the discourse of speculative philosophy.

The linguistic distinction between *Darstellung* (or *Darstellen)* and *Vorstellung* (or *Vorstellen*) is apparent in Hotho's reconstituted *Lectures on Aesthetics* and in the *Lectures on Religion*,[7] and it is already clearly in play in the *Phenomenology*. For example, in W3: 514/M 702, where Hegel is writing about the absolute art object, he uses the term "*Darstellung*" twice. On the other hand, when discussing the content of communal worship, later, in Revelatory Religion, he repeatedly uses "*Vorstellen*." For example, he writes, "This form of representation (*Form des Vorstellens*) constitutes the determination in which Spirit becomes conscious of itself in its religious community [*Gemeinde*]" (W3: 556/M 765). The introduction of representational language actually precedes and anticipates the move from art to Revelatory Religion. Indeed, the first instance of representational language (*Vorstellen*) occurs in the communally shared and celebrated Homeric epic. Hegel writes, "The external existence of this *Vorstellens*, language, is the earliest [sacred] language, the epic as such" (W3: 530/M 729). It is this notion of language as the "external existence" of Absolute Being (*Wesen*, also translated as "essence") that comes to inform the religious community of worship (*Cultus*) through shared doctrine.

The linguistic representations (*Vorstellungen*) of church doctrine (e.g., the Nicene Creed) are much better suited to the indwelling of spirit than are the individual, always finite works of art, a truth illustrated by the fact that worship is both communal and temporal: The creeds are invoked, chanted, and sung together, discursively, in a community of believers. We might say that the temples erected by the architectural *Werkmeister* (W3: 512/M 699), which were left empty by the death of the individual artform,[8] are once again filled. However, such places of communal gathering are no longer populated with beautiful stone sculptures but rather inhabited by living celebrants, sharing and incanting sacred phrases and pronouncements. The "objectivity of representational language (*Vorstellens*) ... is the life of the community" (W3: 557/M766).

Consequently, the move from art to Revelatory Religion, from *Darstellung* to *Vorstellung*, allows us to grasp how the essential finitude – the end of the singular, beautiful art object – is enfolded into a greater structure of meaning. The presentation of *the* individual art object (Christ) has been revealed to be absolutely singular, whose end informs the discursive, historically temporal language of Revelatory Religion. We might say that whereas the singular art object manifests itself as a word (Christ, the word [logos] made flesh), the language of communal worship enfolds singular words into meaningful sentences and propositions. This linguistic move into propositional language is also a necessary step in art's philosophical vocation, where its history is further embraced in the systematic, speculative narrative (logos) of Hegelian Science.

However, the finite nature of the individual artform is also responsible for its on-going, modern (in the Hegelian sense) actuality, which can be read as an apparently endless pursuit to find (again) the perfectly adequate embodiment of absolute essence/meaning that defines beauty. In other words, it is the essentially finite nature of the art object that fuels the apparent progression of its continuing history. The fact that we are still happily caught up in artistic activity, creativity, history, criticism, and so on does not contradict the end of art scenario but rather depends upon it, if we understand "end" as the finitude of individual art products themselves. I want to now discuss this on-going, putatively never-ending artistic activity as participating in what Hegel calls "actuality (*Wirklichkeit*)." Rather than understanding this important ontological concept according to the reassuringly idealistic mantra of "everything that is actual is rational" and vice versa, I present Hegelian actuality as fundamentally unfinished, as the crucially *human* pursuit of *something* absolute that always escapes it. The actual is indeed reasonable, but it is precisely its grounding in (human) reason that condemns it to what both Kant and Fichte conceived of as an endless approximation of an intuitively present but actually absent "beyond." Consequently, artistic actuality arises *after* artistic beauty has been achieved in the most accomplished Classical artwork (Christ), whose individual form was perfectly adequate to the universality of its content. To be once again beautiful is nonetheless what the actuality of modern (Romantic, post-Classical) art yearns for, while remaining a consummation devoutly to be wished; for such an accomplishment can never be realized *in actuality*, as Hegel conceives it. Rediscovered beauty will thus remain out of reach for human, all-too-human artistic striving, fundamentally divorced from the revelatory agency of the Absolute. Only the conceptual interplay between reason and revelation can bring about the adequate discursive structure of meaning, carried out in the fully syllogized beauty of Science. But for now, let us come back to earth, to the world of actuality.

Certainly, the fact that artistic activity is ever-present, everywhere, and ongoing seems to contradict any idea that art itself may have somehow ended or become insignificant with the essential finitude of the last, singularly beautiful, Classical art object. In order to avoid such a conclusion and to come to terms with the crepuscular aspect of art, in Hegel, some commentators embrace an avowedly modernist turn: the idea that Hegel only forecloses on a specific, *démodé* (Classical) kind of art, leaving room for the flowering of art in the modern and indeed contemporary expressions that we are familiar with today. Hegel may thus be recognized and thanked for having opened philosophical doors onto modern and even post-modern artistic creation, an essential element of how we generally conceive and define our humanity.[9]

It is undeniable that contemporary artistic activity forms an important feature of our own actuality. Artists have obviously not stopped producing their art. Galleries, theatres and publishing houses are full of it to overflowing. Certainly, today more people are producing art, presenting it, experiencing it, thinking about it, writing about it than ever before, a statement that Hegel himself could even have accurately made, two centuries ago, in Heidelberg and especially in the vibrant cultural setting of Berlin where he spent the last chapter of his life, going to the theatre, the concert hall, the opera, and the like. Furthermore, art's history is generally studied and taught according to a narrative that seems to celebrate its present novelty and continuing progress. Has no one informed the world that art is dead, that it is insignificant, that people should abandon the theatres and galleries, and get to church?

The relation between the absolute dimension of art and its worldly, human practice is necessarily ambiguous, as we have hopefully seen by now, with art expressing, as it does, the comingling of human and absolute agencies. Indeed, when I first presented the *Encyclopaedia Logic* in a graduate seminar, I used art as an example of "actuality," the ontological category that Hegel presents in the eponymous chapter of his work and which I discussed at the outset, in chapter 1. However, some years later, when I went back and reread my notes in preparation for another go at the EL, I scratched out the art example and replaced it with the idea of written political constitutions, as better expressions of the type of reality that Hegel means by *Wirklichkeit.*[10] Art, it seemed to me, was too elevated, too absolute a form of spirit to be a feature of human actuality and its limits, as I discussed in chapter 1. Briefly, actuality reflects, above all, the agency of human reason in its never-ending, earthly striving rather than the revelatory instantiations of art. However, when I looked again at the Additions to the "Actuality" chapter in the EL, I found that Hegel does indeed refer to art there, albeit in passing.[11] How can that be the case when "Art" per se is only specifically evoked much later in the *Encyclopaedia,* in the last section, on Absolute Spirit? Upon discovering a reference to art in the "Actuality" chapter, one might wonder how artistic productions and political constitutions are ontologically alike. The answer is that, from the point of view of actuality, they are both expressions of spirit that are once again, "all too human," in that they bracket the revelatory agency of the Absolute.

What the *Logic* demonstrates is the ontological similarity, within the category of *Wirklichkeit,* between the *human* strivings involved in artistic production, and political jurisprudence. As features of actuality, both artistic production and political constitutions (and law generally) are examples of what Hegel qualifies as *Objective* as opposed to *Absolute* Spirit. Taking place in the world and aspiring to something greater that remains stubbornly beyond, both the productions of contemporary artistic activity and the penning and amending of political constitutions are condemned to be endlessly works-in-progress. Both spheres of activity represent unending approximations of something absolute, something beautiful, true, and good, akin to the Platonic forms, presupposed by the pursuit itself and yet never fully attained.

On Hegel's reading, there will never be a peaceful, just, cosmopolitan world order underscored by the perfect constitution, just as there will never be *another* perfectly beautiful art object. The *Logic* shows that actuality may be more ontologically meaningful than natural contingency; it is undoubtedly a level of reality that is informed by human reason and in which reason may recognize itself. However, actuality, in its historical progress, can do no better than reiterate bad infinities, unending attempts in search of systematic completion. Such closure (*Schluss*) is only afforded by the Scientific (systematic) point of view where art is speculatively or conceptually enfolded into the historical narratives of (the philosophies of) art, religion, and philosophy. However, we are not there yet. For now, let us say that the finitude of actual, individual art objects guarantees their never-ending re-iterations in modern artistic actuality.[12] Indeed, art seems to end in its own endless progress, whose (bad) infinity is a direct consequence of the finite nature of its own man-made products. Consequently, observing ever-present, ongoing, present-day artistic activity does not contradict the notion of art's essential finitude but rather helps us see it as a feature of Hegelian *actuality*, comprehended in terms of infinite striving and approximation.

I do not mean to imply that, for Hegel, continual artistic activity qua modern, post-Classical art is somehow bad or spurious nor that its narrative of progress is a self-delusional fiction. As is the case with political constitutions, the manifold expressions and schools of modern art may indeed be conceived as a progression, one that adds the excitement and challenge of the new and original. However, without an encompassing ("absolute," "systematic," "speculative," "Scientific") narrative of presupposed "wholeness," to use William Desmond's term,[13] the progress of art has no meaningful purpose nor end; it is literally going nowhere. Constantly inventing new figures, caught up in an endless series of new expressions, new flavours, new forms, and new personalities, the only thing definitive in artistic actuality is the evanescent character of "newness" itself. Along with the endless striving for lost beauty, the constant and continual reiteration of "the new" is another recognizable feature of late Romantic, ironic art, which is arguably our present-day art.

In my book *The Anti-Romantic*, I show how Hegel sees Romantic irony as characterizing his present-day artistic actuality, where the incessant search for new forms breaks down into the individual, critical pronouncements that Hegel associates with Friedrich Schlegel's ironic hypercriticism.[14] As the expression of his contemporary actuality, Hegel sees the "art" of Romantic irony as the *Vereitelung* ("vanitization") or rendering vain[15] of all that is truly objective, of all that is systematically coherent and Scientific. The fact that Hegel's most explicit polemic against Romantic irony is found in his later Berlin lectures, two decades after the demise of the Jena circle, demonstrates the persistent, on-going character of the actuality that Hegel attributes to ironic forms and the contemporary challenge that their fragmentary, critical iterations present to his own systematic view of Science. Nonetheless, the essential emptiness and vanity of Romantic irony's artistic expressions are already powerfully prefigured in the Religion chapter of the *Phenomenology of Spirit*, where Hegel's pronouncement of the death of God in the world is followed by some of his most evocative prose: images of vacant, dead artforms, statues, empty temples, formerly beautiful individual artworks that are now void of essence or meaning.[16] As we saw above, only in the representational language of Revelatory Religion (and in later expressions of Absolute Spirit) will these empty "temples" be discursively and temporally re-inhabited by now-absent, essential content, where the human and the divine come together in forms of worship.

Ironic art has given up on essential content altogether, whether artistic or religious, and it has filled this absolute void with the hollow form of its own individual subjectivity, which has consequently been promoted to absolute status. That is why Hegel uses Fichte's foundational formula of "*Ich bin Ich* (I = I)" as the paradigmatic expression of Romantic irony's empty and vain self-reflection (W13: 93). In modern irony, as read by Hegel, there is no distance between the form/content of artistic expression and the form/content of the living, "creative," modern individual. Viewed in a contemporary light, I might say that my blog comments, Twitter feed, Facebook page, Reddit writings, and so on are as "artistic" or creative as anything else in the world, simply because they are the reflections of my own subjective vanity (*Eitelkeit*).

One could end the story of art here, and simply say that Hegel's critique of Romantic irony is a critique of (post)modernity, and that in our current celebration of artistic actuality, irony seems to have had the last word.[17] However, the "wholeness" that Hegel assigns to the story of art must somehow be embraced within the systematic body of Science, and the narrative closure that it implies, the on-going and, indeed, never-ending actuality of art's progress. In other words, rather than ensure the integrity of his philosophical system by simply rejecting and repulsing the fragmentary discourse that is inimical to it, Hegel's audacious project seeks to incorporate the "ending" that stands against it as its absolute Other: the end of artistic actuality in Romantic irony, in the on-going performance of art's infinite finitude.

In order that the endless actuality of art's progress be conceived as folding into a systematic narrative of wholeness, it must be accorded an end that is more discursively meaningful than its ending in Romantic irony. The (bad) infinity of art's never-ending iterations of individual artforms must itself be made finite and singular. Hegel accomplishes this feat by comprehending the actuality of Romantic irony as a critical *moment* of dialectic negativity within his systematic account. In so doing, he is taking Friedrich Schlegel's self-declared hypercritical enterprise at its word, thereby incorporating it and indeed harnessing its dialectical negativity into the systematic Hegelian discourse of Science.

In the Hegelian story of art, critical negativity is necessary in order to break down the recalcitrant, repetitive particularities of modern art's actuality, its endless "progress" through different schools and "isms" and, one supposes, the stultifying dogmatic discourses found in "history of art" manuals. Such critical negativity thus appears as the solvent, cometary element in the story of art, as we discovered it above, in chapter 3 on Hegel's presentation of comets and moons. The fluidifying aspect of negativity allows us to go beyond, question, and even overturn dry, bookish accounts, thus giving life to the philosophical narrative of art, ensuring its organicity. Indeed, by incorporating the Romantic/ironic actuality of art into the body of Science, Hegel's project is to save art from its own incessant and futile finitude, according it a new (spiritual) life. He can only do so by putting an end to the endless strivings of art, while nonetheless preserving the dialectical character of its progression, reborn as critical negativity within the narrative of Science.

In Hegel's introductory *Lectures on Aesthetics,* we see how this works. Several pages before his scathing attack on Friedrich Schlegel as the father of irony and vanity, Hegel refers to Friedrich and his brother August in a relatively positive light. They are acknowledged in this context for introducing a new sense of freedom into German art scholarship, and for their critical openness to other cultures in history (e.g., Indian). In the Schlegel brothers' critical theories, writes Hegel, the old "rules and theories have been overturned" in a way that involves "a clever polemic against the traditional views." Most importantly, the thrust of the Schlegel's recent art criticism participates in a broader (Hegelian) philosophical project, by making possible a "deeper way" of grasping the truth of artistic beauty, by subverting the standard theorizing on the history of art.[18] To what extent Hegel succeeds in thus incorporating the terminal nature of ironic criticism into his systematic narrative remains, of course, an open question, one that perhaps testifies to the openness of the Hegelian system itself. In any case, modern art's narrative of meaningful progress depends on the incorporation of criticism into the presupposed wholeness of Science.

The incorporation of ironic actuality into the holistic account of art, as its essentially critical moment, is not idiosyncratic. The same dynamic is replayed in Hegel's introductory *Lectures on the Philosophy of History,* where we find "Critical History" presented as a dialectical element allowing us to move from the dogmatic "reflective" historiography, and particularly its calcified moralizing expression in "pragmatic" historiography, to the lively systematicity of philosophical history. Indeed, as we saw in chapter 3, it may be possible to find the cometary agency of critical negativity at play throughout the *Encyclopaedic* system, where it appears as the "second" moment of particularity (for-another), within the general Hegelian syllogism (*Schluss*) of Universality, Particularity, and Singularity.

The systematic narrative that Hegel develops, where the Schlegels' critical activity is briefly acknowledged, is historical in its account. Indeed, in presenting irony as a critical "moment" and as a necessarily modern feature within a historical development, Hegel has already presented it as *past*, as a late chapter in the story of art, a twilight episode that can only be truly comprehended according to the *philosophy* of art, which, in Hegel, is necessarily historical in its configuration (pre-Classical, Classical, Romantic-modern). In other words, artistic actuality finds its meaning through its historical outcome, which, in turn, shows itself to be philosophical, that is, running on the syllogistic lines of the Concept.

In historicizing artistic activity, Hegel brings it into the narrative realm of Absolute Spirit as presented in the *Lectures on Aesthetics* and in the *Encyclopaedia*, where art is revealed as the complicit expression of both Absolute and human self-knowing. It is the human aspect that characterizes Hegel's idea of *Geist* (spirit) in general, the idea that the Absolute must temper and temporalize its revelatory activity, must not pour itself out in one punctual, singular instant of *Anschauung* (intuition), even if endlessly reiterated. The articulations of (human) spirit must rather build upon themselves progressively, pedagogically, through developing forms of human consciousness,[19] instantiated in the corresponding historical moments of artistic activity, then to be taken up in the representational discourse of Revelatory Religion and finally, in philosophical Science.

From the point of view of the revelatory agency of the Absolute, which I introduced at the outset as essential to understanding art in Hegel as more than purely anthropological, every beautiful, individual art object is a form of incarnation. However, incarnation, in its eternal instantaneity, is radically *non*-historical. As an instance of the embodied Absolute, each individual instance of *schöne Kunst* has the status of a singular word, as I wrote above, which may be taken as immediately invested with sacred content, but whose finitude nonetheless calls for greater discursive structures of meaning. Universal content always surpasses the finite artform that embodies it, leaving it behind. Even the beautiful Classical sculptures of the Ancient world are never fully adequate to the liveliness of their divine content, a fact illustrated by the serial reiterations of each *particular* godly statue; there can never be just one sculpture of Athena, no matter how beautiful. Introducing historical temporality into art, through the discursive realities of revelatory religion and philosophy both recognizes and overcomes art's essential finitude, that is, the punctual embodiments of universal content in beautiful, singular (Classical) forms, and the endless, modern production of individual objects striving for such lost beauty. Finally, in historicizing art, philosophy spiritualizes and humanizes it, making it something that is "by us" and "for us," within the larger pedagogical structure of meaning that Hegel calls *Geist*. The heroic project of Hegel's philosophy of art, in enfolding its essential finitude into greater narrative structures of meaning, is to save art from its own incessant and ultimately ironic endings, to make sense of the obsessive, compulsive character of artistic modernity by comprehending its always revolutionary "progression" into systematic, historical accounts.

Such salvation finally takes place within the narrative body of philosophical Science itself: the completed (*vollkommen*) outcome of Hegel's grand syllogism, which passes from the Universal, through the Particular, into the universal Singularity, into the one that is all: to the mediated corpus of the Idea. Thus, at the end of the *Philosophy of Spirit*, the last book of the *Encyclopaedia of Philosophical Sciences*, the Ideas of the True and the Good are presented in a way that leads us to expect their culmination in the apparently missing third "Platonic" element: the Idea of Beauty. Instead, in its place, Hegel presents the Absolute Idea itself, the Singular recapitulative embodiment of everything that has come before.

If we accept the intimation of the Idea of Beauty here, in the culminating position of Science, beyond the Ideas of the True and the Good, then it becomes possible to see how Hegel meant the *Encyclopaedia* to realize the project of the seminal "Oldest System Program of German Idealism," which he worked on with his friends Schelling and Hölderlin around 1797. Indeed, in that early manifesto, we find that "*truth and goodness* are united like sisters *only in beauty*."[20] If one were to object that this early writing is far removed from the mature Hegel of the Berlin years, I would answer that Hegel's lifelong philosophical project consists in bridging the radical divide between the domains of the theoretical (the True) and the practical (the Good), a division that is grounded in the then-dominant philosophies of Kant and Fichte. And how else to conceive the union of the two apparently separate pursuits of the True and the Good than in the reconciling Idea of the Beautiful?[21] If the *Encyclopaedia of Philosophical Sciences* is indeed the embodiment of universal content, and the Singular reconciliation of the Ideas of the True and the Good, should we not then see it as a beautiful artform?

The claim that Hegel's *Encyclopaedia of Philosophical Sciences* may be viewed as the ultimate artwork, the Singular incarnation of Beauty, may appear to be just as outrageous as the notion that the perfect art object took place in the individuality of Christ. In fact, the two propositions are intertwined. Both forms are perfect (*vollkommen*) Singular embodiments of the human and the Absolute. Their difference lies in how the immediate *individuality* of the incarnated and disincarnated Christly art object has been given, in Science, a mediated narrative, in which the punctuality of absolute Revelation has been deployed through the discursive, historical, and *anthropological* figures of spirit. Nonetheless, in both the living individuality of Christ and in the accomplished Singularity of

Science, the Absolute reveals itself in "human form," allowing for reciprocal recognition, where humanity is conscious of itself in the Absolute and the Absolute knows itself through human spirit, forming what Hegel refers to as Absolute Spirit.[22] In the Scientific exercises of art, religion, and philosophy, the divine and the human can be said to comingle in greater, historical forms of discursive meaning, which are no longer instances of finite revelation but are truly infinite. Whereas the human element embodied in the Christly art object was that of natural man, the humanity of Science resides in the fact that the *Encyclopaedia of Philosophical Sciences* is both the fruit of human spirit and destined to be *for* humanity, through its vocation as a book of philosophy and a teaching manual that was meant to be read and studied within the *Cultus* of the state university.

The final expression of art's finitude, in Hegel, is perhaps nothing other than the *Encyclopaedic* articulation of his own system, taken as the ultimate work of *schöne Kunst.* As is the case with the beautiful work of art whose finitude bespeaks an essential end within greater structures of interpretation, taking the *Encyclopaedia* as a fulfilled work of art invites us to a critical reflection on its meaning, thereby overcoming the hard individuality of its systematicity, opening onto new interpretations of its singularity.

8
The Hermeneutics of Worship

We have seen how Hegel viewed his epochal late-Enlightenment moment in spirit as falling under the sign of *Verstand* (understanding) and its fixated incapacity to perceive how the apparently opposed discourses of reason and revelation should be comprehended as binary expressions of immediate knowing, each demanding the reciprocal mediation of the other. The immediate forms of cognition, which we explored in chapter 4 on "insight," are features of the hard, lunar nature of *Verstand*, which is reluctant to abandon the exclusive binarity of its positions. Briefly, the understanding does not recognize the speculative truth that lies within representational discourse and the conceptual destiny of the judgment form. The culture of *Verstand* clearly represented a pressing, contemporary challenge for Hegel, when he was pronouncing his courses on religion, in Berlin, a fact made explicit in his preface to Hinrichs's *Religionsphilosophie*, which I introduced in chapter 1. Since I have been presenting this historical cultural moment in the linguistic terms of representation (*Vorstellens*) and judgment (*Urteil*), it is not surprising that the contemporary danger of a recalcitrant (lunar) culture of *Verstand* should have hermeneutical implications, that is, relative to a way of interpreting sacred text.

In the last chapter, we saw how one way of comprehending the finitude of art in Hegel is through the passage from artistic *Darstellen* (presenting) to religious *Vorstellen* (representing). I discussed this passage in terms of absolute revelation, recognizing that both art and religion are expressions of Absolute Spirit. Whereas, in beautiful art, the Absolute presents itself in finite, intuitive, individual embodiments, in revelatory religion the individual "words" of art are enfolded into broader narrative structures. Church doctrine and dogma are the realization of such structures, within the language of representation. Of course, it is up to Science to recognize the speculative (Scientific) nature that lies, unacknowledged, within the representational discourses of church doctrine. As we saw in chapter 6, this recognition means comprehending that doctrine, as a linguistic form of representation, is not the embodiment of heteronomous positivity, inimical to the self-liberating struggles of human reason, but rather shares with the latter a vocation for freedom.

Consequently, we might say that Hegel's goal is to liberate church doctrine, as representational language, from the bi-polar hermeneutics of the understanding by substituting a speculative form of interpretation. The speculative hermeneutics of Science means recognizing the discourse of religion as a form of Absolute Spirit that shares with artistic beauty, as we saw in the last chapter, an essential complicity between human and divine agencies. Human religious worship (*Cultus*) may thus be considered as the real, shared celebration of the divine (revelation) and the human (reason), taking place, *bien entendu*, in the language of representation but grasped "by us" speculative philosophers, within the broader (broadest?) logos of Science. In order to show how Hegel means to save religious doctrine from the dominant culture of *Verstand*, I want to return to Hegel's preface to Hinrichs's *Religionsphilosophie.* In the preface, we discover a kind of genealogy of *Verstand* as it pertains to religious doctrine, thus temporalzing its bi-polar hermeneutical approach and rendering possible, even dialectically inevitable, its overcoming. This outcome will allow us to apprehend the Scientific destiny of religious doctrine and its *Cultus* (worship).

Before discussing the preface to Hinrichs's now largely forgotten work, I want to make a few further points. First, the text is particularly significant because it was actually written and published under Hegel's eye, and therefore escapes any philological reservations pertaining to the authenticity of the *Lectures on the Philosophy of Religion*'s contents. As well, in re-articulating the main thrust of the criticism found in the *Principles of the Philosophy of Right*, the text refutes claims that Hegel's apparent religious conservatism, that is, his anti-liberal, anti-individualist position, was largely circumstantial and politically expedient. In fact, in revealing the hermeneutical mistreatment of doctrine at the hands of the contemporary theology of *Verstand*, Hegel not only presents the centrality of doctrine in religion, he expands his view to show how such mistreatment resonates in political demagoguery, terrorism, and repression. The political aspect of biblical hermeneutics therefore comes to the fore, and the danger that I discussed above, notably in chapters 5 and 6, with respect to the bifurcated culture of the *Verstand*, comes home to roost. Given the performative nature of discourse generally, as I have been considering it in Hegel, it should not be surprising that the language of religious doctrine should have actual socio-political purchase. After all, the community of worship can be thought of as the performative reality and the social, celebratory embodiment of shared doctrinal words.

Second, the preface also provides us with a hint to a positive program of reconciliation between faith and knowledge through teaching, a brief refrain that, once identified, can be found echoing throughout the *Lectures on the Philosophy of Religion*, although this motif has, to my knowledge, gone largely unheard. Religious doctrine is fundamental to Hegel's philosophy of religion to the extent that theological content must be taught and learned. The doctrines (*Lehre*) of the Church are literally teachings, and this is how their real words participate in *Sittlichkeit*, in philosophy and, finally, in Science. As Hegel writes in his preface: "[T]he true content [of religion] comes to the mind first in words and letters" (W11: 44).[1] Of course, this content must be *aufgehoben*, negated by thought and raised up. However, rather than discounting its status as substantial content and its essential centrality, the sublation of doctrine into Science confirms it.

Church doctrine is essentially text, and this is what we are discussing when we refer to the representational thought that comes to form religious truth. In the same way that philosophy of history must rely on different levels of historical text or historiography, philosophy of religion reflects upon, speculatively, religious texts that exist in the form of church doctrine. Indeed, it may be helpful to see religious doctrine in the same light as Hegel's treatment of historiography in the opening pages of his *Lectures on the Philosophy of History*, where original, reflective (universal, pragmatic, critical) and philosophical historiography become the *aufgehoben* content of the philosophy of history. Religious doctrine forms philosophical content just as do historical accounts. In both cases, we recognize that philosophy does not produce its content a priori; it reflects on the texts that it provides itself with, in such a way as to bring them into the narrative of Science.

Regarding religious doctrine, there are two problems associated with the hermeneutical approach that I am putting forward. First, while Hegel refers repeatedly to the *Lehre* of religion, he rarely, if ever, actually cites the doctrines he has in mind. Second, commentators on Hegel tend to be philosophically allergic to the very mention of church doctrine or dogma, which is generally associated with obscurantism and superstition, an attitude already in evidence in Hegel's own late-Enlightenment time, when doctrine was associated with the positive, heteronomous aspect of religion. As I mentioned above, however, Hegel's mission is to show how doctrine, as the linguistic, representational (*vorgestellt*) material of Revelation, is above-all revelatory of, and recognizable as, absolute agency. Acknowledging this reality allows religious doctrine to be reciprocally recognized by reason, since both actions are revelatory of freedom. In Hegel's words from the *Lectures*, "It is in God's nature, in his perfect autonomy, to exist for the spirit of man" (W17: 383).

In his preface to Hinrichs's work on religion, we discover a brief Hegelian genealogy of doctrinal hermeneutics: how theology has treated sacred text and church doctrine, from Scholasticism, through the Enlightenment, to the present age (1821), a year after he publishes his *Philosophy of Right.* I use the term "genealogy" because the narrative that it presents may be seen as leading to and diagnosing a contemporary condition of malaise, in a way that anticipates Nietzsche's and Foucault's use of the method. This unhappy condition is characterized by the paradigmatic or symptomatic figure of Schleiermacher, whose "religion of feeling" represents, for Hegel, the ultimate mistreatment of sacred text and doctrine. As I showed in my earlier references to the preface, Schleiermacher embodies, for Hegel, the exclusive binarity that he associates with the contemporary culture of *Verstand.* Thus, the genealogy "leading" to Schleiermacher's hermeneutical approach to doctrine can be read as the genealogy of this culture.

The brief story begins in the religious context of the pre-Renaissance, late-Medieval world, where ratiocinating understanding is under the sway of positive religion and entirely taken up with the casuistic concerns of Church scholarship. In this context, the representational language of reflective thought finds absolute truth in the doctrinal objects of faith, in the immediate and finite objectivity presented as "the stories, events, circumstances, and commandments" (W11: 46) of positive religion. The truth of these revelatory elements is imposed dogmatically. In fact, the "holding-for-true" (*Fürwahrhalten*) of finite things that is characteristic of Scholastic understanding is cognitively identical to the dogmatic empiricism Hegel ascribes to Jacobi, as we saw above, in chapter 5: empirical reasoning grounded in religious faith, where both express forms of immediate knowing. The truth of what I perceive is guaranteed by my faith in God. However, here, the empirically received "finite things (*Dinge*)" that Hegel is referring to are of a textual nature, viz. to the "stories, events, circumstances, and commandments" that are recounted or written. In other words, reflexive understanding, in the religious context, does not involve direct perception of revelatory objectivity. Although the Apostles may indeed have born direct empirical witness to the miraculous events they recount, just as Thucydides may have indeed observed Pericles's speeches, scholastic theology treats the words of the biblical accounts themselves in a factual way, where the words are taken as true, as immediately representing the singular facts that they recount. In reflecting upon these doctrinal accounts, Scholasticism both holds them for true and positions itself as detached from them in its reflective discourse.

The language of scholasticism is one of "sterile erudition and orthodoxy," (W11: 48) where dogmatic understanding takes the "letters" *(Buchstaben)*, of an "external, historical account (*aüsserliche Historische*)," as the "last word (*Hauptwort*)" on divine truth (ibid.). In this portrayal of traditional theological hermeneutics, Hegel is presenting the unilateral position of dogmatic faith, as a certain historical moment of thought when the data of Revelation, as original text, was accepted as true in an immediate, nominalist fashion, in order to form the material for theological judgments. Such judgments are the grammatical form of reflective thinking that is appropriate to the ratiocinating understanding.

The actual judgments of scholastic understanding are themselves textual in nature and the texts, although "external," form a new, more reflective level of Church doctrine than the original biblical accounts that they reflect upon. This is particularly true regarding the Lutheran Augsburg Confession, which seeks to ground in scriptural references the teachings of earlier ecumenical doctrines, namely the Apostles', the Nicene, and the Athanasian Creeds. In all these liturgical professions of faith, we find articulated the core tenets of Christianity as a religion of Revelation: the Trinitarian nature of God, the divinity of Christ, the reality of Holy Spirit, and the possibility of salvation. For Hegel, it is this doctrinal content that allows the representational language of Christianity to be grasped speculatively, in the language of Science.

Regarding the question of linguistic content and its relation to the Scientific narrative, we can therefore associate the doctrines of positive religion that I just mentioned with the level of historiographical discourse that Hegel presents in his introductory *Lectures on the Philosophy of History* as "reflective history." In both cases, original accounts have been reflected upon and consequently made present to contemporary, philosophical account. In taking church doctrine as content, we see how the Hegelian "middle," characterized by the discourses of the understanding, representation and judgment, is always ambiguous: as the middle term of the systematic syllogism, it is essential and contentful (*gehaltvoll*); as a moment of *Verstand*, it represents a constant danger of fixation in sterile, stubborn ratiocination and the unreconciled opposition between reasoning and faith, a danger fully realized, for Hegel, in the contemporary culture of *Verstand*.

According to the preface's speculative (dialectical) genealogy of *Verstand*, dogmatic, orthodox theology is the architect of its own demise. The frenetic casuistic activity of theological erudition in Late Scholasticism releases the "infinite energy" (W11: 48) of pure thought, which is inherent in reflexive thinking and synonymous, in Hegelian terms, with abstract freedom. As such the activity of thought performs the cometary negativity that we discovered in chapter 3, which powers dialectical movement, overcoming fixed, sclerotic positions, dissolving them into systematic movement. Consequently, we can say that reflexive understanding turns on itself, or rather, the frenetic activity of its disputations turns back on its own dogmatic and orthodox approach to the finite objectivity represented in sacred text. Historically, the power of thought promoted in Scholasticism is unleashed in the Enlightenment. Hegel presents late-Scholasticism as a kind of bacchanal of free thinking, where thought turns against its own hitherto held dogmatic approach to doctrine, replacing it with a thoroughgoing skepticism regarding the content of Revelation.

In theological terms, the "histories," "commandments," and doctrines are simply not taken as true anymore. In linguistic terms, the words of these accounts and embodying their sacred meanings have been sundered in two, leaving, on one hand, empty signifiers and on the other, pure essence or thought. Biblical texts are no longer invested with sacred content, and are now treated hermeneutically as a system of linguistic signifiers divorced from their meaning, which becomes arbitrarily assignable. According to this new way of looking at things, the data of Revelation as represented in original, Biblical accounts endure the same fate as does worldly objectivity at the hands of subjective idealism. All facts are reduced to subjectively determined and formulated appearances; essence as true meaning is now an unattainable (through *understanding*) thing-in-itself.

The radical skepticism that always haunts reflexive understanding and accounts for its cometary restlessness, is expressed, as in Kantian empiricism, in the assertion that the truth, as the thing-in-itself, cannot be *known* but only apprehended immediately through subjective intuition or feeling. Schleiermacher's religion of feeling appears precisely in this light, as the corollary to his hermeneutical approach to religious doctrine, where, as he expresses it in his *Speeches on Religion*, "all sacred text is a mausoleum for religion, testimony that a great spirit has passed through but is no longer there."[2] In Schleiermacher, according to Hegel, theology is "reduced to historical [i.e., hermeneutical] erudition and then to the deficient exposition of certain subjective feelings" (W11 50). Thus, Schleiermacher is presented as one of those "ratiocinating theologians [...] who set religion in subjective feelings" (W11: 51).

Far from representing an idiosyncratic curiosity, the theologian of feeling appears as a "contemporary representation (*Zeitvorstellung*)" of "the culture in our time" (W11: 51). This is the culture of the *Verstand* that we have returned to repeatedly in the present book. In Hegel's preface to Hinrichs's work, we see how ratiocinating reason has collapsed into skepticism, as Jacobi had predicted, leaving only intuition or feeling. As we have seen, Hegel sees this culture as a condition of malaise, a condition where unilateral positions of immediate knowing, qua *Einsicht*, are sclerotically fixed and therefore impediments to the life or movement of thought and ultimately to the holistic conception of the state, spirit, and, ultimately, Science. This condition of malaise is manifest in what Hegel refers to as the three "absolute presuppositions" or "truths" of "our time" (W11: 52), which I introduced in chapter 1, all of which are represented in Schleiermacher's theology of content-free feeling, and which can therefore be comprehended as hermeneutical positions with regard to doctrine.

The first contemporary presupposition is the skeptical assertion that "man knows nothing of the truth" (W11: 52). This attitude is deduced from the empiricism of Kantian critical philosophy which "has presented to understanding the correct consciousness of itself: that it is incapable of knowing the truth" (ibid.). However, Hegel is not here presenting a general observation in the theory of knowledge. This modern skeptical attitude is significant because of its approach to religious text, that is, to doctrine as taking place in the meaningful, sacred words of representational language. As we saw historically, in the Enlightenment's approach to such language, the bacchanal of doubt overturned and emptied the doctrinal discourse of Revelation of its truth, leaving behind empty words or rather signs, what Hegel calls *Buchstaben* or *Namen*.

The skeptical attitude to absolute truth leads directly to the second universal presupposition of our times, "that spirit [...] can only deal with appearances and finite things" (W11: 54). Hermeneutically, this meant that the culture of *Verstand*, as practised by Schleiermacher, reduces sacred text and doctrine to arbitrarily determinable texts, "a mausoleum for religion", which may be used to refer to the individual, historical events of what was once the sacred story. Christ himself thus becomes a purely historical individual (a "creature", rather than begotten of God, contravening the Nicene Creed). As Hegel writes, "The intelligence when occupied with religious doctrines, [now] must restrict itself to their aspects as appearances, throw itself into their external circumstances and become interested in their narrative, where spirt has [only] to do with things past, with something remote from itself in which spirit itself is not present" (W11: 55). This type of theological hermeneutics is always open to arbitrary, subjective interpretation and may consequently be compared with Hegel's polemical take on critical historiography, productive of "monstrosities of pure imagination" and "subjective fancies" (W12: 18–19).[3]

We might say that, in broader ontological terms, generalized skepticism brings about an entirely empirical reality, where the world, emptied of all significant content, is reduced to a swarm of *inherently* meaningless things, to subjectively determined appearances. However, it is not my contention that the fate of all worldly things is what Hegel is concerned with in his diagnosis of the contemporary malaise of *Verstand.* Rather, what is of significance for him is first and foremost the reality of spirit and its place within Science. Since both of these crucial Hegelian elements are fundamentally textual in nature, depending upon an idea of concrete, contentful, and fulfilled (*vollkommen*) logos, the hermeneutical emptying of religious doctrine, of that which represents a form of Absolute Spirit, where the divine and the human comingle in forms of communal worship, has grave import.

Out of the empirical and skeptical hermeneutical attitudes towards doctrinal truth arises the third "universal prejudice" of the present age, "the opinion that feeling constitutes the veritable and even sole form in which religiosity conserves its authenticity" (W11: 56). In other words, Schleiermacher's theology of feeling is symptomatic of a modern condition where the informed, revelatory truth of text has been reduced to empirical, subjectively determinable sense data in the form of arbitrarily interpreted linguistic signs, where "rational" skepticism is generalized and where intuitive feeling is seen as the only way to experience a truth that is necessarily grasped as beyond.

The preface shows us how the hermeneutical approach that Hegel discovers in Schleiermacher reflects a generalized malaise of the late-Enlightenment Berlin epoch, one that spills out beyond the realm of Absolute Spirit (art, religion, philosophy) and onto the "earlier" realm of what Hegel treats, in his *Encyclopaedic* system, as Objective Spirit, that is, the human project of Reason (versus Revelation) as it has culminated in the ethical-political actuality of the times. Anchored in the aporia of reflexive, representational understanding, caught between the horns of skepticism and feeling, consciousness cannot escape the destructive dichotomy between the dogmatisms of faith and reason, the opposition that both Lessing and Kant had already seen as politically dangerous to the Enlightenment project of human freedom, and which we discussed in detail, in chapter 5. Indeed, it is precisely this contemporary culture of *Verstand* that gives rise to Karl Sand's act of political terrorism and brings about the subsequent state-imposed repression. For Hegel, it was no accident that Sand was a student of theology. The link between the contemporary culture of individual feeling and political violence and repression is clearly enunciated (with a little tweaking of the translation) in Hegel's manuscript from his *Lectures on the Philosophy of Religion.* Indeed, Hegel complains how "the content of religion" and "objective faith" has been replaced by an "empirical consciousness" along with the "deification of oneself," where "truth as objective" has perished in the face of "religious feeling." He then remarks that "violence and repression necessarily appear if consciousness is no longer open to objective faith" (LR1: 240).

We find the same theme iterated in the preface to the *Philosophy of Right* (PR) where Karl Sand's mentor, the post-Kantian, anti-Semitic, nationalist "ringleader," Jakob Friedrich Fries is denounced by Hegel as representing "the philosophy of recent times," according to which "truth itself cannot be known" (Hegel's first general presupposition of the times) and where everything depends on individual, arbitrary feeling. Thus, Hegel remarks that in Fries's famous speech at the nationalist Württemberg rally, "the constitution" is treated in the same way that Schleiermacher mistreats Church doctrine. In each case, the words of contentful linguistic expressions (e.g., the constitution) are emptied of all meaningful content, leaving only empty signs (*Buchstaben*) on one hand and subjective (nationalist) sentiment on the other (W7: 17–18).

Before continuing with what I described above as the positive program hinted at in Hinrichs's preface, I want to make two brief remarks concerning our own contemporary difficulty in grasping the relation between Hegelian philosophy (or philosophy generally) and religion. It is entirely possible that our difficulty arises from the fact that we fall squarely within the modern culture that Hegel describes, one that is largely defined by reflective, analytical thinking and which is defined by, to quote Peter Hodgson again, "the reigning dogmatisms of our time," that is, "philosophical agnosticism and religious fundamentalism."[4] Our contemporary reliance on subjective feeling and the eschewal of doctrinal content is the perfect expression of "our one-sided relation" to God (W17: 382), how we have reduced religion to our own personal experience, making it all about us, forgetting that the whole idea of revelation, whether expressed in the representational language of religion or in the speculative discourse (logos) of Science implies an agency whose "nature it is to exist for human spirit, to communicate with him" (W17: 383).

Does the refusal of revelatory agency indeed impoverish our own present-day actuality, as Hegel wants to demonstrate? Certainly, an argument can be made that many of the religion-driven, tribal conflicts in today's world are driven by or nourished by arbitrary, sentimentalist interpretations of the divine and its agency. Further, Hegel's hermeneutical critique of feeling-based theology helps us understand how the general undermining of forms of language and discourse, whereby the performative meaningfulness of text is sacrificed or etiolated in favour of arbitrary assignments of subjective individual feeling is ethically and politically dangerous. In that language grounds, structures, and performs the worlds that we live in, the substance that we accord to our laws, constitutions, literatures, doctrines, acts, accords, treaties, and so on, has real ramifications on our shared realities and our ability to live together.

Modern theology, according to Hegel, has become divided between two seemingly opposed, yet strictly complementary positions: on one hand, scripture and doctrine are viewed as external accounts, as empty text, as the purely positive, orthodox trappings of religion and, as such, the object of skepticism; on the other hand, feeling is seen as the only way to God. The preface arrives at this conclusion and yet also provides a glimpse of how this contemporary condition may be overcome. Just as the fixated theological impasse spills over into the social-political realm, giving rise, in the worst case, to extremist violence and repression, the proposed solution has real political implications. For us, contemporary readers of Hegel, just as radical expressions of religious fundamentalism may be viewed as pernicious to contemporary forms of law-based, liberal, democratic governance, we may also look to the preface's proposed solution as salutary in our own context.

Clearly echoing Lessing's goal of uniting revelation and reason, in his essay, "The Education of the Human Race," Hegel sees education as overcoming the opposition between subjective feeling (with its attendant position of skeptical empiricism) and the positive doctrines of religion. Quoting the Hinrichs preface, "I consider belief, according to the genuine, ancient sense of the term [i.e., not as mere subjective conviction – *Gewissheit* or *Furwahrhalten*] as involving both phases, the one just as much as the other, and I place them together, bound up in a relational unity" (W11: 43–4). Consequently, "natural feeling and natural will" are certainly "immediate to man." Likewise, "the true content [of religion] comes to mind externally at first, in the word and the letter." However, "religious education brings about the unity of the two, so that the feelings ... lose their force, and what was the empty letter grows into its own living spirit." It is important to see that Hegel's idea of education here presents a radically different hermeneutical approach from the one he associates with Schleiermacher and the understanding, which promotes "the same reverence for, and the same belief in, finite histories, events, circumstances, mental images, commandments, etc. as there is in absolute Being and eternal history" (W11: 46). In this contemporary condition, "the frame" is promoted over the "dignity of the work of art within" (ibid.).

The hermeneutical approach espoused by Hegel accepts doctrine as language that is inherently invested with *meaning* or essence, which is ultimately conceived as the truth of Revelation: "Because truth simply is, it must appear and it must have appeared; this manifestation of truth belongs to its eternal nature itself" (ibid.). Divorcing doctrine from its revelatory idea "degrades its content to an empty abstraction," where text becomes empty letters, "*Buchstaben*" (W11: 48). While Hegel's promotion of doctrine may seem symptomatic of orthodoxy, the opposite is, in fact, the case. In education, the language of doctrine (*Lehre* as "teachings") is remembered, internalized, *aufgehoben* in such a way as to be determined and thus made "mine," where I am liberated from the external positivity of its linguistic reality by having recognized myself in it.[5] In that religious education is initially a communal affair, the liberation it affords is at first communal. However, since theology is an essential content of philosophical Science (as the philosophy of religion) and scientific education is ultimately a state affair, the immediately communal celebration of doctrine is overcome and taken up into the organic state. We can thus understand Sand's extremist political act as symptomatic of bad state education, at the hands of teachers like Fries, who maintain the opposition between subjective feeling and expressions of meaningful language as simply empty, arbitrary letters, and thus condemn their students to heteronomous tutelage. In that specific case, expressions of communal, exclusive nationalism were allowed to supplant the organic configurations of the Hegelian state and its idea of the university. I want to briefly examine the relation between state education and political freedom by referring to several passages from Hegel's *Lectures on Religion* where he discusses the centrality of doctrine as teaching.

In the *Lectures* of 1827, we find doctrine developed within the Christian (Protestant) community as "something presupposed and finished," as something that has been "brought forth and developed in the church" (LR3 334/VR3 257). Even though such doctrine is historically and contingently determined, "developed out of other concrete contents that are intermixed with impurities," in the church it is "present to hand and must then be preserved" (ibid.). The preservation of doctrine happens through its teaching. "[In the church] that which is doctrine must also be taught. It is, it exists, it is valid, it is acknowledged and immediately presupposed." Through doctrine, "spiritual truth" becomes known, "and the fact that spiritual truth appears" is "precisely that it is taught" as doctrine. Which allows Hegel to affirm that "the church is essentially a teaching church, by virtue of which there is a teaching office whose function is to expound doctrine" (LR3 335).

While "human beings" experience doctrine as pre-existing, as already present to hand, as something they are "born into," such truth initially strikes the individual free subject as something external, heteronomous and imposed – "as authority," as "something distinct from me" (LR3 335). Indeed, in presenting itself, through teaching, "as something valid" that must be learned, doctrine is first experienced as authority. The truth of doctrine first appears as simply there, as something that must be "put up with," like the existence of the sun, remarks Hegel. However, through the process of actually learning doctrine, of memorizing and interiorizing it, its truth is "taken up by individuals into themselves," They come to "assimilate" and "appropriate" truths that initially appeared to them as external authority. This process of learning the teachings of the church can therefore be understood as a liberation from "absolute otherness," where "this otherness is [now] posited as something overcome, as already conquered." The truth of doctrine is therefore the pre-supposed possibility of freedom, within the community of the church where, in Hegel's words, individuals are both "born into freedom and to freedom" (LR3 336). What I ultimately recognize as my own in the initially authoritative, external teaching of doctrine is *myself* as spirit, in a process by which "one's rational [i.e., free human] spirit is brought to consciousness" as "something objective" (ibid.).

The teaching of doctrine, within the church community (*Gemeinde*), initially takes the form of "custom," "habituation," or "cultivation." Initiates and children learn doctrine like the Nicene Creed by heart, as a profession of faith to be acquired by rote and memorized. However, as with habituation generally, in Hegel, this type of learning already represents a liberation from other forms of natural determination. Just as the dancer liberates themself from the strange, immediate recalcitrance of their body, through habitual practice, in order to attain the lively freedom of the performing artist as an ensouled body, the community reciting the learned doctrine of truth comes to actually embody spirit. I have been emphasizing the linguistic aspect of doctrine. In that context, habituation means the progressive investment of what were first empty linguistic signs, simply phrases recited by rote and found already there. Gradually, the empty signs come to gain meaning, one that is shared in the shared rites of worship, where the signs have become meaningful words participating in greater structures of significance.

Such a vision of the spiritual community as an ensouled body instantiated in the living verb is powerful and seductive. I believe it represents the stage that we reach, in reading the *Phenomenology*, when we finish chapter 6, the comforting evocation of community as the "I that is we," of perfect reciprocal recognition of individuals, in the "Yea" of reconciliation within a homogeneous group. As we know, however, the immediate self-knowledge of community must be "overcome" and differentiated in order for it to be raised to the level of Science, just as the teachings of truth through doctrine must become philosophy. This "raising" can only happen through the recognition that doctrine represents the predicative agency of an absolute Other, bespeaking a reality beyond that of human actuality (*Wirklichkeit*) and its limitations.

Taking *Lehre* in this way already anticipates the recognition of its post-religious, philosophical vocation. As we find expressed in the *Lectures on the Philosophy of Religion*, "[T]he doctrine of faith is first of all constituted in the church, then later it is thinking … which later asserts its rights in the matter … by way of philosophy" (LR 334). We cannot ignore the fact that the philosophical overcoming and raising up of doctrine is again, like doctrine itself, essentially a matter of teaching, through language. Philosophical teaching raises the actuality of spirit above and beyond its embodiment in the community, to the reality of the fully articulated, scientific state. To put it another way, just as Hegel presents the teaching of church doctrine as the substantial, constitutive discourse of the free Christian community, of its truth, he presents the teaching of philosophy as a constitutive discourse whose "church" is the state university, and whose form of worship (*Cultus*) is the hermeneutically shared, celebrated, and critically ("cometarily") questioned discourses of Science.

The move or progression from the simple, homogeneous community to the ideal (Scientific) state involves the "decay" of the former, the word Hegel employs in his *Lectures on the Philosophy of Religion*, describing the current state of the *Cultus*, which he likens to the decadence of Rome. The decay of the community of worship is described in similar terms to those we found, above, in Hinrichs's preface, where the polarity of reflective thinking and subjective feeling has turned religion into an arbitrary play of "virtuosities," a reference to Schleiermacher's concept of religious mediators as virtuosi. In the *Lectures*, this state of affairs is explicitly related to the hermeneutical destiny of doctrine, which I described above: "[T]he decay within the state of religion" has taken place "[a]t the point where the doctrines of religion have become representations, mere factual data" (LR 160). The "fading away (*Vergehen*) of the community" that Hegel refers to here has been brought about by having "allowed reason and religion to contradict themselves" (LR 161). Significantly, the possibility of transforming the *Vergehen* of the community into an *Übergehen* (transition) thus lies in the reconciliation of reason and religion in philosophy. "Religion [must] take refuge in philosophy," where it may find "sanctuary" (LR 162) in the teaching of the philosophy of religion, and specifically through Hegel's own lectures: "These lectures have attempted to offer guidance to this end [i.e., to the reconciliation of reason and religion]" (ibid.). And, of course, the lectures themselves took performative place within the Faculty of Philosophy at the (State) University of Berlin.

9

Philosophy and Its Scientific Conclusion (*Schluss*)

Hegel's thoughts on the history of philosophy can be found mainly in the form of posthumously published notes, either his own sparse lecture notes or, more copiously, from the notebooks of the students who attended the courses that he taught on the subject at the University of Berlin between 1820 and 1831, just before his untimely death. The outline of some of his ideas on the history of philosophy can also be found in his *Encyclopaedia of Philosophical Sciences*, in the final sections of Absolute Spirit, where he deals with philosophy itself as the highest human spiritual pursuit, following those of art and religion, which we have been discussing in the last two chapters. Of course, one might also argue that fundamental ideas for his history of philosophy are anticipated in his earlier *Phenomenology of Spirit* (1807), which recounts the epic journey of human thought through time. However, as we have seen, this human, all-too-human epic, which I have been associating with "reason," ends at the *Phenomenology*'s chapter 7, on Religion, where the reciprocal, absolute agency of revelation is presented.

Hegel always began his courses, whether on art, religion, states (world history), or the history of philosophy, with introductory lectures. His published introductions usually deal with common misconceptions but also with common sense intuitions that turn out to be founded, albeit in ways that go far beyond common sense. Above all, Hegel's introductions generally show how the material presented relates to his notion of Science (*Wissenschaft*) as systematic philosophy, that is to say, how the element under discussion fits into and participates in the organic whole. I will rely mainly on Hegel's introductory lectures on the subject, in order to examine how the history of philosophy is related to his idea of Science, where "love of wisdom" is meant to have become wisdom itself.[1]

The problem is this: If we believe that the history of philosophy must be undertaken before we can apprehend what philosophy truly is (as Science), then we are left in the strange position of studying the history of an object that we do not know. Conversely, we cannot know what philosophy truly is without having first studied its history, without knowing how it got to be what it is. In other words, only the true, accomplished notion of philosophy puts us in a position to comprehend its history, and yet the true notion of philosophy only appears as a result of that history. In fact, this apparent paradox is what makes the history of philosophy special, distinguishing it from other histories. For example, the histories of mathematics, states, art, and so on, all presuppose the knowledge of their objects (the artwork, numbers, states, religions ...). How can we study the history of philosophy without knowing its object (truth)? In fact, the temporal logic of the present perfect, which we discussed above, in chapter 4, helps us see that the "Now," at which point we begin, is already fully informed with its historical becoming.

Although, in Hegel, the introduction may have a rhetorical vocation, it is not the arbitrary construction of the author. Rather, as is the case with Hegelian philosophy generally, the truth is assumed to be already known, immediately or intuitively, but must nonetheless be found out (again) or demonstrated systematically. It is a method that echoes Plato's solution to the Eristic argument: We must begin with an innate but inchoate truth, which must be subsequently carried out, developed, or demonstrated dialectically, in an argued fashion. Hegel's introduction to the history of philosophy presupposes the true conception of its subject matter, philosophy, while assuming that its search for truth has already been accomplished in the culminating point of Science, where love of wisdom has actually become wisdom itself: absolute self-knowledge. Philosophy becomes wisdom (Science) when it knows itself, and it knows itself through the knowledge of its history, according to the temporal grammar of the *Perfekt* tense of "having been." In other words, when philosophy recognizes its history as its own, and recognizes itself in its history, then it is Science. This adds an even deeper dimension to the history of philosophy: By revisiting that history, we are actually involved in the process of Science; we participate in philosophy's self-knowledge.

However, as we have seen, such human self-knowledge qua spirit is only possible because it recognizes itself in the reciprocal self-knowing of the Absolute. Briefly, human self-knowledge must acknowledge itself as partaking in and of the Absolute's self-revelatory agency. Reason must become conscious of itself as complicit in revelation. Reason comes to comprehend that without truth being given (revealed), there is no truth to be known, and conversely, without the human knowledge of truth, there is no actual truth at all. In more obviously Hegelian terms, self-knowledge is only accomplished through mediating otherness, whereby thought recognizes itself in the Other, and the Other in thought. Humanity and the Absolute are each reciprocally, the Other of itself, whereby subjectivity is comprehended as substantial and substance is recognized as subject.

The end of the history of philosophy is a point where philosophy recognizes itself in its past articulations and sees these as integral to what it is and has always been. However, since this wisdom of self-knowledge is accomplished through the reconciliation with absolute otherness, we have to look back at the strivings of human philosophical reason in this light: as the progressive coming to terms with itself as revelatory (and revelation as taking place through human rational agency). The idea of "the end of history" has been at least as much debated, in Hegel studies, as the terminal nature of the other form of absolute spirit that we discussed in chapter 7: art. Similarly, the history of philosophy does imply the end of philosophical activity and the summarizing of its actuality. However, just as art's ending in religion portends and guarantees the enduring significance of its actual strivings, and religion's ending in philosophy guarantees the lasting significance of its doctrinal teachings, "saved" by philosophical thought, philosophy comes to term in the systematic narrative of Science. There, philosophy's actuality, which means its actual teaching as history of philosophy, has arrived at the eternal "Now" that was necessarily there at the outset, in the form of Science.

Science is the culmination of the philosophical narrative, and just as art and religion had their own discursive forms (*Darstellen* and *Vorstellen*), the logos of Science speaks in the speculative language of the concept, whose most accomplished form is syllogistic. Rather than seeing such systematic closure (*Schluss* = syllogism) as typical Germanic folly, I have been presenting it in narrative terms, where meaning is provided through the coherency, wholeness, and culmination of the account. Without such a summing up, without such a sense of achievement, historical accounts, as with any other account, tend to be nothing more than the recounting of an endless series of meaningless, and ultimately, boring events. One thinks of how children tend to tell a story, "This happened, then this happened, then something else happened, then this happened ..."

The principal interest of any history at all, it may be argued, involves the thoughtful relating of past events with the present, with "us." But what constitutes the "events" within philosophical history, and who are the protagonists of its story? Hegel calls them "heroes of thought." By the power of their reason, they have "penetrated into the being of things, of nature, of spirit, of God, providing treasures of thought" (H 210/W18: 20), for us, students of that history who may come to recognize ourselves, as philosophers, in it. The so-called events of philosophical history do not take place in the physical world but rather in thought itself, in the realm of universal concerns. This means that the less attention the history of philosophy pays to the personal, particular aspects of the "hero's" life, the better. What matters is the philosopher's thought, not their personal idiosyncrasies. The past "acts of thought" that we reflect upon may appear, at first, foreign to us, things of the past, but "in reality, we are what we are through history" (H 210/ W18: 21). Our awareness of this is what Hegel calls "the possession of self-conscious reason."

The process by which philosophical thought inhabits and informs the "being of things" has a determined linguistic dimension. Indeed, the things that philosophy deals with are fundamentally linguistic representations (*Vorstellungen*). For example, the "heroes of philosophy" do not reflect directly on the immediacy of natural things themselves. Natural scientists have already "thought over" or considered the things of nature, taken its raw, immediate signs and invested them so that they come to represent the discourses that make up the natural sciences. It is this textual material that philosophers further think over. The result is a discourse on a discourse. The philosophical content of Hegelian Science is conceptual or speculative because it embraces the representational language upon which it has reflected as the particular moment within syllogistic systematicity. In making its objects into its own content, the discourse of Hegelian Science does not add anything to their formative discourses but rather recognizes within them the conceptual movement that lies latent and unrecognized therein. While philosophy recognizes itself in the linguistic contents that it has reflected upon (e.g., from the natural sciences), the truth of this state of affairs is only revealed in Science, in the culminating view of what philosophy, through its history, has always been about.

While the past iterations of philosophy have indeed espoused the predicative language of judgment, expressing the binary ontologic of the understanding, for example in the oppositional discourses of faith and knowing in the pantheism quarrel, the speculative truth of Science allows "us" to see how immediately exclusive positions carry within themselves the seeds and resources for their own overcoming and mediation. If philosophy has a meaningful history, it is one that can only be grasped in retrospect, and, crucially, in the reconciling form of the speculative discourse of Science. Once again, the logos of Science is no more than the discursive recognition of what philosophy has always been up to, and acknowledgment of the onto-grammatical nature of its judgments.

The process or progress of reason (human self-consciousness through the "otherness" of the past) informs, as we have seen, the present "Now" of Hegelian Science. However, in fact, the same can be said with regard to every philosophical "present," – every philosopher in the history of the domain has taken the material (of thought) that has been passed on, has rethought it, and made it his/her own in their present "now." In doing so, the "otherness" of past philosophical knowledge has been constantly reworked, transformed, preserved, and yet invested with the spirit of those reflecting upon it. Thus, philosophy can be seen to "rise in relation to previous philosophy ((H 210/ W18: 21)," in a way that bespeaks progress. Such progress should not be seen as strictly linear but rather, to use Hegel's strong metaphor, it is a story that "swells like a river, the farther it gets from its source (ibid.)," incorporating the philosophical contributions of all those who, in the past, have reflected on "their" history and so invested it with the spirit of their time.

As historians of philosophy, the "events" we have before us are human philosophical systems, produced by human spirit. They are textual in nature. On another level, however, the history we have before us is that of thought itself, in the form of the Absolute (or the Idea), which becomes real and comes to recognize itself through the historical articulations that it shares, within the province of Absolute Spirit, with human reason. I will return to this absolute dimension below. For now, let us reiterate a principal theme of this book: the revelatory nature of absolute agency. This fundamental metaphysical notion is perhaps best comprehended (historically) in Neoplatonic terms, where Plato's highest Form or Idea (the Good) becomes immanent in the world, giving rise to the respondent human desire to know its source. As we saw in chapter 4, absolute agency expresses itself in the ahistorical "Now." The historical nature of scientific cognition is actualized when humanity is involved, through the history of philosophy. As we have seen, the end of this history involves the absolute dimension of Science and its self-knowing wisdom.

The dynamic encounter between the absolute aspect of Hegel's Science, as the whole, fully recognized Truth, and the historical immanence of human philosophical endeavour is problematic, as we saw above, in chapter 4. The Truth, as absolute, must be eternally present. Otherwise, it would not be the Truth. However, as such, how can it have a history? What is the relation between the historical truths of philosophy and the Truth itself? If the Truth is the fully developed whole, what is the truth status of its parts, of the "events" that make up the history of philosophy? Are they errors? If so, how can the whole Truth be made up of errors? What is the relation between the whole Truth and the particular fields of human thought, for example, the natural sciences and religion? These are central questions that Hegel deals with in the introductory lectures to his *History of Philosophy*, and which I have addressed by referring to the grammatical temporality of the *Perfekt* tense.

The apparent contradiction between the Truth as eternal and history as transitory, changing, and therefore untrue implies that philosophy, as a historical pursuit, cannot gain its object, Truth. This problem appears to be reflected in the history of philosophy itself. Whereas other sciences seem to progress calmly, gradually gaining truth and expanding knowledge, philosophy seems to undergo constant upheaval, where earlier contributions are contradicted and dismissed. Thus, a common idea regarding the history of philosophy is that it is only an accumulation of opposed opinions. Just as world history seems to recount a series of contingent actions, across time, the history of philosophy is seen to recount contingent thoughts. Both pursuits appear characteristic of the limits of actuality, as presented in the first chapter of this book. In this regard, philosophy becomes a series of senseless follies, or, at best, culturally useful information that may be possessed as helpful erudition. Already for Hegel, the fact that this tends to be the contemporary view of philosophy is the reflection of a present-day climate of opinion generally. The opinionated world simply sees itself reflected in the history of philosophy: a vast multitude of opinions, spread out for the arbitrary choosing.[2] As is the case with worldly actuality generally, and as we observed it in modern artistic practice (chapter 7), philosophical actuality seems to be never-ending, constantly and continually engaged in an endless approximation of a Truth that remains stubbornly beyond.

If the actual culture of opinion is the climate for beginning a discussion of the history of philosophy, the result will be the finding out of particular, isolated ideas that appear foreign to the philosophical apprentice because they appear removed and distant. The history of philosophy thus appears to simply subject us to a mass of strange opinions. However, this common view runs counter to what the history of philosophy truly is: the free movement of thought, in which we may recognize ourselves as thinking and free. As historians of philosophy, and thus as philosophers, we must follow this past movement, working it out for ourselves, making it truly our own. There are no shortcuts, in spite of the spurious promises of our current culture of the *Verstand* and its bipolar forms of immediate knowing: skeptical reasoning and personal feeling.

Common opinion does not recognize the philosophical process and its progression, and indeed, the events of the history of philosophy seem to challenge the very idea of process. Just as history per se can be seen as the thankless rise and fall of individuals and civilizations, the history of philosophy can similarly be seen as an endless, meaningless account of "the dead burying their dead," a "battlefield covered with the bones of the dead" (H 224/W18: 35), where each new philosophy is presented as the right one, consigning others to the philosophical graveyard. On this view, each philosopher builds and creates their new system, one that shows all previous attempts to be wrong. However, as Hegel argues in the introduction to his *Phenomenology of Spirit*, a system of philosophy that is absolutely true cannot leave anything out; otherwise, it would neither be true nor absolute.[3] Even "error" must be included in such a system. In fact, it is these past "errors" that are historically incorporated into the holistic view of philosophy that is enfolded into Science as its "having been." The history of philosophy is integral to the Truth. If indeed "the Truth is One" (H 225/W18: 36), it is because the systematic One incorporates diversity rather than excluding it. The diversity and number of past philosophies do not refute philosophy. Rather, Science teaches that the diversity of "error" is philosophy's *own* history, through which it comes to *be* what it has been.

Consequently, the different philosophies of the past are not "a collection of chance events" that are disconnected. Rather, "in the movement of the thinking spirit, there is real connection and what there takes place is rational" (H 238/W18: 50). Once again, the term "rational" is much misunderstood, in Hegel. Rather than implying that history (in general) runs on some kind of occult, pre-determining, dialectical program, designed by a transcendent "software" designer, "rational" describes a relation wherein thought has come to recognize itself in worldly otherness, precisely because it has thought through that otherness. In the case of history, "rational" means that human reason (spirit) has come to recognize itself in what was initially historical otherness.

Because thought, for Hegel, is characterized by movement, the syllogistically articulated history (of philosophy), as rational, will follow the movement of the Concept. This movement is not linear and never-ending but rather can be seen as a development that is circular, and deepening, like a spiral, where the endpoint is already pre-conceived intuitively at the beginning. The development between beginning and end must be seen as one of enrichment, of struggle, and above all, as free. To get the point across, Hegel, in his introductory *Lectures on the History of Philosophy* refers to Aristotle, through the terms of potentiality and actuality, and metaphorically to the development of the seed into the actual tree. Such development is driven by the final, actual (in the Aristotelian sense) form, which must be presupposed as already there, at the start, in the potential of the seed. In the present context, the movement of philosophical history is driven by its final form, as Science, and yet this destiny must be already present at the beginning, as an intuition of the achieved whole, the wisdom of philosophical self-knowledge. As we have seen, through Karl Löwith's reference to Aristotelian time in Hegel, in chapter 4, the truth of Science resides in the eternal "Now," which is thoroughly informed by the historical content of human thought or spirit.

Referring to the metaphor of the tree (H 244/W18: 56), we can say that the history of human spirit, recounted in the history of philosophy, is not a system of external, mechanistic necessity but a system carrying out its *own* potential; as the story of its *own* necessity, the history of philosophy is the story of its freedom. The metaphor of the tree helps us see how philosophy is both a complete system while at the same time being in development. Just as the development of the tree may appear as an accidental process, where branches and twigs seem to grow at random, the stages of historical development may seem chaotic. However, from the point of view of the fully realized tree, we comprehend that the apparently contingent, haphazard growth actually makes sense. In the case of philosophy, we come to recognize that the unifying theme of the story is, and has always been, the realization of human freedom. If such a history is rational, it is because "our" (free) thought recognizes itself in its past moments, by revisiting and reflecting upon the process of what has brought us to the point of such retrospection. The end is the self-knowledge of spirit, which, as we find it in chapter 8 of the *Phenomenology*, is Absolute Knowing only because it involves recognition of the revelatory agency of the Absolute, and its complicity in the human story of freedom.

As Hegel argues in the introduction to the *Phenomenology of Spirit*, the philosophical "errors" of the past become the actual content of philosophical Science as a whole (i.e., of philosophy as it is embraced within Science). If past philosophies have passed away, it is not because they are wrong, but rather because they are not yet complete or fully accomplished "*vollkommen*," according to the syllogistic movement (*Schluss*) of the Concept. The grammatical forms of their judgments have not yet realized their ontological potential. Philosophy is only complete, as Science, when form is adequate to content, where the accomplished form embraces all past forms as its particular content. In Science, all past forms are preserved as present content, affirmatively contained as elements in an organic whole. As preserved, each past philosophy has only surrendered its pretention to be final and absolute, a pretention which, in fact, constituted its "error." Nonetheless, it is the very finite nature of each "past" philosophical form, its "error," which reveals its significance, its meaning. Indeed, according to the Hegelian idea of essence as arising from what has been (*Wesen ist gewesen*), it is only because finite things vanish, give up their ghost, that they are meaningful within a grander narrative structure of *Geist*.

Consequently, each past philosophy must be taken as the full expression of its particular "present," within spirit (in the progress of humanity).

For example, Cartesian philosophy is the full and adequate expression of a mechanistic (geometrical) view of nature and the self that conceives it as such, current at the time of Descartes (H 244/W18: 57). However, his philosophy is insufficient to fully explain later organic chemistry or the romantic-expressive conception of selfhood. In a way, we can say that the history of philosophy does not deal with the past but with moments that have been *present*. The content of philosophy is always "true" with respect to its moment in time, its moment in spirit, and yet constitutes an "error" or is incomplete and finite with regards to the whole of Science. Consequently, we must not regard the history of philosophy as simply dealing with the past. "In time, it is always true and for each and every time (H 245/W18: 57)", as Hegel remarks. Our project, as historians of philosophy (i.e., as philosophers) is to rediscover the "presence" in the past forms. In doing so, we make those forms significant "for us"; or to put it another way, we ourselves become present in those past forms, which, once again, is what Hegel means by "reason." Consequently, reason in history, defined as thought's recognition of itself in (historical) otherness, implies that the history of philosophy ultimately does not deal with what is gone, but with what forms the truth of the human living present as an expression of thought, which is to say, for Hegel, an expression of freedom.

Each philosopher has their place in time. History of philosophy has mainly to do with finding this place or rather the time, the moment in spirit, in the progress of humanity. This method is a sign of maturity. As with individuals, it is a mistake, a sign of immaturity, to try to relive one's youth or one's childhood. Rather, the mature individual looks back on the different stages of their life, grasps each in its place, while both recognizing themself in these past moments and recognizing this past as constituting the person one has become. This is the process Hegel refers to generally as "remembering" (*Erinnerung*). It does not mean yearning nostalgically for past forms because they are "simpler," more natural, purer, and so on. Such nostalgic yearning for simplicity is a feature of the culture of *Verstand*, its reliance on feeling, and the endless dogmatic striving for lost essence, which we have associated with theoretical, political, artistic, and moral actuality (*Wirklichkeit*). Hegel is opposed to the romantic idea of the past, presaged by Rousseau, developed in Herder, where history is seen as a kind of falling away or decadence from an original state that was somehow truer and better because it was closer to a natural source of the Good. Against this trend, Hegel maintains that the earliest forms of philosophy are, in fact, the poorest, the most abstract, falling into general, unilateral categories of idealism or materialism. Conversely, the later philosophical forms (barring anachronistic expressions) tend to be more concrete, precisely because they have reflected upon and taken earlier forms into account. The ultimate (last) philosophical form is Science, where the love of wisdom is finally requited. It is nothing new, but simply the realization of what the search has always been about: the collaboration of human reason and absolute revelation in the performative reality of their reciprocal self-knowledge. The wisdom of Science thus accomplishes the injunction of the oracle: Know thyself!

If we take spirit as the movement of human thought through historical moments in time, and we accept that philosophy is the highest manifestation of thought, then philosophy must have an essential bond with the spirit of its time. We might then ask how philosophy arises within a given culture, at a certain time. For example, it is usually said that philosophy arises when physical conditions of ease and luxury allow people to think beyond their immediate needs, to indulge in philosophical contemplation. However, for Hegel, the idea that physical conditions influence spiritual (or mental) manifestations is wrong-headed. In fact, the opposite is true. Because spirit, in general, is the process of thought overcoming, determining, and negating nature qua "physical conditions," it is rather the universe of physical occurrence that is conditioned by philosophy. For example, it is the subjective idealism of Cartesian philosophy that determines its natural world as mechanical, geometrical, and devoid of spontaneous animation.

Given that philosophy, as the highest articulation of thought, embodies the overcoming of natural life, and liberation from natural determination, the consequence is that a culture's philosophical truth manifests itself when that culture's original "robustness of life" is in a state of decline (H257/W18: 71). In fact, philosophy (as thought) hastens the decline! Philosophy, as the negating agency of thought, shakes up and even destroys status quo reality. Philosophical agency, within the holistic narrative of Science, can be comprehended, at least in part, as a form of cometary negativity, as I presented it in chapter 3. Hence, the best philosophy accompanies the downfall of civilizations. As Hegel famously expresses the crepuscular nature of philosophy, in the preface to the *Philosophy of Right*, the owl of Minerva takes flight at dusk. As examples, in the introductory *Lectures on the History of Philosophy*, Hegel cites Socrates and Plato, whose philosophies arose in the period of Athenian decadence, when the city was past its prime, its freshness and youthful vitality faded. Indeed, Socratic questioning hastened that decline. Similarly, the best of Roman philosophy (Stoicism, Epicureanism) appears with the decadence of Rome, and the zenith of Ancient philosophy, in general, appears with the Neoplatonists at Alexandria. Similarly, the high point of modern philosophy (Jakob Böhme) is contemporaneous with the decline of the Holy Roman Empire. It is significant that the philosophical apexes of both the Ancient and Modern philosophical epochs espouse a Neoplatonic form. The reason for this is that Neoplatonic thought is the closest that philosophy can come to the syllogistic Truth of Science, according to the Concept, where the universal (Good/Idea/Absolute) lets itself go into the otherness of natural substance, which is comprehended as subjectively revelatory through the reciprocal human agency of reason qua spirit. Hegel's *Encyclopaedia of Philosophical Sciences* is the systematic reiteration of the same conceptual form found in Neoplatonism (and in Jakob Böhme). We are thus invited to ask whether the appearance of Hegelian Science presages the decline of modernity, a question that I will leave open, for now.

Philosophy is the love of wisdom. In Hegel, wisdom is the self-knowledge of spirit as absolute Truth. However, philosophy is not the only form of human thought that has acknowledged such truth. What makes philosophy the highest form of absolute spirit? If we answer that philosophy is a form of *absolute* spirit, a form of knowing where human reason comingles with the revelatory agency of the Absolute, then we may also wonder what distinguishes philosophy from the penultimate form of absolute spirit: religion, which we have already shown, in chapter 7, to be the outcome or truth of art.

Given what we have seen regarding the absolute vocation of philosophy as systematic Science, we cannot merely exclude religion as that which is opposed to it, for then Science would not be absolutely true. In fact, the exclusion of religion reflects the unilateral Enlightenment view of reasoning over against faith and the agency of Revelation. As we have seen, however, the binary, exclusive approach to reasoning and faith, proper to the *Verstand*, relies on taking each form, in its immediacy, as requiring reciprocal mediation, where reason acknowledges that what it knows is the "given" as revealed, and revelation, as taking place in the doctrine of religion, acknowledges its role in the teaching of humanity. Each expression is accorded its pride of place in Science. Nonetheless, from a historical point of view, it is true that philosophy has distinguished itself from religion over time. Indeed, the very conditions for the beginning of philosophy certainly involve opposition to previously existing religions. Such a historical opposition, culminating in the crisis of the *Pantheismusstreit*, does not refute the reconciliation of reason and revelation but rather is its underlying condition. In fact, as we have seen, the fundamental opposition between faith and reasoning, in Hegel's contemporary culture of *Verstand*, presents itself to him and indeed to his age as a cultural imperative: the present overcoming of the bifurcated state-of-affairs.

As we saw in the last chapter, in religion the Absolute is experienced as a Beyond, as the Other, but one which may be reconciled with man through communal worship. As the shared recognition of the complicit relation between God and man, worship should consequently be taken as a collaborative expression of reason and revelation: the self-recognition of human and absolute thought in otherness. As we have seen, in religion, such recognition is expressed in the linguistic form of representation (*Vorstellens*), that is, as the doctrinal language affirming Christ as the human God and the godly human in a linguistic form that outstrips the singular finitude of art. It is the language of doctrine that is celebrated in the communal reality of worship. Philosophy, in its aspiration for the (revealed) Truth has always participated in the same collaborative enterprise between the human (Reason) and the divine (Revelation), instantiated in its *logos*, a correspondence that has allowed me, already in the first chapter of this book, to present the idea that philosophical Science may itself be seen as a form of worship – as the celebration of and in shared language, within the "temple" of the modern state university. The specificity of philosophy over against religion lies in the nature of philosophy's language qua *logos*. Whereas church doctrine is representative, the language of philosophy is inherently speculative (espousing the movement of the Concept), although the line between the two expressions may be ambiguous. For example, on Hegel's view, the Gospel according to John is inherently speculative whereas the unilateral, exclusive discourses of the *Verstand* (e.g., Jacobi or Mendelssohn) tend to be representative. How can we establish the difference, particularly since the representational discourse of religion and the speculative language of philosophy are both articulated in the grammatical structure of judgment or predication?

Throughout this book and elsewhere I have insisted upon the ontological nature of the grammatical form of judgment in Hegel's notion of Science, for example in chapter 2 on the metaphysics of the copula in Hegel's *Logics*. Central to the idea that Hegel sees the judgment form as evolving into the syllogism, through the fulfillment of the copula (the verb "to be") between subject and predicate, is the comprehension of *Subjekt* both grammatically and psychically. I have traced this fundamental insight back to Hegel's apprehension of the elemental Fichtean *Tathundlung* (factual action) of *Ich bin Ich*, where we do, in fact, have a *Satz* (proposition) in which the grammatical subject is also a self-positing self. I have also introduced the idea that Hegel's fundamental insight is further informed by Hölderlin's aphoristic and brilliant interpretation of the Fichtean *Grundsatz* in the text *Urteil und Sein*, where Hölderlin demonstrates that the Fichtean addition of a *Nicht-Ich* is not necessary since the judgment form is, in itself, not only a statement of self-identity but, by positing itself as "other," equally a statement of self-differencing. This idea is crucial to what Hegel understands as "speculative": the identity of identity and difference. Judgment can be considered "speculative" not because it changes form but simply because it is understood as expressing both identity and difference within a singular grammatical form. The reality of identity and difference is not an added result to the judgment form but actually takes place in the copula "is," whose ful-filled existence is realized in the middle term of the syllogism, that is, in the contentful moment of particularity, where things are what they are because they *are* also not what they are not.

Before concluding the present chapter, I would like to add another dimension to Hegel's idea of the speculative proposition, which is nothing more than a particular way of grasping the common form of the predicative proposition, a way that is proper to Science, enabling it to "read" the history of philosophy as developing iterations of its own Concept or syllogistic completion (*Schluss*).

The dimension that helps us complete the picture, enabling us to distinguish between the speculative grasp of predication and its representative cousin, is found in the preface to the *Phenomenology of Spirit*, where Hegel discusses briefly what he means by the "speculative proposition" or sentence (Reid 2021).[4] The speculative approach to the proposition (or judgment) sees that when the onto-grammatical subject posits itself into the predicate, the predicate (as substance) actually has selfhood conferred upon it, in such a way that now the predicate can be seen as subject, and where what was formerly subject should now be seen as the predicate. This reciprocal, "speculative" predicative action is described by Hegel as involving a "*Gegenstoss* (counter-thrust)," wherein the "Subject has passed over into the Predicate" (W3: 57/M 60). Whereas Fichte had relied on a "not-I" in order to guarantee a "counter-thrust," Hölderlin had shown Hegel that such reciprocal action could be contained within the judgment form itself. The lesson learned: the speculative *Satz*.

Given the ontological nature of the subject-predicate relation, the speculative proposition constitutes its own grammatical ontology, observable in the way the copula is now conceived. Whereas in the reflective grammar of representative language, the predicative content of the unilaterally subjective and self-identical "I" is described in terms of "vanity" and "futility," the *speculative* proposition brings about a "harmony" of both identity and difference, a "floating centre" (M61/W3, 59) of meaning. In the speculatively grasped copula, as Hegel puts it in fittingly ambiguous terms, "meaning has become different from what it was meant to mean" (M62/W3: 60). In other terms, whereas the reflective proposition of representative language expresses the unilateral, dogmatic opinion of the subject/self, which it imposes upon the predicate/object, the speculative proposition allows the predicate to speak for itself. The result is an ambiguity of meaning that takes place *in the copula*, which now articulates the dialogical relationship between subject and predicate. This relationship is one where identity is fully enlivened by difference, and whose multiplication of meaning involves an essential openness to interpretation (Reid 2021).

On the absolute level of Science, the speculative proposition implies the reciprocal, mutual determination between human reason and absolute revelation, where, from the former's point of view, it is substance (nature) that has been determined by the positing of human thought into otherness; then, from the latter, revelatory point of view, it is the Absolute (substance qua subject) that posits and reveals itself through human knowing. Science comprehends that this is indeed what philosophy has always been carrying out – knowing *what is revealed*, but without being fully aware of its own reasoning complicity in the act of revelation itself. If the discourses of religion and the positive sciences can be qualified as representational, it is because they do not recognize the onto-grammatical complicity that lies inchoate in the copula of its own judgments. On one hand, religious conceit takes doctrine as pure revelation, in the form of positivity, excluding human reason. Conversely, the representative discourse of dogmatic reason figures that it can and must determine everything, including God. The world is its oyster, to crack open and consume! The "vanity (*Eitelkeit*)" that Hegel refers to regarding representational language is the fitting expression of a predicative act that is entirely one-sided, refusing the reciprocal free predication of the other. It is simply self-reflection, the I = I in its non-speculative sense.

In the last chapter, we saw how Hegelian Science proposes a safe harbour to religion by adopting its doctrine as revelatory, thus sparing it the dismemberment that contemporary hermeneutics reserves for it. We have also seen how absolute revelation is essentially ahistorical, how it seeks to pour itself out in the eternal "Now." Likewise, the representational language in which religious doctrine takes place tends to eschew dialectical negativity and movement, tending toward dogmatic utterances of "what is." Nonetheless, religion and its doctrines certainly appear to have a history. Indeed, in their common eastern origins, in the Church Fathers, in later Scholastic philosophy, we find religion and philosophy mixed together in historical moments. Indeed, theology and philosophical metaphysics have never been entirely exclusive. Given this ambiguously shared past, the question becomes, to what extent should the history of philosophy, as practised within Science, take past forms of religious thinking and its representational language into account?

Although philosophy recognizes religion as having a shared goal, it is crucial to note that the representative, symbolic nature of religious discourse does not allow it to be, *in itself*, historical. The "eternal" aspect in religion is never more than an ever-present revelation. In fact, if religion were itself historical, it would be the free self-movement of thought, that is, it would be philosophy. In fact, when religion claims a history, it becomes something else: mythology. In his introductory *Lectures on the History of Philosophy*, Hegel finds he must therefore distinguish mythology from philosophy, an increasingly pressing task given the on-going efforts of his old friend (and rival) Schelling, whose work seems to be moving toward a position where philosophy itself is taken as the ultimate, rational form of mythology!

Mythology, for Hegel, reflects only the external aspect of religion, that is, its presentation in artistic objects, which may appear to have some sort of historical movement, through pre-Christian epochs, involving different forms of myth: African/Egyptian, "oriental," Greek, and Roman. However, while mythologies may *seem* to evolve historically, in fact they are always anchored in artistic symbolism, which is essentially non-historical. Indeed, the nature of artistic symbolism means that the religious "Beyond" is always immediately incarnate in the finite expressions of art that mythology employs, as we saw in chapter 7, on art. By putting aside the mythological, symbolic aspect of religion, we put aside any historical elements that it may appear to have, in its choice of culturally specific art objects (animals, pyramids, temples, statues ...). When religion is allowed an actual history, in Hegel, it is only after its crucial beginning – at the catastrophic end of the most beautiful art object: Christ, and the beginning of the *philosophical* narrative that Hegel refers to as spirit. Of course, as we have seen, the human agency of spirit ensures its historical unfolding in time, where revelatory expressions of the Absolute, in art and religion, are embraced, and made meaningful, in and through the history of philosophy, the third moment of absolute spirit. Consequently, it is only in the philosophical realization of Science that expressions of revelation are conceived as having unfolded, according to the historical narrative of Reason, one that is humanly teachable, knowable, and meaningful. Briefly, art and religion are historical because they are presented in the philosophies of art and religion.

In the last chapter, on religion, we discovered the idea of worship as a communal celebration of text, in the form of religious doctrine. I also emphasized the idea that church doctrine (*Lehre*) has a pedagogical function; it is a form of teaching. While the educational and, therefore, liberational aspect of doctrine may not be immediately evident, it is certainly the mission of Hegelian Science to acknowledge the speculative and non-dogmatic tenor of the church's teachings. This truth is the substance of Hegel's *Philosophy of Religion*, as he taught it in his university courses on the subject. It is only in this context that the revelatory nature of religion can be comprehended as unfolding historically, in terms understandable within the narrative of human reason. The same dynamic may now be witnessed in Hegel's teaching of the history of philosophy, where the highest form of revelation, that of the Idea, can be truly grasped as unfolding within a historical account wherein it is absolutely complicit with the agency of human reason. The result is what Hegel refers to as Absolute Spirit. Just as the empty temples of art become filled with the shared celebration of sacred text, philosophy has its own form of worship: the philosophy class within the state university. It is in this living context of Science that the texts of philosophy find their performative truth, where they are read, discussed, interpreted and, above all, found to be meaningful expressions of the on-going complicity between human reason and absolute revelation. Only thus do we learn what the history of philosophy has to teach: knowledge of human freedom and the certainty that there is indeed something true to be known.

PART FOUR

After the *Schluss*: Da Capo al Fine

10
Organic Systematicity and Its Excremental Challenge

Systematic Stakes

Recent Hegel scholarship readily acknowledges the organicity of his system of philosophy, also known as Science (*Wissenschaft*). For example, Karen Ng begins her book *Hegel's Concept of Life* by noting that "throughout his philosophical system," Hegel describes "the activity of Reason and thought in terms of the development and activity of organic life."[1] Indeed, acknowledging the organic trope has several advantages for presenting Hegel's thought. It allows the essential systematicity of his philosophy to be seen as living rather than as a dead, mechanistic configuration of nineteenth-century metaphysics. Representing Science as organic also allows it to skirt accusations of systematic, totalizing closure. Organic systems are "holistic" and open to otherness. The system as a living organism also puts it into movement, even self-movement, thereby overcoming charges of historical ossification. The living, organic philosophical system as open and self-moving may even claim a degree of progression, without actually claiming to tell a tale of "progress," an idea largely discounted or avoided in contemporary intellectual narratives. Perhaps best of all, the organic paradigm evokes a self-moving articulation of difference within identity, where the parts are holistically and vitally integrated into the whole, which, in turn, gives life and meaning to the different, incorporated parts or organs. Finally, we cannot ignore how the positive associations that we tend to lend the term "organic," as an expression of what is natural and therefore essentially authentic and good, according to the deep-seated romantic-expressivist tenor of our times, gives Hegel's systematic intellectual enterprise a more positive branding than it might normally have. I see my students visibly relax when I refer to Hegel's conception of the state as "organic."[2]

To the extent that the elements, parts, or members of the Hegelian system are themselves expressive of syllogistic movement, it is not too much of a stretch to conceive of Science as an organic individuality, whose life is present in the purposive, dynamic inter-relation between the whole and its constituent organs. As Hegel puts it in the *Encyclopaedia*'s *Philosophy of Nature,* "in an organism, each member is both an end [in itself] and a means [to an end]" (PN 356/W9 459). Above all, the organic trope pertains to the lively activity of the Idea, whose life is embodied in the highest accomplishments in spirit, and, above all, in the expression is philosophy itself.

> Spirit, just as it is something true, is something living, organic [*organisch*], systematic, and it is only through the knowledge of that nature as its own that the science of spirit is equally true, living, organic, and systematic. (ES 379 Add., W10: 15)

Most commentators who recognize the organic nature of the system rightly conceive the organism of Science as a dynamic individuality that is open to externality and animated by internal difference: The living, organic system is the identity of identity and difference, "capable of containing and enduring its own contradiction" (EN 359 Remark/W9: 469). However, the question that I want to raise is whether such features of internal differentiation within individual embodiment are sufficient for an organic comprehension of Hegel's philosophical Science. Given the power of the organic trope in comprehending Science's systematicity, I believe it is beholden upon us to look closely at how Hegel actually conceives of the living organism, beyond the reassuring generalities that I mentioned at the outset. Indeed, if organicity is meant to characterize the Hegelian system, then should we not investigate how Hegel presents the animal organism itself, particularly, the animal organism, which alone possesses the self-moving, vital complexity that is apparently so essential to his philosophical system?

There has been marked contemporary interest in Hegelian biology, as attested to by a recent issue of *Hegel Bulletin* devoted to the subject.[3] However, to be clear, my intention is not to maintain that Hegel conceives of his system as actually *being* an animal organism. I want to examine features of organicity that Hegel clearly attributes to his own philosophical system, through his discussion of the individual animal organism. Doing so, brings to light aspects of Scientific systematicity that have gone unnoticed. Crucially, as we will see, the animal whose biological organicity is of primary interest to Hegel is the human being, the animal endowed with subjectivity, consciousness, and reason but which remains vitally tied to its organic functions.

Specifically, I want to look at that aspect of the animal organism that is generally ignored: excretion. While those advancing the idea of systematic organicity are quite happy to imagine speculative Science as open to the upstream content of "immediacy," in its various forms, whether as raw, undigested nature or as the "content of the positive sciences" (W4: 423), the question of "downstream" systematic effluent is avoided, either because it is judged distasteful or because it is simply too difficult to relate the idealistic heights of Hegelian Science to something as base as feces. Regardless of the reasons for such "systematic" neglect, Hegel's organics, in the *Philosophy of Nature* do contain substantial pages, often in the Remarks and Additions, not only on the animal digestive process but on its excremental results. It therefore seems to me that we should consider such essential organic end products as relevant to the organic conception of the system of philosophical Science. The question is ultimately, if we accept the organic nature of Hegelian Science, then should we not ask, "What does the system leave behind?" Or more bluntly, "What does the system excrete?" In order to answer these questions, we must "hold our nose" (W2: 541) and look closely (there is no delicate way of expressing this) at how Hegel conceives animal digestion and its faecal outcome.

If discussions on digestion and excretion were confined to the *Philosophy of Nature,* they would be of limited or discrete interest to Hegel scholars. However, these elements resonate to the highest speculative reaches of Hegel's Science. Indeed, the digestive/excretory function of the "Absolute" itself is acknowledged in the culminating chapter of the *Encyclopaedia Logic* (EL 213 R) where the life of the Idea confronts "inorganic nature" through a process of "assimilation" and "reproduction" (EL 218), a process described in the paragraph's Addition in the digestive terms of bilious "irritability" and "reproduction." I write "digestive" because, as we will see, it is as a pre-sexual instance of "formal" reproduction that animal excretion appears in the *Philosophy of Nature,* as distasteful (or Freudian?) as we might find such a notion.[4] The digestive elements of "irritability and reproduction," shared by individual animal organisms and the life of the Idea, involve aspects of self-objectification and self-unification (*Zusammenschliessen*) that Hegel presents in terms of excremental superfluity and individual purposiveness.

A few timorous Hegel commentators have followed to its excremental conclusion the animal digestive process that Hegel presents in the *Philosophy of Nature,* and I have referred to their findings in Reid 2022. What is missing from these rare accounts is the further step that I want to take. Having established what the living, animal (self-moving) organism actually excretes, how does the biological end product apply to the organically conceived Scientific system itself? One exception to the general reluctance to consider systematic excrement is Slavoj Žižek who, in his exuberantly scatological "Hegel and the Object, Or, the Idea's

Constipation,"[5] reads the Idea's "*sich Entschliessen*," at the culmination of the *Logics*, as a healthy act of ideal defecation. In order to maintain this, Žižek presents the system according to the "third" syllogistic configuration, Spirit-Logic-Nature, where the "act of releasing the other [i.e., Nature] is thoroughly *immanent* to the dialectical process, its conclusive moment, the sign of the conclusion of a dialectical circle." While the idea is provocative, it is highly problematic since what is "let go" at the end of the *Logics* qua Nature is not released as something expulsed *outside* the system, as we will see is the case with animal feces, but rather the predetermined natural object of the subsequent *Philosophy of Nature*. While, as we will discuss, there is indubitably something "natural" about the system's excremental remainder, what is "disclosed" or "desyllogized" (*entgeschlossen*) by the Idea at the end of the *Logics* can hardly be likened to the extra-systematic expulsion of excrement as it is discussed by Hegel. Žižek's reading does not refer to the digestive-excremental process as it occurs in the "Animal Organism" section of the *Philosophy of Nature*, which is crucial to understanding both the constitution and the significance that Hegel attributes to animal feces.[6]

Particularity of Poop: Superfluity, Individuality, and Purposiveness

As Jane O'Hara-May points out in her article "Measuring Man's Needs,"[7] the qualitative analysis of human feces was, in Hegel's time, rather innovative. Previously, the approach had been generally quantitative, through studies motivated by institutional, economic factors: How much food did a soldier, sailor, inmate require in order to survive and carry out their duties? Measuring the quantity of excreted material was an important benchmark in these studies. Against this current, Berzelius was a pioneer in the qualitative approach, employing a chemical analysis of feces in order to understand the processes involved in digestion and assimilation. One can only suppose that, here again, the practical applications had institutional and economic reach: *What* must be eaten to ensure a person's survival, growth, strength, and so on; for Berzelius's research was primarily focused on *human* digestion and excretion. This is significant since, in Hegel, we are ultimately interested in the *human* animal, that is, in the development of the animal's subjective relation to its digestive processes and their result, as we see in his reference to children's feces in the Remark to EN 365, and to Berzelius's experiments on human feces in the Addition. The anthropological specificity is particularly meaningful, for our purposes, because we want to be able to apply the organic aspect of excretion to the Hegelian system itself, which, like the human animal, is meant to be an organic system endowed with consciousness qua *Geist.*

Hegel's repeated references to the work of Berzelius clearly show that Hegel is actually discussing human feces here, and not, initially, something more speculative. Hence he states that "human excrement contains undecomposed bile, albumen, biliary gum, and two peculiar substances, one that looked like glue ..." In more detail, "the human body evacuates through the rectum, bile, albumen, two peculiar animal substances, biliary matter, sodium carbonate, sodium chloride, and sodium phosphate, phosphate of magnesia, and phosphate of lime" (EN 365 Add./ W9: 492). The important conclusion, for Hegel, is that "all of these materials are not merely heterogeneous, inassimilable matter" but, above all, they are elements found in the organism itself. Indeed, "many of the substances [found in feces] also enter into the composition of the hair, others into that of the muscles and brain" (ibid.). Consequently, following the empirical research of Berzelius, it is wrong to conclude that the excretory result of digestion is simply surplus ingested but unassimilated material or the fact that "a larger quantity of matter is assimilated than the organs to be nourished by it are able to appropriate" (ibid). Again referring to Berzelius, Hegel remarks that "closer inspection reveals disparities between the constituents of food, the assimilated material, and the substances excreted [which] render this assumption untenable" (ibid.). The upshot, for Hegel, is that what the animal organism excretes, "the bile, pancreatic juice, etc. is nothing else but the organism's own process which it gets rid of in material shape." It is this conclusion that will allow Hegel to view animal excretion as syllogistically superfluous, a "form of abstract, formal repulsion" (ibid.) where what is excreted is above all the organism's own mediating digestive process, thus reproducing (formally) the individual animal's subjective purposiveness.

Let us look more closely at this process, as reflected in its excremental result and specifically in its "principal ingredients," which are "substances originating from gastric juices."[8] Understanding how Hegel views this organic process is essential to apprehending the true nature of organic and thus systematic excretion. Further, if what the organism excretes is principally the elements of its own animal process, then our examination of excretion should lead us to understand how the whole, purposive "organism" of Science stands in relation to its own *particular* processes.

In Hegel, it is always helpful to know where we are in the syllogistic unfolding of the narrative. This is especially important within the economy of the *Encyclopaedia*, where the syllogistic structures are more pronounced than in the *Phenomenology of Spirit.* In the EN, the paragraphs dealing with digestion and excretion are found in the section on the animal organism (EN 350–75). Within that tripartite section, we find ourselves in the second, mediating sub-section, entitled "Assimilation." The first sub-section is Shape [*Gestalt*]); the third section is on the genus process. Looking closer, within the three sub-moments of Assimilation where we find ourselves, digestion takes place again in a middle, mediating sub-section, entitled the "Practical Relation," which follows the "Theoretical Relationship" and anticipates the "Constructive Instinct." Consequently, the section on digestion and excretion occurs in the most "middle," internal moment of Hegel's presentation of the animal organism, in the middle of the middle. In more conceptual terms, we find ourselves in the particular moment of the particular moment, if we take the general, syllogistic form of the concept's dialectical movement as passing from the Universal, to the Particular, to the Singular.

The Hegelian moment of particularity is generally characterized by opposition between different binary configurations that present themselves as mutually exclusive: something has a specific particularity because it is *not* something else. Of course, the dialectical truth (outcome) is that in order to be what it particularly *is*, something must be *both* what it is and what it is *not*. That is, true self-identity must involve difference. This is why the fundamental dialectic of identity and difference, in Hegel, takes place in the middle, "particular," moment of the *Logics*, in the second book, on Essence. Of course, the *accomplishment* of essential truth is carried out in the third, reconciling moment of the *Logics*: in the "Doctrine of the Concept." For now, I want to emphasise the *particular* nature of digestion as a binary, oppositional process within the animal organism, along with a bilious, dissolvent element that overcomes static opposition, putting it into movement. Grasping particularity as informed by both opposition and solvency will help us analyze the significance of the excreted product in relation to the organic system, which is what we are after. Let us begin with the particular oppositions at play in digestion. First and foremost, we find the opposition between the organic and the non-organic.

By "non-organic" ([*Unorganisch*] EN 365 Add.), Hegel does not mean "inorganic" or mineral but rather, that which the organism "confronts" and "assimilates" (cf. EL 219 Add.), that is, consumes as food. Indeed, both the vegetable and animal material that the living animal consumes are "in truth organic structures." However, in terms of the digestive process of assimilation carried out by the living, animal organism, they are of "non-organic" nature because they are determined as food "for this animal" (EN 365 Add./W9: 484). The non-organic is determined as something having "no enduring existence of its own." It is a "nullity as soon as it comes into contact with a living being (ibid)" that eats it. The transformation involved in digestive assimilation is simply the "revelation of this relationship" (ibid.). The fundamental opposition involved in assimilation and digestion is thus between organic nature and its "non-organic" object, and the "state of tension" that this relation involves (EN 365 Add./W9: 483). Furthermore, the "alimentary process" is essentially the "melting of the non-organic into organic fluidity" (ibid). In other words, at the most fundamental level of digestive opposition, between the organic and the non-organic, the goal is the fluidification and breakdown of that opposition.

Consequently, the mediation that characterizes the particularity of the digestive process involves the fluidification of the fixed, established opposition between organic and its Other. Significantly, the terms of the opposition (organic versus non-organic) do not in themselves have the resources of negativity necessary for its overcoming and fluidification. The second element of particularity is necessary: solvent negativity, which is provided, in digestion, by bile. Bile (*Galle*) is thus "animal fire" (EN 364/W9 480) and the liquid "anger" or "irritability" (cf. EL 218 Add.) required for the overcoming of the fundamental opposition between organic and non-organic, which is brought about in the digestive process. It is the cometary element we found in chapter 3.

Other, subsidiary internal oppositions arise within the particularity of the digestive process itself. This is because the external relation to the non-organic and the "entanglement with outside things" (EN 365 Add.) has been brought inside, internalized in the mediating process of digestion, a process whose result is then produced as excrement. Once again, what is excreted is the particularity of the process itself. In the syllogistic terms that Hegel employs,

> the syllogism of the organism is, therefore, not the syllogism of external teleology, for it [i.e., the organism] does not stop at directing its activity and form [i.e., negativity] against the outer object but makes this very process ... into an object [of excrement]. (EN 365 R)

Digestive excretion is thus presented in terms of "the second premise of the universal syllogism of purposive activity," where the "outward process" brings about the animal's "uniting of itself with itself" (ibid.), which we will discuss below as its individual purposiveness. Here, Hegel refers significantly to the *Encyclopaedia Logic* (EL 209), a paragraph where he deals with "subjective purpose as the power over [mediating] processes." Syllogistically, this involves the internalization of the "first premise" (EL 208), where the subjective attitude to the object was an "outward-directed activity," for example, in taking possession of food. Importantly, the incorporation or internalization of the outward-directed activity becomes, the "second premise," that is, the particular moment of the syllogism, which brings about, in EL 209, the opposition between the two earlier articulations of natural purposiveness from the section on teleology: mechanism, and chemism. Returning to the EN, the internal distinction between the mechanical and the chemical now appears as another *particular* opposition within the digestive process. I want to look at how this new opposition, within the particular moments of organic assimilation, is shown to again not have the resources of negativity necessary for its own overcoming and how its reliance on the solvent element of bile becomes a principal element of excretion.

Before proceeding, I would like to remark briefly on how the articulations of thought (*des Denkens*) or the Concept (*des Begriffs*), as grounded in the *Logics*, stand in relation to the particular processes evoked in the *Philosophy of Nature*'s discussion of digestion. I take the relation to be metonymic rather than metaphorical.[9] What is meant by this is that, according to Hegel, the life of the organism, that is, what constitutes its "purposive activity" (EN 365 R/W9: 482)[10] is the actual movement of the Concept, which might be conceived as the "soul" of the living thing, its unconscious "subjectivity" (EN 365), the breath that animates it (animus) as a living whole. Anyone with a better explanation of what animates organic life, of why the mere sum of different parts does not, in itself, constitute a living, purposive, individual animal organism or why and how, in death, life leaves that physical embodiment, is welcome to supply one. For our purposes, we can simply affirm that the metonymy between the *philosophies* of nature and thought runs both ways; dialectical thought informs organic processes, which, in turn, express the agency of thought. Consequently, a discussion of natural organics can and should inform the study of systematic organicity, a study that I am undertaking here. Once again, I am not maintaining that, for Hegel, Science *is* an animal. I am exploring to what extent the (human) animal and Science are conceptually organic. Whether or how this metonymy is apparent in other particular aspects of the system, for example, in the organic state, I will leave aside. Let us return to our discussion of digestion's internal, particular oppositions and their bilious overcoming, now, by looking at the opposition between mechanism and chemism. Examining this opposition will allow us to present the crucial notion of immediate assimilation, which, in turn, will help us see how the particular processes of animal digestion may be conceived as superfluous while giving rise to subjective purposiveness.

In the late eighteenth and early nineteenth centuries, theories of animal digestion and assimilation were generally divided between two main ideas: the mechanical notion that nourishment was extracted from food through physical, gastric processes of squeezing, pressing, grinding, and the like, over against the chemical theories, which explained digestion as the chemical dissolution of food, rendering it organically assimilable. Again demonstrating how his philosophy of nature is really a philosophy of the empirical or positive sciences of nature, Hegel takes each approach into account. He refers, in this context, to the work of Lazzaro Spallanzani, whose experiments were meant to find out "whether digestion is effected by solvent juices or by trituration performed by the stomach muscles or by both" (EN 365R). The Hegelian response is that neither unilateral approach per se can explain digestion. By conceiving of digestion in these oppositional terms (mechanical or chemical), one can never capture its truth.

> All chemical and mechanical explanations founder ... Neither chemistry nor mechanics can follow empirically the alteration of food to the point where it is changed into blood, no matter what methods they employ. (W9: 484)

Regarding the controversy between the mechanical and chemical approaches to digestion, Hegel seems to favour the former explanation, but on the condition that it be understood as enacting the *immediate* assimilation that expresses the fundamental truth of the digestive process in animal organisms. Briefly, in the mechanical digestive action, "the violent pressing and pushing of the walls of the stomach" that Spellanzani had noted, enact proximate contact between the non-organic and the organic, making possible the "triumph over food which has entered the environment (*Dunstkreis*) of the living animal" (EN 365R/ W9 491). The question is how this feature of mechanical immediacy fits into the narrative of digestive particularity that I am putting forward.

First, while one might suppose that Hegel would favour the chemical explanation over digestive assimilation, since it is closer to contemporary, "true" notions on the subject, this is not the case. First, Hegel's refusal of the chemical explanation is because his notion of chemistry is not molecular but rather, we might say, alchemistic, fundamentally informed by the interplay between acidic and alkaline substances (cf. Schelling). Accordingly, the interaction of different chemical compounds always arrives at states of equilibrium or neutrality: the more acidic substance interacting with the more basic or alkaline substance, producing a third, relatively inert result. Thus, if "the relationship [between the organic and the non-organic] would only be chemical ... the effect would be nothing more than a neutralization, where nothing more than, 'a thick slime [would be] formed,'" states Hegel quoting Treviranus's *Biologie* (W9: 488).

In Hegel's view, the truth of digestion can only be got at through the speculative recognition of the presupposed and culminating identity between the organic and the non-organic Other, where the former has triumphed over the latter. Only when the truth of this speculative unity is recognized does the mediating process of higher organisms come to make sense. Thus, the immediate relationship involved in digestion is simply the fundamental recognition of the ultimate identity between the organic and the non-organic, the fact that "what is particular and external has no enduring existence of its own, but is a nullity as soon as it comes into contact with a living being; and this [digestive] transformation is merely the revelation of this relationship" (EN 365 Add./W9 484). Rather than presenting this speculative notion of transformation as a theoretical a priori given, Hegel refers to the biology of immediate digestive assimilation as arising from the mechanical nature of digestion.

The immediate assimilative relationship between the organic and the non-organic, where the latter is "transformed directly and at a stroke" is thus "fundamental" (ibid.), a "direct melting of the non-organic into the organic" (ibid.), which takes place throughout the animal realm. This essential relation can also be understood in terms of substance and accident. In that sense, the non-organic is no more than an accidental "shape which it immediately surrenders" (ibid.). Biologically, this immediate assimilative relation between the organic and the non-organic Other can be found in "lower animals" like "worms and zoophytes," as well as in "hydra brachiopoda and vorticella" (ibid.). In all these cases, assimilation takes place directly, through physical contact, where what "has hardly been swallowed is changed, transformed into a homogeneous mass" (ibid). These primitive organisms are devoid of mediating digestive organs, and one "cannot differentiate between oesophagus, stomach, and intestines" (ibid). Importantly, in terms of our investigation into the significance of excretion, what is excreted in these primitive organisms devoid of mediating digestive processes is indistinguishable from what is ingested: "the polyp opens its mouth again and evacuates part of the ingested food along the same way in which it entered the hydra's stomach" (ibid.). In other words, immediate assimilation is devoid of particularity. To the extent that "immediate assimilation" (ibid.) is a feature of digestion generally, as the presupposed truth of the determinate relation between the organic and its Other, we can say that it is universally present in living things. However, whereas primitive animal forms excrete nothing other than the nugatory result of immediate assimilation, higher animal forms like humans excrete the particular results of the digestive process itself, which may appear as superfluous with regards to the speculative truth of digestion: the "triumph" (ibid.)

of the organic over the non-organic, as witnessed in immediate assimilation. This "triumph" gives onto the purposive individuality of the living animal, an important finding that I will explicate below, and apply to the organic system of Science.

For Hegel, the speculative truth of immediate assimilation means that it underlies digestion generally, even universally. Consequently, even the particular features of more complex animal organisms rely on some degree of immediate assimilation through the mechanical workings of their surfaces, where, for example, "the stomach and intestinal canal are themselves nothing else but the outer skin, only reversed and developed and shaped into a peculiar form" (EN 365 Add.). The importance of immediate or direct assimilation explains why Hegel details at length cases where thirsty sailors have apparently absorbed water directly through their skin, minus the salt; where opium "rubbed in the shoulder" has been assimilated into the organism. Hegel again cites Treviranus, whose experiments apparently demonstrated that digestion, qua direct assimilation, can take place in animals outside their stomachs, for example, that "bones, flesh and other animal parts [introduced] under the skin of live animals" were found to be "completely decomposed" (ibid.). In all of these cases, the essential action of digestive assimilation takes place: the transformation of the non-organic into "animal lymph," the "universal element of animality" (ibid.).

Given the fundamental, indeed universal importance of immediate assimilation throughout the digestive process and within the animal organism generally, one might indeed wonder whether all the mediating, particular structures of digestion, in higher animal organisms, are not entirely superfluous. It is precisely this superfluity that is expressed in and through animal excretion. However, the introduction of "separate stages" and the "intermediation of several organs" is absolutely essential for the strength, movement, and "actuality" of the complex animal organism itself, which must test itself against non-organic otherness, not in "one stroke" but through the mediating structures of its own digestive processes.

> This complex arrangement of digestion through the intermediation of several organs is, for the non-organic, indeed superfluous, but it is not so for the organism which progresses through these moments within itself for its own sake in order to be movement and consequently actuality. (ibid.)

Hegel goes as far, again in the lengthy Addition to EN 365, to associate the vigour of digestive overcoming, "progressing through these [mediating, digestive] moments for its own sake," with the vitality of spirit, "just as the strength of spirit is measured only by the extent of the opposition it has overcome," an outcome that presents itself as the animal's individual purposiveness.[11]

Before returning to our examination of the particular lineaments at play in the oppositional mediations of the digestive process, it is important to recall that according to Hegel's reading of animal digestion, what is excreted is "significantly" the particular digestive elements involved in the process of the animal itself. Only in this sense do we grasp why excretion is presented as the "first, formal (EN 365)" reproductive level of the animal organism. That is why, in the Remark to EN 365, Hegel likens the "superfluity [*Überfluss*]" of the "characteristic product" of animal digestion (i.e., feces) to the production of seeds in the plant. The crucial difference is this: While it is the whole plant itself that is demonstrated as superfluous in its purposive production of seeds, for the organically organized animal, it is the mediating processes alone that are demonstrated as superfluous through the production of feces. In any case, the superfluity of excrement is not, as we saw above, based on the animal having eaten more than it could digest but rather, on the animal's own digestive encounter with the non-organic Other. Let us return to the lineaments of the particular "*Momente*" (EN 365R) of the mediating animal digestive process, which will form the substance of excretion and allow us to grasp the truth of its superfluity.

Although Hegel's explanation of animal digestion is far from simple, in spite of his assurance that it is "not very complicated" (EN 365 Add./W9: 490), there are two principal elements that appear throughout: On one hand, an element that is variously presented as "sluggish," "inertia," "neutral," "being-in-itself"; and on the other hand "inflammable," "anger," "active," "attacking," "destructive," "being-for-itself." The first relatively passive element is associated, although ambiguously, with chyme (the product of gastric digestion), as well as with pancreatic juice, the spleen, the liver, and the venous system. The second active "cometary" element is above all associated with bile. Indeed, "chemical analysis of the bile yields nothing more specific than that its tendency is to inflame" (ibid.). The bile's inflammatory character even acts on the "passive" organs normally associated with its production, for example, the spleen, which is initially a "being-in-itself" and "sluggish," but "ignited" (*befeuert*, ibid.) through its production of bile. Similarly, pancreatic juice, when associated with bile, "attacks" the chyme. Bile even serves to help bring "the inertia of the venous system to a focus in opposition to the lungs" (ibid), as attested to by the fact that shame and anger both bring about changes in blood flows, such as "blushing of the face and bosom" (EN 365 Add.).

Against the universal certainty of immediate assimilation, which underlies digestion generally, particularized, mediated digestion necessarily appears as a superfluous error, as a "false opinion" (ibid.). Consequently, "the main point is that the organism, although exercising a mediating, distinctive activity, none the less remains in its universality …" (ibid.). And further on: "Because the animal is involved in a struggle with the outer world, its relation to the latter is untrue, since this outer world has already been transformed, in principle (*an sich*) by the animal lymph" (ibid.) Most decisively, "The animal, in turning against its food, fails to recognize its own self [in it]" (ibid.). Of course, as readers of the *Phenomenology of Spirit*, we know from the introduction that error is not something to be feared but rather to be embraced as constitutive of the Truth, and the same logic applies in the "lowly" function of animal digestion. Consequently, we must understand the organism's digestive struggle with its non-organic Other as a constitutive process of purposive animal individuality itself. Therefore, what the animal is really struggling with is not an outer thing but the animal reality of its own digestive process. "What the organism has to conquer is therefore its own process, this entanglement with the outer thing" (EN 365 Add.).

To "return into itself," as a universal self-relating purposiveness, the individualized animal must "repudiate and reject that means" or that "mediation which consists in involving itself with the non-organic" (ibid.). It is in this rejection and repudiation of its own digestive process, of its own digestive particularity as seemingly superfluous where we discover the reproductive aspect of animal excretion, which involves the "positing of itself as immediately self-identical," that is, as the affirmation of its animal wholeness and self-related, living individuality (I = I). The living animal is thus "reproducing itself in this self-preservation" (M404). Briefly, in excreting as superfluous "this [erroneous] entanglement with the outer thing," the individual animal affirms and reproduces itself, albeit in a way that is entirely "formal" or subjective.

The subjective "oneness" (EL 217) or individuality that arises from digestive struggle is not to be confused with what is actually excreted. Although the actual feces can be seen as a reproductive positing of the organism, akin to the seeds of a plant, it is not the truth of formal reproduction. Rather, through the excretion of its particular struggle with non-organic objective otherness, the living animal (re)produces itself as purposive organic life. Consequently, perhaps the best expression of formal, animal reproduction is the Fichtean formula, I=I, which I used in the last paragraph. Indeed, Hegel often borrows the formula to express unmediated, exclusive, and thus formal subjectivity. As well, using the Fichtean formula to express organic purposiveness highlights the limits of the animal trope when applied to the Hegelian system as a whole, an issue that I will return to below.

The internal entanglement and opposition with the outer non-organic thing is thus an essential element of the particularity that complex animal digestion involves. As such, it falls syllogistically into the mediating moment between universality and singularity, as "the second premise of the universal syllogism of purposive activity [aka life]," as we saw above, in the remark to EN 365. What is more difficult to apprehend, and hitherto unnoticed, as far as I can see, is how, as a moment of particularity, the digestive process must involve not one but two distinct moments. Briefly, it is impossible to grasp Hegel's presentation of animal digestion and assimilation without acknowledging the participation of both the oppositional aspects of this *particular* process as well as the bilious action that dissolves the oppositions. In fact, it is the fiery, fluidifying nature of bile that animates the digestive process, "the active destruction, this turning in on itself of the organism" (EN 365 Add.), that characterizes digestion as a mediating process, as distinct from the vital universality of immediate assimilation. That is why, "as soon as animals acquire a developed [i.e., mediated] nature and do not merely have an immediate digestion or remain simply at the lymphatic stage, they have both liver and bile (ibid.)." Bile is the essential solvent element of digestion, ensuring the "organic relation of differences" that are essential to systematic organicity generally. In other words, the elements of digestion involve the active coordination between solvent "animal water" and bilious "fire" (EN 364) over against "heterogeneous, inassimilable matter" (EN 365 Add./W9 492).[12] These elements, as discovered by Berzelius, form the substance of animal excretion, as the excreted means of digestion or the "repudiation and rejection of that means" (ibid.).

Animal excrement consists of the expulsed remains of digestive particularity: the otherness of non-organic material but, more significantly, the trace of solvent negativity (watery albumen and fiery bile). This is the "anger" that characterizes the digestive process, over against its "one-sided" opposition "toward the object" (EN 365R/W9: 483), the "fact that the animal turns in anger against what is external" (EN 365 Add./ W9: 490). However, because bilious anger is expressed *within the animal itself* and constitutes its own process, what was digestive anger against the non-organic is, in truth, anger that the animal has turned against itself. In fact, the animal "is angry with itself for getting involved with external potencies, and it now turns against itself and its false opinion" (ibid.). Ridding itself of this "superfluous" false opinion, its "involvement (*Verwickeltsein*) with the outer thing" (ibid.) is "repudiated and rejected" (ibid.) as animal excrement. However, the act of excretion, as the negation of a negation or as anger against anger, is necessarily understood as a positing, one which takes the form of a "double determination" (ibid.): on one hand, excretion is the organism's exclusionary "positing of itself as immediately self-identical" (I=I) but also, excretion represents the organism's "reproducing itself" through this "preservation of itself [*Erhaltung seiner*], ibid.) (I=I). Briefly, it is the animal's self-production or purposiveness, its "oneness," that is the speculative truth of the excremental rejection of its entanglement with otherness. The *moments* of particularity appear as superfluous to the self-affirmation of the organism in its enduring, purposive individuality, "the formal process of simple reproduction of its own self, into the uniting of itself with itself [*in das Zusammenschliessen seiner mit sich*]" (EN 365). To grasp how animal excretion stands with regards to the animal organism and to systematic organicity generally, I will now turn to the aspects of individuality and purposiveness that arise through the reproductive aspect associated with excretion.

Animal Individuality and Purposiveness

Individuality. In the Addition to EN 365, Hegel refers repeatedly to the animal organism as an individual. First, in its bilious behaviour to the non-organic individual object (*zu Individuellem*, W9: 491), "it has proven itself to be as an animal individual (*als animalisches Individuum*" ibid.). Thus, the animal has now become, through the carried out process of digestion and its excremental conclusion, "in a real way, for itself, i.e., individual" (ibid.). While one might argue that the *Encyclopaedia*'s Additions should not provide the basis for precise textual analysis, the insistence here on individuality (*Individuum, Individuelle, individuell*) makes it unlikely that those transcribing Hegel's lectures, constituting Michelet's *Zusätze*, could have missed Hegel's point: Digestion and its reproductive excrement constitute the organism as an animal *individual*. This is significant given Hegel's take on individuality generally, which must be distinguished from what he means by singularity (e.g., *das Einzeln*), a distinction that is not always made in the translations and commentaries. In general, Hegel uses the latter term when referring to the syllogistic destiny of the singular, in its inevitable collapse into universality when it does not have the privilege of being "saved" by particularity. In that case, the finite (natural) singular thing is taken up into the generalizing particularity of genus or species, allowing the singular thing to participate, in a humble way, in the Singularity of the fulfilled Concept (the Singular universal "filled" with particular content). The unmediated singular per se can do nothing but vanish into the indeterminate universal, as we witness in the *Phenomenology*'s chapter on Sense-certainty, where singular sensations collapse into the empty indeterminacy of the "here" and the "now." On the other hand, *Individualität*, in Hegel, presents the "singular" insofar as it resists its conceptual destiny, holding onto its "for-itselfness," which it seeks to anchor by assigning itself particular properties. Continuing the reference to the *Phenomenology*, we can say that the object of perception, with its properties, is "individual," as opposed to the singularity of raw sense data. In the Addition to EN 365, Hegel refers to the "animal individual" as having posited itself *(sich gezetzt)* as "real being-for-self (*Fürsichsein*)" (W9: 491).

Although Hegel describes the animal individual here as possessing subjectivity, we should not get too excited by the introduction of this term, as if Hegel were describing the essential genesis point of *human* consciousness as arising from digestion. The level of subjectivity involved in digestion and excretion is strictly animal, and only as such is it applicable to the human, that is, to the extent that human beings are always also individual animals. Animal subjectivity does indeed manifest itself, in digestion, through the overcoming of its non-organic Other, within itself, as a "self-relation" that involves self "diremption and division" (EN 365 Add.). However, the essential outcome here is the constitution of subjectivity as an *animal* individual, which only happens through the animal's "repelling of itself from itself" (ibid.).[13] This action is excretion: "The differentiation does not take place only within the organism itself; on the contrary, the nature of the organism is to produce itself as something external to it," that is, as excrement, the necessary moment of self-differencing within formal "reproduction" (EN 365).[14]

As I mentioned above, individuality, for Hegel, generally involves exclusivity, the exclusion of what is "not-I," leaving the formal I=I. In the present context, the animal organism, in order to constitute and, above all, maintain and conserve itself ("*in dieser Erhaltung seiner*," W 9: 491) as a self-relating *individuality*, must expel its internal differentiation, its "entanglement (*Verwicklung*)" with otherness in the form of "superfluous" excrement. Through the expulsion of its entanglement with otherness, what is formally reproduced is the *self-produced* (formal) reality of individual wholeness that characterizes animal life. For our investigation, we are left with the following questions, which I will return to below, along with the question of systematic superfluity: Does the system of Science, qua organic, indeed present itself as an individual, and not only as a syllogistically accomplished Singular (universal)? And if so, what form of systematic excrement might perform and even guarantee such self-reproductive, self-maintaining, exclusive individuality?

Purposiveness. The third organic element that arises through the acknowledgment of the excretory function of the individual animal organism is purposiveness. Of course, the question of "purposiveness" cannot help but evoke its elaboration in Kant's third *Critique*, in his discussion of that regulative idea as ideally active within nature, underlying both its holistic beauty and its scientific comprehensibility. As I mentioned above, Karen Ng's recent book strikes me as exemplary in its investigation of the notion of life, in Hegel, as tangential to the Kantian notion of purposiveness, and indeed Hegel himself recognizes the Kantian notion as simply subjective idealism's approach to what is, in fact, the agency of the Concept. Here, I am concerned with how organic purposiveness arises through animal excretion, and further, how the biological concept may be applied to the system of Science as an organic whole.

At the end of the substantial Addition to EN 365 that I have been referring to throughout, Hegel states, "In truth, the activity of the organism is purposive" (*zweckmässige*, W9: 493). This "truth" is arrived at because, as is usual in Hegel, its certitude has been there from the start. What is rejected or expulsed in animal life, relative to the pre-conceived and realized end or purpose (*Zweck*), is therefore the *means* to that end: the "repudiating and rejecting [of the] means" of the digestive process, as "superfluous" with regards to the general certainty of immediate assimilation "in itself," which we visited above. That is why Hegel, somewhat surprisingly, talks about "Reason" in the Remark to EN 365. The "satisfaction" that the animal experiences in excreting the elements involved in its digestive means to an end "conforms to Reason" because, as the *Phenomenology* has taught us, Reason is the "certainty of [individual] consciousness of being all reality" (W3: 179/M 233). Here, the certainty is that of immediate digestive assimilation: "the immediate action of life as the power over its non-organic object (EN 363 Add.). This power over the non-organic Other "presupposes" that this Other is "in itself identical with it," a certainty appearing as "ideality and being-for-self (*Fürsichsein*)." In syllogistic terms, which Hegel employs in the remark to EN 365, the expulsion of the trace elements of particularity (solvent bile and the stuff that it was opposed to) as excrement, leaves behind the pure ideality of Universality and Singularity, in the form of subjective animal individuality. It is this "purposive activity," in digestion and excretion, that realizes its end or "purpose [*Zwecks*]" (EN 365 Remark/M397) in the "union [*Zusammenschliessen*] of the organism with itself" (ibid.). The culminating *self*-uniting that constitutes the purposiveness attained through digestion and its outcome is one of *individual* ideality. It is a *Schluss* (conclusion, syllogism) devoid of its own particularity, which the animal organism has expulsed, voided as the superfluous entanglement with non-organic otherness.

The purposiveness attained through animal excretion is presented by Hegel as a self-affirmation or "self-confidence [*Zuversicht*]" (W9: 492) on the part of the organism, which has not only triumphed over the outer non-organic object but, more importantly, has triumphed over its own digestive entanglement with that object. Purposiveness, in this light, is certainly an affirmation of life but only if we take this affirmation as the "satisfaction" of Reason, that is, of its truth: ideality as the achieved identity between the organic and the non-organic, "the subjective [...] identity of its concept and its reality" (EN 365 Remark/W9: 483). Such a truth results from the animal organism's actual overcoming of its "one-sided [oppositional] subjectivity" and "anger towards the object" (ibid.), an anger now expulsed as excreted bile. However, one must not expect too much from the digestive "*Schluss*" or syllogism. It only attains the formal "*Zusammenschliessen*" devoid of mediating particularity, which it has expelled as "a false opinion" (W9: 490), rather than as a constitutive error. That is what I believe Hegel means when he writes, "The syllogism of the organism is, therefore, not the syllogism of external teleology" (EN 365 R). As opposed to this "universal syllogism of purposive activity" (ibid), which takes the form of U-P-S, where the particular moment constitutes the essential content of the whole, the behavior of digestion is only "expounded in the second premise," that is, in the moments of particularity, which, when excreted, present the organism solely as a "uniting of itself with itself [*Zusammenschliessen*]," which I have presented according to the Fichtean formula, I=I.

Nonetheless, in excreting its involvement with non-organic otherness as a means to an end, the animal organism affirms itself as that end qua pure ideality, which is the essence of its purposiveness. If, through digestion, the organism "takes and wins nothing but chyle" (ibid.), it is because chyle is the same as "animal lymph" and blood, and the biological essence of each is to circulate. Briefly, we may surmise that the result of mediated digestion is circulatory fluidity within the organism. The power that drives the inner circulatory movement essential to the animal organism, that which animates it and constitutes its anima, is the purposiveness of pure ideality, the power of the idea, which posits the excreted digestive process as superfluous to its immediate truth or self-certainty.

However, we can also say that the end of the digestive process, as ideality, as the self-confident self-affirmation of the organism, is the immediate feeling of its individual life as a truth that is more than the sum of its internal, animal processes, which it has excreted as superfluous. From this point of view, the upshot of the process, as a pure *Zusammenschliessen*, is therefore characterized by a feeling of "satiation, the self-feeling which feels completeness in place of the previous lack" (EN 365 Add./W9: 493). Douglas Finn's reading of purposiveness (although he does not refer to it as such) as "the unified organizational activity of life" which refuses to "be reduced to any one of its processes," captures the general idea of the feeling of organic satisfaction that Hegel describes, as arising from the process of excretion. In excretion, purposiveness is thus presented as a feeling of organic satisfaction and wholeness, of self-assurance resulting from the expulsion of the organic individual's self-doubt, the false opinion that arose through its entanglement with the non-organic. In excretion (defecation), the animal is affirming: "That's not me! I am more than that! I am more than the functioning of my particular digestive organs!" However, as pure ideality, exclusive of particular process, the feeling of self-confidence, of jubilant, self-organizational power or vitality must also be one of emptiness, of renewed hunger. While this is not apparent to the satisfied animal, as philosophers of nature we know that the truth of the animal's feeling of completeness is really an immediate form of self-certainty, which, as *natural* feeling can be nothing other than fleeting, for hunger is, like excretion, a fundamental element of life: "Only what is living feels a lack," as Hegel succinctly puts it, in the remark to EN 359.

Animal Organicity and Science

Recall that my intention is to explore the limits of Hegel's own notion of animal organicity as it is heuristically applied to his system of Science, an application that he himself invites us to make, for example, by describing that system as "*organisch*" (ES 379 Add./W10: 15), as well as in presenting the life of the Idea in organic terms in the EL, which I quoted at the outset of the chapter. My investigations into Hegel's presentation of the excremental dimension of animal organicity has revealed crucial aspects of superfluity, individuality, and purposiveness. I would like to now briefly apply these elements to the organic systematicity of Science, shedding new light on it. Nonetheless, as we will see, the excremental elements also reveal the limits of conceiving Hegel's systematic project solely according to the trope of animal organicity.

First, regarding superfluity, as we have seen, what the animal excretes as superfluous are elements of its own animality qua the particular, mediating processes of digestion. Is it possible to read this notion of superfluity into the system of Science, where the mediating process of particularity per se is found to be "de trop" and expulsed?

Such systematic excretion must contain the two fundamental elements of particularity that we have discovered, together but no longer in a dynamic, interactive relation. They are elements to be analyzed, as Berzelius did, in the fecal material itself: solvent bile and non-organic material (i.e., material to which the organism has stood opposed). I believe we can establish that, from the point of view of the system of Science, what is excreted is essentially linked to the understanding (*Verstand*) as a type of abstract thinking that stands apart from and opposed to its object. In this sense, *der Verstand* indeed represents false opinion and may be judged repulsive[15] to the scientific organism. My affirmation is supported by the last lines of Hegel's Addition to EN 365:

> The *understanding* pretends to know more than speculative philosophy and loftily looks down on it; but it remains confined within the sphere of finite mediation [i.e., particularity], and vitality as such is beyond its grasp [my emphasis].

Of course, we know that the *Verstand* is absolutely essential to the organism of Science. The understanding's reflections provide the mediating, particular content of Science, the locus and process of systemic "digestion," whereby Science proves itself to be "*inhaltsvoll*." However, the *Verstand*, as a process does operate according to the binary logic of particularity, involving both the subjective (bilious) negativity of reflective thought, along with its "one-sided" (W9: 483) approach to its object as Other. Further, we can also affirm that the *Verstand*'s action is digestive, breaking elements down, analyzing them and producing abstract judgments that cause us to "hold our nose" when they "come out."

> "All men are mortal; Caius is a man; therefore, he is mortal." I at least have never come up with anything as boring. It must be produced in our gut, without our consciousness. Certainly, many things are produced in our gut, for example the production of urine, and still worse, but then when that comes out, we plug our nose. The same goes for such an argument.[16]

In fact, Hegel's detailed presentation of the animal digestive system, with its references to the empirical sciences of the day, is a perfect example of the understanding at work within Science, along with its (small c) concepts or judgments. However, the *Verstand* itself tends to remain fixed in its own oppositions, for example in the "external relationships [that are alternately] mechanical and chemical in nature" (M406), which we discussed above. Thus, taken outside the purposive, systematic context, the understanding and its work appear as repulsive, "disgusting,"[17] and superfluous. Perhaps, at this point, we can venture that what appears as superfluous and repulsive to the organic system of Science is its own necessary reliance on the understanding and its concepts and, more explicitly, on the common language grammatical forms of predication in which the meaningful mediation of its "digestive" process takes place.

Briefly, what the system of Science expulses and finds repulsive may well be its own "entanglement" in the representational language and judgment forms of the understanding upon which it relies for the particular content that enlivens its syllogistic life.[18]

Let us move on to the notion of individuality as it comes to light in the context of animal excretion and consider how it might appropriately apply to the organic system of Science. As we saw above, in its digestive comportment toward "the individual thing," the animal "has proven itself to be an animal individual" (EN 365 Add.). This individuality is subjective or "for-itself" because "the organism in constituting itself a subjectivity is immediately a repelling of itself from itself" (ibid.). Briefly, the animal has "in a real way ... become an individual" through the action of expelling the constituting otherness of *itself.* Individuality is thus formed in the "self-relation" (ibid.) that has excluded its own internal difference. In this way, "the organism produces itself as something different from itself" (ibid.), which is the essence of animal reproduction. However, as "the form of abstract, formal repulsion" (ibid.), what excretion produces is subjective individuality itself, devoid of mediating characteristics (I=I).

Although "abstract," excretion is nonetheless a fundamental moment of animal reproduction per se, underlying the subsequent stages of the constructive instinct and the genus process. Regardless of how distasteful we might find this idea, the comingling of the excretory and the reproductive is physiologically presented in the fact that "in the animal organization, the organs of excretion and the genitals, the highest and lowest parts, are intimately connected" (ibid.), or where "... speech and kissing, on one hand, and eating, drinking and spitting, on the other, are all done with the mouth" (ibid.). Similarly, as "formal," excremental reproduction remains an exercise in *self*-production, as we have seen. This conclusion is important when we turn to the Scientific dimensions of organic excrement.

It is clear that Hegel's idea of animal excretion as a form of reproduction, when applied to the organicity of the system, presents that system as an individuality, one which is for-itself and hence subjective. The philosophical system, thus presented, is not merely a singular, nor even a universal Singular, according to the ontological elenchus of the "universal syllogism of purposive activity" (EN 365 R/W9: 482); it is an *Individualität,* and as such should be seen as an organic, self-preserving identity that maintains and affirms itself through the expulsion of inner differentiation. However, assigning the characteristic of self-preserving or maintaining to Science does not immediately imply that the system is self-conscious in actively seeking its own preservation, as the human animal might be said to do. While the fully accomplished *Encyclopaedic* system may indeed be self-aware or self-conscious, at the "animal" level of Science, that is, as an excreting, self-moving organism, self-preservation might be construed as instinctual, pre-reflexive and immediate. The Scientific individuality arising from systematic excretion may be conceived as self-preserving simply because that is what it means to be an individual animal organism. From this perspective, we might simply remark that the fact that the Hegelian philosophical system has maintained and preserved itself for almost two centuries is sufficient proof of its organic individuality. Further, if the amount of scholarly activity in Hegel studies testifies to the system's vitality, then we may certainly judge the Scientific "animal" to be alive and self-maintaining.

The ongoing actuality of Hegel raises an important consideration: If we take the organic aspect of his system seriously, and recognize that, as an organic individual, it has maintained itself over time and is thus alive and active today, with its digestive system fully functioning (i.e., within all the dialectically treated particular content of Logic, Nature, and Spirit), then we might ask ourselves: What might be recognizable as present-day excreted material? While it may be tempting, particularly to those who have no taste for Hegel, to see all of us who write on him as excrement produced by the organic system, the Hegelian analysis of fecal matter has shown us that this is not necessarily the case.[19]

Animal excrement, as we have seen, is essentially made up of bile and non-organic material, a binary configuration that we have likened to Hegel's grasp of the *Verstand*. Given this, what the organic system of Science excretes are forms of philosophy that conceive of mind as an individual, subjectively reflective exercise that is biliously aimed at understanding, that is, at solving, analyzing, explaining, and so on, a self-subsistent material reality over against which mind stands. Such basic requirements might therefore include thinkers in the neo-Kantian tradition, in logical positivism, in realist empiricist traditions, and perhaps in analytic philosophy generally. Above all, what the system excretes is any form of thought that does not recognize the prefigured, ideal complicity between the "organic" and the "non-organic," between thought and its Other. While I cannot develop the idea further here, excreted figures of thought look a lot like forms of natural consciousness as Hegel presents it at the outset of his *Phenomenology of Spirit*!

Finally, let us look at the purposive aspect that we discovered above, in our examination of Hegel's presentation of animal excretion. There, purposiveness appeared as pure ideality, as an immediate *Zusammenschliessen*, a self-confident self-affirmation resulting from the excretion of the mediating digestive process as "superfluous." In the animal organism, the feeling of such purposive ideality qua vitality and satiation nevertheless opens onto an inevitable resurgence of hungry lack, and a rapacity that is tantamount to organic life itself. To be an animal organism is to assimilate the non-organic, to excrete, to feel satisfaction, and to be hungry for more. If we conceive of the organicity of the Hegelian system in this way, then its self-maintaining individuality and its purposiveness should be expressed as the vital self-affirmation of its own ideality, and perhaps of idealism generally. Further, the same ideality might now be conceived not just as an openness to new content, an idea of open systematicity that often accompanies the use of the organic trope in Hegel studies, but as a systematic *hunger* for content, derived from the very affirmation of its ideal vitality and the "triumph" over its entanglement with digestive otherness. Briefly, the idea of systematic excretion presents us with the idea of an organic philosophical system that is self-maintaining through an actual hunger for new content.

The purposive element of self-affirmation and hunger is easily observable in the constantly expanding areas of Hegel studies, where the philosopher's thought has been applied to virtually all areas of contemporary ethics, natural science, logic, law, education, history, art, religion, biology, including animal excrement! The organic approach to Hegel implies that it is the purposiveness of the individual system itself that demands such content, such food for thought.

One cannot escape the feeling that there is something monstrous about such a philosophical animal, satiated, self-affirming, triumphant, and yet constantly hungry for new content, excreting forms of thought that it finds repulsive.[20] And this monstrous aspect is perhaps especially the case for forms of thought and culture that refuse being conceived of as "non-organic" food and resist assimilation into the organic system. Rather than avoid or shy away from this issue, which arises through our discussion of organic systematicity, it must be fully recognized as an unfortunate element of the organic trope, one which has nonetheless come to light through our discussion of systematic excrement. However intriguing, necessary, and certainly enriching we may find such critical considerations into the monstrous nature of an organic philosophical system, I will leave them suspended for now.

The excreted forms that "are repulsive" to the system are nonetheless meant to bring about a form of organic reproduction. Rather than seeing this as an unreconciled contradiction or irony, Hegel invites us to acknowledge the essential ambiguity of reproduction itself: the fact that it must involve "products" that are both ours and not ours, both "us" and "not us." Anyone with children understands this without further explanation. The reproductive aspect of excretion is the final element that needs to be approached when the organic trope is applied to Science. On the level of systematic Science, how might we understand excrement as an ambiguous form of reproduction?

It should be stressed that I am not following through Hegel's discussion of reproduction, in its later stages: the constructive instinct and finally, reproduction through the sexual relation, productive of the genus. While it may be tempting to apply these reproductive features to the scientific organism, for now, I must leave it to the reader to imagine what "nests" the system of Science might construct and, above all, how it might meet and mate with other organisms of thought!

Here, I simply want to apply to Scientific reproduction what we have learned about animal excrement. If what is excreted consists of forms of *Verstand* (bilious, abstract thought over against a self-less reality), then how can this result be seen as Hegelian Science's reproduction of *itself*, particularly when the excreted material is presented as polemically opposed to (and repulsive to) the organic system? Perhaps the answer here might involve taking such expulsed forms of thought as nonetheless attributable to the system, and that, for the very reason that they have often come about in opposition to the metaphysical, systematic demands of Science. More succinctly, the organic system of philosophy will naturally produce forms of thought that are inimical to the claims of Hegel's organic system of absolute idealism[21] but which are nonetheless engendered by that system. Can we not therefore say that these reactionary forms stand as excreted (re)productions, ambiguously begotten by the system of Hegelian Science itself? Do they not represent, in other terms, as Hegel presciently wrote at the end of the preface to the *Phenomenology*, "the feet of those, already at the door, who will carry you out" (W3: 67)?

Conceiving the organicity of Hegelian Science in light of the animal organism's formal reproduction as individual purposiveness (I=I) seems to condemn Science to endlessly juxtapose itself to the other philosophical systems that it both excludes and posits. In other words, the individuality of Science seems to contradict the integrative universality that it claims. Hegel addresses this problem in the introduction to the *Phenomenology* (W3: 71/M 76), where individual philosophies of the understanding present themselves as an "empty appearance of knowing." The problem, of course, is that "Science, just because it comes on the scene, is itself an [individual] appearance" (ibid).

The response to this apparent contradiction is only to be found by moving beyond purely animal organicity and recognizing that the Absolute Idea, which completes the system of Hegelian Science, only comes on the scene when the "Life" (EL 216) of the Idea has been supplemented with "Cognition" (EL 223). Only then may we speak of Science as espousing the animal form that Hegel is finally interested in: that of the rational, conscious human being. For consciousness involves the dynamic, reciprocal relation with otherness that goes beyond that of animal digestive assimilation.

Our investigation into Hegel's conception of the excremental activity of the animal organism has shown that it does not contradict his systematic grasp of Science. Rather, recognizing the animal production of excrement shows how the system is meant to be individual and purposive. However, to round out and complete the organic conception of the Idea in its Scientific configuration, we must acknowledge the limits of the purely animal trope. The crucial elements of human cognition and reason (aka spirit) have yet to be demonstrated, as do the revelatory aspects of absolute revelation (aka absolute spirit). Only then, has "this life [become] the absolute Idea" (EL 235), the "One Totality," an organic configuration that is individual, purposive and, above all, capable of conscious self-knowledge.

11
Reason, Revelation, and the Big Bang

When we consider Hegel's account of the Absolute Idea, its dispersal in nature, and its self-re-appropriation into the systematic conclusion (*Schluss*) of Absolute Spirit, we are reminded of certain elements found in contemporary Big Bang cosmology theory. In 2007, in my *Real Words*, I included reflections on this theme, under the ironical, Kierkegaardian heading of "Concluding Unscientific Post-scriptum." I would now like to revisit those considerations, not because the universe itself has changed over the past 13-odd years, although of course it has, but simply because my understanding of both Hegel and Big Bang cosmology have developed since then.

Why bother with such an anachronistic juxtaposition?[1] My reason is the following: this book deals with Hegel's metaphysics. Metaphysics has three traditional objects: the self, the world, and God, which are essentially inter-related, as Kant showed in his *Dialectic of Pure Reason.* We may start with either concern, and when we push our thinking to the limit, we cannot help but encounter the other two. For example, reflection on the cosmos (world) opens onto questions of determinism, freedom, and selfhood. When we reflect on the universality of the universe and the conditions for its absolute beginning, we are confronted with ideas of creation and something we might refer to as godly or divine. Big Bang cosmology allows us to begin with a contemporary reflection on the world taken as an extra-phenomenal entity, as an idea of Reason, as Kant would say, and thus, as an object of metaphysical reflection. This step is philosophically important since it allows us to bring Hegel's metaphysics of the Absolute "down to earth," to make them "relevant" in today's distinctly anti-idealist, materialist, empiricist culture. Similarly, the reader may recall, I expressed the idea of absolute revelation in the more currently digestible terms of contemporary phenomenology, as what has become known as "givenness." Let us begin by looking together at some theoretically and empirically established elements of Big Bang cosmology.

Big Bang theory postulates the existence of a singularity, out of which the universe exploded and then grew into its current, ever-expanding state, an expansion that has been increasing exponentially over the past 4 or 5 billion years and that will continue to do so, driven by postulated black matter/energy. An early and short period of generalized hyper-inflation (well within the first second of the universe's life) introduced a fundamental element of regularity, homogeneity, structure, and comprehensibility into the universe as we know it today.

Accounts of the Big Bang tend to look backwards towards the beginning or origin of the universe and therefore toward the original singularity. We begin in the macrocosmic realm that we are best acquainted with, governed by the theory of relativity, and then move back in time. This retrospective look, which is also a look further into space, leads inevitably to considerations of the microcosmic realm, governed by the strange principles of quantum physics. As we approach the original singularity, looking back in time and further in space, it is generally agreed that the "laws" of physics "break down," to use the words found in most vulgar accounts of this state. Although physics attempts to reach further back toward the singularity, creating super-dense matter in particle accelerators, in the belief that science will one day find the laws that govern matter at such high densities, the conditions of inflation and the original singularity remain beyond all accounts.

Indeed, regarding the singularity, there is nothing more to say about it than what can truthfully be said about the Parmenidean One: it is. The reason for this aporia is simply that if the singularity is the absolute beginning of time/space, it makes no sense to enquire into the physical conditions or causes that gave rise to it and that might explain it, otherwise the conditions or causes would precede the singularity. And if that were so, then the singularity would no longer be the beginning of time-space, thus postulating an "earlier" singularity, and so on, in an infinite regression that would bring about the theoretical nullification of all that is, as Aristotle understood in his deduction of a first and final cause. So Big Bang theory must simply begin with the singularity as an axiom. This is another way of saying that physics can never demonstrate why or even how the Big Bang occurred. Faced with such an apparent impasse, we might adopt a Heideggerian approach and simply celebrate the question of Being itself, and dwell within it: the impossible possibility of something rather than nothing. However, if we look at the singularity in Hegelian terms, as the punctuality of the Absolute, perhaps we can find something meaningful to say about it.

The singular punctuality of the Absolute Idea is arrived at the end of the *Logics*. According to their metaphysical mission, which I presented above, in chapter 2, the *Logics* first present the articulations of thought as it thinks objectivity, predicating substantial otherness in such a way that it becomes increasingly invested or informed with subjectivity. In the second part of the *Logics* ("Subjective Logic" in the *Greater Logic*), what was previously "objectivity" or substance, now invested with selfhood, expresses its new-found agency. In the terms that I have been discussing throughout this book, such agency, conceived in its extra-human exclusivity, should be understood as revelatory, and the selfhood of such revelation is that of the Absolute. Briefly put, Being which was conceived in the "Objective Logic" as predicated substance or nature, now manifests itself subjectively as "*Natura naturans.*" The culmination of Hegel's ontological grammar, traced out in his *Logics,* is the absolute identity between objectivity and subjectivity, between (human) reason and (absolute) revelation, between thought and being, between subject and substance. The punctuality of this culmination is an instance of absolute singularity that Hegel calls the Absolute Idea.

At the end of the *Logics,* within such an explosive identity, reason can be nothing other than *raison d'être.* In terms of the ontological argument, essence is so full of itself that it must spill over into existence. In more Hegelian terms, the Concept cannot *not* be, so it is. It is, *because* it is, with the "because" representing the reason it *is.* Being has every reason to be and so, *is.* This moment is expressed in the "*sich Entschliessen*" (the "desyllogizing," "dis-closing") of the Idea, by which nature is "*frei entgelassen*" ("freely let go") at the end of the *Logics* and before the *Philosophy of Nature.* How does this pertain to the Big Bang?

If the cosmological singularity is the absolute beginning, if it can have no cause outside itself, then it also must have its own reason to be in itself. Its principle of sufficient reason (the principle by which, in Leibniz, things are brought into existence) must be within itself. The singularity must be both reason and being or thought and being, as a self-identical unity.[2] If the singularity, like the absolute Idea, is its own reason to be, then it must be. As well, the singularity must *be* absolutely or universally, since it is absolute. There is only one original singularity per universe (I am not counting "singularities" that are observable in black hole astrophysics) and so the being of that singularity will also be universal, as will its *raison d'être.* However, Leibniz's principle of sufficient reason, as interpreted through Hölderlin's short *Urteil und Sein* text, which I introduced above in chapter 2, also teaches us that existing Being cannot rely entirely on identity; being needs difference in order to be. Consequently, we should read the absolute singularity as a self-identity that nonetheless contains difference within itself, in the form of reason-to-be. Thought and being must be there, in uneasy unity, from the very beginning. We can also read the universe's initial inflation as an ontological judgment, as a self-positing into an otherness that turns out, in the end, to be itself.

Depending on whom you talk to, the universe will either continue to expand or collapse back onto itself (Big Crunch), leaving once again a singularity, not in the past but in the future. This ultimate singularity is postulated to happen following the collapse of all matter, energy, information, or entropy into the ultimate, super-massive black hole, one resulting from the gravitational collapse of the entire universe. Of course, we speculative philosophers realize that this future singularity must be the same as the past singularity, since "singularities" are physically indistinguishable. Indeed, universal "Singularities" are the same *one* since there is nothing in them to predicate any difference. In both cases, the entity is a universal singularity; it is absolute in the sense that there can only be one, as Spinoza wrote about the Substance. Consequently, since the future, "terminal" singularity is the same as the past, "original" singularity "both" must embody the identity of thought and being, whose difference may only be conceived of as "having been," at some point in the cosmic unfolding, in counter-distinction or opposition to each other. In other words, the terminal singularity is and *has been* both thought and nature.

This unicity of initial and terminal singularity might explain a problem some contemporary cosmologists raise: the missing information. According to the Big Crunch scenario, the ultimate, universal black hole absorbs all entropy and information within it and then, when there is nothing else to absorb, "evaporates." As I wrote above, nothing can be predicated of it. The question is, what happens to all the missing information, all the perceivable, understandable, graspable quanta of the universe? A Hegelian might answer that it subsists as thought and Being, compressed, once again, into the punctual singularity of the Absolute Idea, whose Being is both its reason for having been and its *raison d'être.* As is the case with the Absolute Idea, which can do nothing other than *be,* to de-syllogize itself, to let itself go as nature, the terminal cosmological singularity cannot help but spill over into existence. The Big Crunch scenario has thus, according to a Hegelian reading, a necessary element of temporal, ontological circularity.

More recently, the 'Big Crunch" scenario has been challenged by the postulated existence of dark matter, and the observable fact that the universe, in its exponentially accelerated expansion, seems to have slipped the bonds of gravitation as a force sufficient to arrest or reverse its course. According to this "Big Chill" hypothesis, the universe will simply continue its course, ever-expanding, at an exponentially faster rate, into a final state of entropy where all energy, matter and time/space have been exhausted, a hundred or so trillions of years from now. However, I would argue that such a chilling scenario does not, in fact, discount the culmination that I described as occurring in the Big Crunch. Indeed, taking the postulated outcome of absolute entropy at its word, there would be nothing to distinguish the Big Chill's terminal state from the singularity that the Big Crunch arrives at (and begins with). In "both" cases, there is no time, no space, no matter, no energy, and no information. Nothing happens because there is nothing *to* happen. There is no possibility of predicating the difference between the two terminal states of Big Crunch and Big Chill, nor between them and the "initial singularity" postulated by the Big Bang because, in all cases, there is nothing to predicate. We can say that the "final" and the "initial" universal singularities, whether arrived at through the Big Crunch or the Big Chill theories, are ontologically identical since there is literally nothing to distinguish "them." This means that the hypothetical gravitational collapse "back" to the original singularity is the same as the hypothetical dark matter/energy pull to the "future" singularity; gravitational force and dark matter/energy fuel the same rush to the same singularity.

Consequently, Big Bang theory inevitably postulates a state of singularity that is both the spatial/temporal beginning and the end. The narrative arc of the existing universe and everything happening within it should therefore be conceived as taking place between two moments of absolute singularity, which are really the same. Reading absolute singularity through the lens of Hegel's Idea helps us see that its cosmological iteration must necessarily carry its reason-to-be within itself, as reason for what is, for what has been and, presumably, for what will be.

In order to explain some of the observable phenomena that seem to throw certain aspects of the Big Bang theory into doubt, *some* cosmologists have come up with the anthropic principle.[3] In its "strong" form, the principle says the universe is the way it is, that is, relatively smooth and flat, because otherwise we humans would not be around to perceive, understand, or grasp it. Indeed, if the universe had developed any differently, particularly during the chaotic first nano-second of inflation, the physical conditions for our existence would be absent and we would not be able to ask the question of Being. Hence, the universe is the way it is, because we are here to observe it, think it, and be conscious of ourselves within it.

Stated this way, the anthropic principle resonates with Hegel's notion of revelation as I have been presenting it in this book: Asbsolute agency that reveals itself as nature or substance is not recalcitrant to our knowing of it but rather is essentially meaningful "for us," rational knowledge-seeking beings, because we can find ourselves reflected in the laws that we discover in it. In Hegel's terms, the notion of Absolute Spirit essentially involves the agencies of revelation and reason. Similarly, the anthropic principle acknowledges the existence of conscious, reasoning (human) beings as an actual feature of the universe itself, and postulates that the universe's constitutive information is *for us* as thinking beings. The notion of Absolute Spirit helps us comprehend that, as thinkers for whom the universe reveals itself, we can hardly stand outside that which reveals itself, looking in from somewhere else. There is nowhere else. Rather, we exist in the universe itself, ambiguously situated as actors and spectators within its unfolding in space/time, between the "two" singularities. Briefly, both the anthropic principle and the Hegelian Idea portray us as constitutive participants in the universe's self-conscious self-revelation.

Nonetheless, our position as knowing, self-conscious beings within the absolute spatio-temporal framework of the Big Bang universe is necessarily temporal and, in fact, temporary and finite. Although the existence of the universe between its "two" singularities may be conceived as eternal, since there is no time outside its existence, which might render it circumscribed and finite, the same cannot be said for us, participants in the universal drama of self-revelation.

Consider this. Since the universe is expanding with a rate of expansion that increases exponentially with the distance between its objects, where further means faster, in about 100 billion years, from our current human position in the Milky Way, all other observable galaxies, with the exception of Andromeda, which by then will have merged with our own, will have receded from view. Their ever-growing distances and speeds will no longer allow light or other energy (information) to reach "us." Such a cosmic blackout will inevitably occur for any other "us" in the universe, since the same cosmic expansion applies to any cosmic observation point. Every point in the universe will be isolated in terms of information. From that moment on, one could argue that any form of universal, absolute revelation "for us" will certainly be impossible, regardless of who or what that "us" might be.

Further and most definitively, according to the Big Chill model, the ultimate destiny of the universe is cold and lifeless: in 100 trillion years, all stars will have consumed their fuel and burned out. Truly dark matter will expand forever, faster and faster, in cold nothingness, which, as I wrote above, inevitably culminates in the unconditioned conditions of singularity. The universe is now about 14 billion years old. Relatively young, compared with 100 trillion years. The anthropic principle recognizes the plain and simple truth that the present physical state of the universe does indeed allow for the existence of life-based, reflective reason, of which we are the empirical proof, even if our case is utterly unique. However, it is undeniable that at some point in the universe's extra-singular epic, at some point between a broadly defined "now" and "then," the physical conditions (energy and matter) for reasoning consciousness, whether in human or other form, will no longer be present. Revelation will be impossible "for us" conscious beings, both because there will be little or nothing to reveal and because there will be no one for whom revelation can occur. The universe will slip into unconsciousness.

On the other end of the universe's temporal spectrum, it is equally indubitable that the conditions for life-based reflective thought did not exist before the formation of stars and planets, following the inimical physical conditions postulated by Big Bang theory cosmology. It is generally agreed that planets are a fairly recent feature of the universe, beginning to form a billion or so years after the initial flash of inflation. There is little chance that primitive planets could hold complex living organisms and later planetary evolution was almost certainly necessary in order to produce the requisite conditions for complex life forms. Consequently, if conscious, reasoning knowledge of the universe implies both an informative universe and someone or something living and conscious for whom that information is revealed, then both reason and revelation are necessarily temporal and indeed finite, occurring only in the cosmological "sweet spot" between the "two" singularities. However, referring to Hegel's "ideal" reading of the Big Bang/Big Chill universe, it is ultimately irrelevant whether conscious life forms constitute an essentially and necessarily finite moment. Even if, outside the cosmological sweet spot, there was no longer the possibility of reason and revelation, precisely because there presently *is* that reality conscious thought will always *have been* an existing feature of the cosmos' narrative arc. In the Hegelian sense of the *Perfekt* grammatical tense, reason and revelation will always *have been*, and so, will always constitute an essential feature of the universe, corresponding to Hegel's notion of Absolute Spirit.

A Hegelian reading of the anthropic principle helps us understand that the Big Bang universe, in its development, reaches a moment where its reason-to-be reveals itself, at least to some extent, to thought, a moment where nature or the cosmos appears to reasoning agents as the universal Other, as all that is to be actively known. Further, to the extent that reflective thought can be associated with an instance of freedom, we may infer that freedom is a feature within the universal narrative arc. Finally, in recognizing that reason and revelation are complicit aspects in the universe's unfolding, we may conceive of its epic self-awareness in terms of the Aristotelian god, whose self-contemplative life Hegel invites us to partake in, at the very end of his *Encyclopaedia of Philosophical Sciences.*

12
Absolute Music and Meaningfulness

Music in Hegel provides a privileged field of enquiry where fundamental questions of selfhood, time, and meaning come into play. As we will see, the vibratory nature of the sound informs musical notes and their essential vanishing, as well as the musical structures of rhythm, harmony, and melody. Tones also inform the phonocentric aspect of language, conferring upon it the possibility of meaningfulness. Indeed, Hegel invites us to conceive music as the Ur-tone of meaningfulness itself, a kind of "background radiation," we might say, through which the universe can make sense. Music is thus essentially ambiguous, which is why it is felt by the listener as meaningful without determining exactly what that meaning is. As pure meaningfulness, music allows us to experience the breath of revelation: always ambiguous, always inviting us to find meaning and make sense, through reason, without telling us explicitly what that sense is. Before addressing these questions, I will defend Heinrich Gustav Hotho's foundational edition of the *Lectures on Aesthetics* (LA), from which I develop most of my material on Hegel and music. The philological beginning is important because it allows Hegel to defend himself against the common scholarly conceit that his comprehension of music was somehow deficient and hence should not be taken too seriously or that, in fact, his recorded thoughts on music were not really his own.

Hegel Knew His Music

In his *Lectures on Aesthetics*, Hegel presents music as one of the romantic arts, following discussions on architecture and sculpture. More specifically, music appears between two other recognizably romantic artforms: painting and poetry. It is well known that the Hegelian *Lectures* are the edited production of his student Heinrich Gustav Hotho, based on the notes he took in the actual lectures as well as those taken by fellow students, as well as from Hegel's own lecture notes. This has fuelled debate on the authenticity of the Hotho edited *Lectures*, that is, to what extent his version of the *Lectures* corresponds to Hegel's own thought. Arguably, the principal actor in the authenticity debate is Annemarie Gethmann-Siefert, whose essay "The Shape and Influence of Hegel's Aesthetics" introduces both the German and English editions of the now published Hotho student *transcript* of the 1823 Berlin lectures on art that he attended.

In the succinct summation of the English-language translator and editor of the transcript, Robert F. Brown, "Hotho had his own theory of aesthetics that differed in some important respects from Hegel's and, in the judgment of Annemarie Gethmann-Siefert, he imposed these views on the materials in ways that made them appear to be Hegel's own" (AT 1).[1] In the words of Gethmann-Siefert herself, the transcript shows the presence of an "original 'Hegel' [and] a conception of Hegel often decidedly different from the published [Hotho] version [of the *Lectures*]" (ibid. 11). This view has taken on a life of its own, reappearing, for example, in Sallis. There, Hotho's "considerable expertise as regards music" is presented as an indication that he took it "upon himself to compensate for the deficiencies that, because of Hegel's lack of expertise, remained in the lectures" (Sallis, p. 372).

I find Gethmann-Siefert's argument unconvincing and even wrongheaded. First, since Hotho's own thoughts and theories on music no longer exist, his *reported* interest in the subject alone can hardly be proof that he somehow reconfigured and transformed the lectures that he attended and transcribed. Second, the Hotho publication cannot reasonably be said to "deviate considerably from Hegel's own lectures" (Sallis, p. 372). A comparison between the transcript and the *Lectures* shows that the latter generally represent a development or extrapolation of the material contained in the transcripts rather than a deviation. Besides, since Hotho drew upon other student notebooks and from Hegel's own lecture notes and writings, and not just from his own transcript, one can easily account for the further development and extrapolation of the material that Hotho finally edited in the published *Lectures*. Further, since both the transcript and the *Lectures* stem from *Hotho*'s pen, is it really possible to say that one is more faithful to the original source than the other?

At least some of the doubt regarding the authenticity of the Hotho *Lectures* rests upon the idea, mentioned above, that Hegel lacked expertise (see Sallis p. 372) in music, and therefore Hotho, the real expert, felt the need to compensate for his master's lacunae. The view of Hegel's musical ineptitude is mainly based on his first-person admission, in the

Lectures, that "I am little versed in this sphere [of music] and must therefore excuse myself in advance for restricting myself simply to the more general points and to individual remarks" (LA 893; W15: 137). I propose a simple explanation for this statement. The comment is perhaps drawn from the 1828/29 series of lectures, attended by Hegel's young friend and musical prodigy: Felix Mendelssohn (Sallis p. 372). Hegel's disclaimer might then be understood as a recorded "viva voce" expression of justifiable humility. For whatever reason Hegel (or Hotho) uttered it, this profession of musical ignorance is largely disingenuous. Hegel was a frequent concert goer, organized concerts in his own home, knew and frequented important figures in the Berlin musical world and, as we will see, had a solid grasp of music theory.

In fact, I would venture that many scholars reading this chapter are unfamiliar with Hegel's coherent musicological references to chords, triads, thirds, fifths, dominants, to time signatures, bars, overtones, scales, keys, syncopation, harmony, rhythm, and beat, relative majors and minors, and so on. How many reading this present chapter are aware of where the accented beats fall in 6/8 time (LA 917)? The assertion that this theoretical material comes from Hotho is again contradicted by the fact that much of it appears in other textual contexts, for example, in the *Philosophy of Nature*'s lengthy *Zusatz* to §301 (PN 141; W9: 177), where Hegel refers to Tartini's work on the science of harmony (Padova, 1754), while discussing harmonic intervals in detail. So, while Hegel may not have learned the counterpoint and the compositional theory that his student Mendelssohn certainly mastered, he was definitely acquainted with the fundamental aspects of music theory and enough of its history to be able to refer knowledgeably to Bach, Palestrina, Durante, Lotti, Pergolesi, Tartini, Gluck, Haydn, Mozart, Rossini, and Handel. I would remind the twenty-first century reader that musical knowledge and taste involved, at Hegel's time, listening to *live* music. Not only does this mean that to hear a composer's works, you had to attend concert performances but if you *wanted* to hear Schubert (or Beethoven) and did not live in Vienna, you had to travel there by horsedrawn coach or carriage.

In fact, the core position underlying Gethmann-Siefert's regrettably influential thesis that Hotho, in his edited *Lectures*, somehow denatures the authentic or original Hegelian thoughts on music appears to rest on what might be called the anti-systematic prejudice in Hegel studies, a prejudice that the book you are reading seeks to correct. Of course, she is far from alone in this "Hegel as neo-Kantian" tendency, which views any systematic pretention as unduly totalizing, closed, metaphysical, absolutist, homogenizing, and so on, all qualifications that fly in the face of a more contemporary view of art as inherently fragmentary, ironic, and generally reflecting the disintegration of "grand narratives" (cf. F. Lyotard). Thus, for Gethmann-Siefert, it is Hotho's "speculative art history" (AT 9) that is presented in the *Lectures,* and not Hegel, an assertion that clearly ignores the fact that for Hegel the term "speculative" is virtually synonymous with "Scientific," "systematic," and "true." It is hard to see Hegel's aesthetics as anything other than *spekulativ.*

While the principal elements that concern me in this chapter, that is, music as it pertains to meaning, selfhood, and time, obviously have systematic and, therefore, metaphysical and absolute repercussions, I want to approach these issues through prior references to the discreet elements that Hegel actually addresses in his discussion of music. Inevitably, these elements will open onto a broader vista, which is only fitting since music in Hegel is a form of *absolute spirit* and it is thus impossible to address the art of music adequately without referring to the Absolute itself.

The Absolute Dimensions of Musical Art

As an expression of *schöne Kunst,* music arises within the province of absolute spirit, as a precursor to Hegelian considerations on religion and then philosophy. Within Absolute Spirit, the final chapter of the *Encyclopaedia of Philosophical Sciences,* art, religion, and philosophy fall under what Hegel, in his Neoplatonic logic, presents as the Idea (of the beautiful, the good, the true). The revelatory *agency* of the Idea is what constitutes the Absolute. As I have been arguing from the outset, and particularly in the third section of the present book, it is impossible to fully grasp the meaning of art without acknowledging its "sacred" or revelatory content.

In the *Lectures,* music takes place within the broader genre of "romantic" art because, for Hegel, any fine (*schöne*) art following the death of God (i.e., the death of Christ) is one where absolute essence or spirit *has been* exiled beyond the world. The classical world of Greek sculpture, where the stone-like gods were present in the temples of the city, is finished. The ultimate, most perfect, most beautiful earthly "artform," the singular Christ himself, is dead, an idea that I explored above, in chapter 7. The best that post-classical and thus "romantic" (Christian era) art can do is endlessly strive, symbolically, to recapture the absolute essence that has been sent beyond, alienated from the world. Art endlessly attempts to rediscover an adequate, finite, and natural form that embodies what has been lost. In its romantic pursuit, therefore, art moves toward human-made aesthetic forms that Hegel considers to be more adequate to the revelatory content or meaning of the Absolute.

These further forms become increasingly linguistic because language is generally more spiritual and has greater possibilities of meaningfulness or essence than other art forms. Thus, for Hegel, music tends towards the verbal, not because he did not understand or appreciate instrumental music, but because art, in the grand narrative of Science, must make way for religion (expressed in the language of doctrine) and philosophy (in its written texts).

More precisely, in the *Lectures*, after music comes poetry. However, what is fascinating in music, in my view, is precisely the fact that it is pre-linguistic, that in music itself we can discover pure meaning or rather meaningfulness itself. Art first seeks to recapture and portray (*darstellen*) alienated essence or meaning symbolically, in painting, and later, in the linguistic representations (*Vorstellungen*) of poetry. Between the two falls music. In other words, in music, we *hear* the breath of the Absolute, and the endlessly indeterminate possibility of meaning (*sens* [Fr.], *Sinn, Bedeutung, Meinung*) itself, before it is embodied, for a time, in words. Art tends towards linguistic articulations because it is in the language of Science that it will find its ultimate, systematic truth and meaning. Music tends toward opera and opera toward epic poetry not because Hegel failed to understand instrumental music but because words are more *determinately* meaningful than pre-linguistic sounds, tones, or notes (both are *Tönen*, in German). So, the question is, how does meaning arise within music itself, before it accomplishes its vocation (calling) in linguistic embodiment?

Of course, besides being revelatory of the Absolute, art is fundamentally human. Its expressions participate in what Hegel refers to as "spirit," which can be broadly defined as human consciousness in its temporal activity of overcoming and reconfiguring nature. Spirit may thus espouse an historical narrative, and indeed Hegel's accounts of the various aspects of spirit (psychology, law, art, religion, philosophy) are all presented as histories of their material. However, in *absolute* spirit (art, religion, philosophy), the human historical agency, broadly known as "reason," encounters and comingles with the revelatory agency of the Absolute, aka the divine.

Forms of absolute spirit thus involve forms of what can be conceived as forms of worship ("Cultus"), communal configurations where the human and the "divine" celebrate and know one another. This is obviously most apparent in Hegel's religion. However, forms of "worship" are apparent in art, whether in the communal and quasi-religious ceremonies of the Ancient world, where the gods, as statues, figured in the frequented temples and rites or in the communal, theatrical celebration of Greek tragedy, and later, in the romantic or modern era, in the communal celebration of music. Musical celebration involves its specific articulations and elements, such as rhythm, melody, harmony, performance, as well as its reception: the powerful and essentially ambiguous effect that it may have on the listener.[2] All of these elements are addressed, in Hegel, through the question of how meaningfulness arises in music.

Meaningful Tones

Music arises in the interplay between elements that are comprehensible with reference to Kant's transcendental aesthetics: first, time and space, then, the presiding unity of subjectivity best known as the synthetic unity of apperception, but which also takes the form of the transcendental imagination. In Hegel's presentation of music, we grasp how these elements cooperate in a lively, dynamic fashion. The essentially temporal nature of music means that it performs the overcoming of space. This is a general feature of time, in Hegel, from the beginning of the *Philosophy of Nature*, where the initial indeterminacy of empty space is first negated or determined by a punctuality that is essentially temporal. Time, in Hegel, is a fundamental expression of ideality, which may be simply defined as the negating agency of thought, whose source is transcendental selfhood.

Music is essentially a vibration or oscillation, and this is how it becomes meaningful. Discovering the source or nature of musical vibration takes us to the very heart of selfhood and its temporal ideality. Indeed, it is the depth of the relation between the self and time that ensures the profound effect that music may have on the inner self or soul (both *Seele* and *Gemüt*) that Hegel emphasizes. In other words, the essentially vibratory nature of temporal selfhood is both at the source of musical creation and that which is animated or sets in vibratory motion in the self that listens to music.

The transcendental source of musical sound occurs in the temporal oscillation between the self as a presiding unity, and selfhood as a self-othering, spatial overcoming activity or ideality. Referring to the transcendental form of time in sound production, Hegel remarks, "At first this self-identity remains wholly abstract and empty" (LA 907; W15: 156). However, as "activity," selfhood posits itself in "externality," as "time" per se. It is as a self-positing unity that the ideal activity of time annuls the indifferent (*gleichgültig*) spatial dimension in which it posits and negates itself. However, the "object (*Objekt*)" that subjective temporality negates is nothing other than the posited ideality of the subject itself, and so the posited "unity" thus remains "abstract" and "empty."

More concretely, in drawing itself together through the temporal negation of indifferent spatiality, the externality of time takes place as the punctual "now," as an "object" that is no more than the temporal instant (*Zeitpunkt*). However, the inner negativity of the subjective unity cannot help but again overcome this posited instant, whose vanishing produces another "now," indistinguishable from the first, and so on. Consequently, in sound production, we can conceive of a "movement" of time in its "externality," a "change" wherein each new point is nonetheless "indistinguishable" from the other. The result of this temporal activity can therefore be seen as a pure oscillation, an "empty movement" that goes nowhere, a simple vibration. An "empty movement of positing itself as 'other' and then cancelling this alteration, i.e., maintaining itself in its other as the self and only the self as such" (LA 908; W 15: 157). Thus, "The self is in time, and time is the being of the subject itself." Further, since "the time of the sound is that of the subject too," the sound of music "penetrates the self, grips it in its simplest being [whereby] the temporal movement and its rhythm sets the self in motion" (ibid.).

More precisely still, the oscillation between the "subjective unity" of transcendental time and its "ideal negative activity" (LA 907) enacts the vibrations at the heart of sound, which first may be conceived as repeated iterations of the temporal, punctual "now." In the musical production of sound, the negating temporal action of time on space necessarily involves the negation of some fixed spatial element: a string, air in a confined space, vocal chords, a drum or cymbal, and so on, setting them into temporal vibration whereby notes (nows?) are produced. Hence, musical notes are themselves manifested temporally, not only determined by vibrational frequency (oscillations over time) but also because notes follow one another in time. Indeed, it is the essential nature of the musical note to appear and disappear or vanish in time (LA 913; W15: 165).

Vanishing is an essential element in understanding meaning (or the essence of things) in Hegel generally, and in music this is specifically the case. I will return to the question below. For now, I want to stick with the generation of notes, as they arise from the inner depths of the musician's temporal soul in order to resonate in that of the listener. To proceed, we must first distinguish between sound per se (*Klang*) and tones (*Tönen*) the term that also designates musical notes.[3]

First, tones must be distinguished from sounds, which, in turn, must be distinguished from noise. Through references to the *Encyclopaedia's Philosophy of Spirit* and to the *Logic*, we see that sound requires vibration, the oscillating movement that we have just visited above, in the *Lectures on Aesthetics*, with reference to the temporal nature of musical notes. A sound (*Klang*) is not a noise (*Schall, Rauschen*), for Hegel, because the latter lacks the crucial element of presiding unity that sound entails. John McCumber uses the example of a hammer cracking and shattering a stone to represent a noise. On the other hand, a presentation of sound can be found in the *Philosophy of Nature*, in the "Physics of Particular Individuality," where Hegel discusses the specific gravity of an individual body in terms of its capacity to produce sound, rather than noise.

> A body has the specific gravity that it does because its inner unity allows it to re-assert its inner cohesiveness under the shock of otherness, setting in motion a vibration that is manifest (*Encyclopedia* §300 *Zusatz*) as sound [*Klang*].

In the *Philosophy of Nature*, as in the *Lectures on Aesthetics*, Hegel presents vibratory sound as an expression of subjectivity, evocatively, as the "plaint of the ideal in the midst of violence" (ibid). As such, sound is already inchoate subjectivity, qua the ideal or the temporal overcoming of outer objectivity in its spatial dimension, under a presiding "unity" and "cohesiveness."

While a further distinction must be made between sounds and tones/notes, it is important to realize that the distinction is not exclusive. Musical notes, as *Tönen*, obviously retain their general sonic qualities. A plucked guitar string emits a sound that is also a musical note, emitted from the presiding unity of the musical instrument and that of the guitarist. Ultimately, what constitutes a musical note is its temporal nature, its transient, vanishing quality, its essential, reiterated "nowness." As Hegel remarks in the *Lectures*, the tone, in its coming-to-be, is annihilated by its very existence and vanishes of itself (LA: 890; W15: 134).

It is the vanishing quality of the tone/note that lends it meaning or essence, which generally for Hegel, only manifests itself in what has been (*Wesen ist gewesen* [W6: 13]). Nonetheless, it is important to note that such essence, to be determinately meaningful, must be grasped within structures of greater meaning. Ultimately, in music, a note is not merely a sound because the note participates in a work of music. It only does so by vanishing temporally within that work. As Hegel puts it: "The note/tone is an expression [*Aüsserung*] and an externality, but an expression which makes itself disappear again precisely because it is an externality" (LA 891; W15: 136). The question of meaning is central to my enterprise here, particularly as it pertains to music. It is meaning that allows us to distinguish between sounds and tones/notes. The latter are meaningful sounds. Meaning arises through the vanishing quality of tones.

Tones are meaningful because they arise from the temporal vibration within subjectivity itself, between the "presiding unity" of the self and its idealizing activity. Given this, we can say that tones are meaningful sounds arising from the innermost depths of the self. Further, and equally important, tones should be distinguished from sounds in terms of their destination or vocation. As I mentioned above, in Hegel, discreet elements draw their determinate meanings from the greater structures (of meaning) in which they take place. In the context of music, we can say that musical notes, as tones, are sounds that are meaningful because their essential vanishing takes place within the greater systematic structure of the musical work, even if that work is as simple as a basic musical scale. Briefly, meaning spills out of musical notes, in their essential vanishing, within structures where that meaning becomes musical. A note is a meaningful sound because it both partakes *in* and *of* a determinate musical context. As we will see, that context necessarily involves other elements that Hegel discusses: rhythm, harmony, and melody. McCumber discovers a supporting quote for this idea in the *Greater Logic.*

> The individual note first has a sense [*Sinn*, meaning] in the relation and connection to another and to the sequence of others; the harmony or disharmony in which a circle of connections constitutes its qualitative nature, which rests upon quantitative relations. The individual note is the tonic [*Grundton*] of a system, but equally again a single member of a system of a different tonic [GL: 355; W5: 421].

Besides providing another example of how Hegel's familiarity with music theory was appreciable and not confined to the Hotho *Lectures*, the quote illustrates the point that I've been making: how the vanishing transience of musical notes or tones is meaningful within greater structures of significance. As an individual self, I may produce vocal sounds and even tones but they are only notes when they are part of a song. Otherwise, my single tone, if it can be considered as such, remains a meaningless sound.[4]

At the Scientific (*wissenschaftlich*, systematic) level, it is within the *Encyclopaedic* whole that art gains its significance (what Hegel calls "its truth"), and it is within art, as an expression of absolute spirit, that music has its true sense. Since scientific sense is best expressed in words, it is no surprise that the destiny of tones should be seen as coming to form the thoughtful vocalizations that inform words. Hence, the third element of McCumber's discussion, following his exploration of sounds and tones is the "word."

Language per se is not my concern here, except to point out that Hegel's supposed lack of appreciation for instrumental music, compared with his evident love of opera, is not necessarily due to a lack of musical sophistication on his part (where he could prefer Rossini over Beethoven, for example) but the acknowledgment of music's vocation: an abstract, indeterminate form of meaning (*Sinn*) whose tones come to inform linguistic signs, thereby determining meaningful words, ultimately, within the context of Science. Thus, in the *Lectures*, the section that follows music is poetry, with references to the epic form that appear anachronistic, considering that poetry is the third "romantic" or modern art form (after painting and music). The reason for such anachronism is simply that language, from a conceptual (i.e., retrospective, Scientific) point of view, necessarily comes "after" the presentations (*Darstellungen*) of painting and the meaningful tones/notes that are the substance of music.

Simon Jarvis explores "the relation between language, music and thinking in Hegel's thought," in his article "Musical Thinking: Hegel and the Phenomenology of Prosody" (Jarvis p. 57). Remarking that for Hegel, thinking generally involves "making-explicit" and "referentiality," Jarvis notes that music forms a kind of pre-referential "preliminary movement towards thinking, a thinking which has left so much implicit as to leave in question whether it deserves the title of thinking" (Jarvis p. 59). Jarvis draws his reference to "musical thinking" from the expression Hegel uses in the "Unhappy Consciousness" section of the *Phenomenology of Spirit* (W3: 168) where it is described as "a movement towards thinking," which "does not get as far as the Concept" (Jarvis p. 58). I take what Jarvis is referring to as pre-referential or "musical thinking" may be grasped as meaningfulness per se or as indeterminate meaning. In music, *Sinn* has not yet attained the linguistic determination of "making explicit" in an actual *Bedeutung*. It is this thoroughly ambiguous indeterminacy of meaning that forms the incantatory content of music, informing the actual musical structures (songs, sonatas, symphonies ...) in the same way, remarks Hegel, that the statues of the gods stood in relation to the temples of classical architecture (LA 894). The devotional, revelatory, and indeed absolute content of music that Hegel alludes to here in the *Lectures* appears, as Jarvis notes, in the "Unhappy Consciousness" section of the *Phenomenology* as "the chaotic jingling of bells or a mist of warm incense" of musical thinking. In both cases, we encounter pure indeterminate meaningfulness. The religious dimension of music leads us to a discussion of how it appeals to the soul. I want to look at how musical content, as indeterminate, ambiguous meaning presents itself anthropologically, as inner feeling, both as it arises from within the musical artist and resonates in the listener.

The Vibratory Elements of Music

We have seen how the production of tones/notes is grounded in the temporal aspect of subjectivity. In musical notes, temporal ideality posits itself "spatially" but then negates this empty self-positing since there is nothing objective for it to grasp onto. As Hegel puts it, as opposed to the representational arts of sculpture and painting, "what alone is fitted for expression in music is the object-free inner life, abstract subjectivity as such" (LA 891; W15: 135). Musical notes are produced from the "ultimate subjective innerness as such," and thus music is "the art of the soul [*Gemüts*]." In fact, music frees us from the "independently free objects and our relation to them," which we experience in painting and sculpture (ibid.). In music we are therefore torn out of our enthralled "independence" to the objective world, where we are always independent *of* something. In the object-free experience of music, we are thrown back on the "free unstable soaring" (ibid.) of our own selfhood. We are captivated by our own "inner subjective life" (ibid), a self-captivation where we are freed from the ambiguous relation that consciousness experiences in its relation to objects. Such object-free captivation is akin to a form of madness, one which Hegel associates with a state of *Gemüt*, and to which I will return.[5]

We have seen how the unity of selfhood presides over this self-positing, ensuring that the temporal movement has something to return to before setting out again. The oscillatory or vibratory nature of the relation between temporal positing and return into unity rings out as tones/notes, which have no determinate spatial reality but are simply evanescent iterations of the "now." However, as we have seen, notes are only such to the extent that they are further determined within greater musicological frameworks, whose "architecture" involves bigger structures of rhythm, harmony, and melody.

While it is not my intention here to explore in detail Hegel's analysis of these fundamental musical elements, I do want to briefly explain how, in the best of cases, they should not be alien to the inner subjective life of the artist or that of the listener. Rather, in music as in fine art, rhythm, harmony, and melody should be viewed as further developments of the oscillatory dynamic at the source of musical sound itself, between a temporal self-positing and the presiding subjective unity and order. The point is to show how beautiful music presents an artistic form that is fully appropriate to its content, and vice versa, an organic notion that informs all instances of artistic beauty (*schöne Kunst*) for Hegel: the perfectly adequate cohabitation of form and content in a singular aesthetic experience. Of course, such a singular cohabitation can never last and nor should it. Indeed, as I have stressed, all artworks are temporal, finite, and vanishing. What music exemplifies, through its own incessant vanishing, is how such vanishing is the ground condition of meaning.

The idea that notes comprise a series of indistinguishable, temporal instances of the "now," each one "passing away [in] the vanishing and renewal of points of time" (LA 914; W15: 165) is not sufficient to produce a beautiful musical artform. Here again, the unity of selfhood presides over the process and determines it: "Contrasted with this empty progress, the self is what persists in and by itself, and its self-concentration interrupts the indefinite series of points in time and makes gaps in their continuity" (ibid), producing rhythm. In the further rhythmic determination of notes or tones, we once again recognize the temporal oscillation that we discovered at the very source of sonic production: an oscillation or vibration between self-positing activity and stable selfhood that we likened to the Kantian synthetic unity of apperception or his transcendental imagination. The first architectural element of music, the bar or measure, results when the "indefinite variety of particular quantities ... running riot" is again "contradicted" by "the unity of the self" (LA 914). The musical bar or measure appears as "an ordering of the arbitrary manifold" (LA 915), where, Hegel states, the "unity and uniformity" that "solely belongs to the self [...] is inserted into time by the self for its own self-satisfaction" (ibid.). Indeed, "in [selfless] nature this abstract identity does not exist" (ibid).

Even within the unifying regularity and "uniformity" of the bar, oscillating temporality again arises. For although bars share a repeated time signature (4/4, 3/4, 6/8 ...), which Hegel acknowledges, within each bar, notes still have varying and apparently arbitrary durations. Thus, the "definiteness" of the bar or measure "must absorb the variety into itself and make uniformity appear in what is not uniform" (LA 916; W15: 167). Indeed, while the bar (*Takt*) or measure (*Gleich* in Hotho's student transcript) may share some of the regularity of classical architecture and its uniform columns (LA 915), bars still incorporate different note lengths and quantities that fall within their time signatures. It is this tension and diversity that begins to make music interesting and artistic.

The rhythmic result of the vibratory oscillation between unity and diversity within the musical bar is further instantiated in the "accent" or "stress" that occurs within the bars. Here, the German makes it difficult to distinguish between the bar (*Takt*) and the beat (*Takt*). However, what Hegel is clearly referring to is the fact that different time signatures involve different beats within their regularity, some "strong" and some "weak" (LA 917; W15: 168). As an example, Hegel refers to 6/8 time as having two dominant beats, "the double accent emphasizing the precise division into two halves" (ibid.). Again within the regular repetitiveness of the bar, syncopation provides a further "counter-thrust between the rhythm of the bar and the melody" (LA 918; W15: 170), allowing music to escape the "barbarism of a uniform rhythm" (ibid.), enjoying "freedom from the pedantry of metre" and its "dullness" (ibid.).

Harmony and melody further enact the lively oscillation at the heart of rhythm and beat, the vibration between the subjective aspects of order and temporal freedom, which now are presented in the more general aesthetic terms of freedom and necessity. Indeed, while harmony tends to be governed by the quantitative "laws of harmony" (LA 919; W15: 171) and the "inner necessity" of the scale with its "keynote" and the harmonic elements of the "third and fifth" or the more "contrasting" notes of the "second and seventh" (LA 925; W15: 180), melody, "in its free deployment of notes does float independently above the bar, rhythm and harmony" (LA 930; W15: 186). Melody is the "free sounding of the soul in the field of music" (ibid.). As in all expressions of *schöne Kunst,* beauty in music arises from the playful collaboration between freedom and necessity, aka between thought as the free ideal, and heteronomous nature. Just as Schiller's playful (*Spieltrieb*) idea of beauty involves the interplay between freedom (*Formtrieb*) and necessity (*Stofftrieb*), Hegel's music presents the concept of *real* freedom as the beautiful marriage between the two:

> The close link between harmony and melody does not forgo its freedom at all ... For genuine freedom does not stand opposed to necessity as an alien and therefore pressing and suppressing might; on the contrary, it has this substantive might as its own indwelling essence (LA 930–1).

It is this "indwelling essence" that I am presenting as the meaning (*Sinn*) of music, its essential content.[6]

Let us further reflect on the question of musical content as it pertains to meaning. We have followed the production of sound, from the oscillatory nature within subjectivity itself, between unbridled temporal positing and the unifying, ordering activity of selfhood. It is the lively vibration between these elements that sounds out through tones/notes, rhythmic structures and then in harmony and melody. While these notes and the music that they produce occur in the vibrations of vocal cords, strings, wood, drum skins, or in confined columns of air, they are performed there by the subject qua musician. This is a crucial point. While sound and notes arise in instruments of music, including in the vocal cords themselves, their source lies elsewhere, in the ideal depths of the subject, which Hegel refers to as the soul (*Seele*) or the heart (*Gemüt*). So, while Hegel may refer, in the *Philosophy of Nature,* to the sound produced from the struck object as "the plaint of the ideal" (W9: 174; PN 300 Add.), it would be a mistake to see music as arising from within nature itself and its things. It is the musical self that strikes the drum, which, as a natural thing is itself devoid of subjective voice. Thus, for Hegel, birds may produce pleasing sounds, even notes, but these are never music. The reason: They are missing the subjective content of soul or heart, which, as we have seen, involves temporal ideality.[7]

Music and Soul

Before further discussing this important aspect of the musical experience, it is necessary to remark on the distinction between *Seele* and *Gemüt*, although both are often rendered as "soul." The German terms have, in Hegel, distinct technical meanings. Briefly, "*Seele*" is the object of Hegelian anthropology, as presented in that section of his *Philosophy of Subjective Spirit* within the *Encyclopaedia of Philosophical Sciences.* Within that context, *Seele* is certainly presented as the seat of subjective "ideality" (ES 403; W10: 122). As Hegel remarks in the addition of the previous *Encyclopaedia* section: "We have finally arrived at the individual soul which posits its determinateness as an ideal moment." Or again, "Nowhere so much as in the case of the soul … if we are to understand it, must that feature of 'ideality' be kept in view, which represents it as the negation of the real …" (ES 402).

In fact, the discussion of the *Seele* in music best refers to the "Anthropology" sections on the "Feeling Soul" (1830), or the "Dreaming Soul" (1827),[8] where we are no longer dealing with the soul as it first appears in the fetus and the newborn child, but later, within the mature conscious individual who has learned to draw upon and refer to their unconscious mind (*Seele*), at least to a certain extent. The contents of the soul "belong not to their actuality or subjectivity as such, but only to their implicit self" (W10: 123; ES 404). Thus, Hegel continues, "under all the superstructure of specialized and instrumental consciousness that may subsequently be added to it, the individuality always remains this single-souled inner life [*Innerlichkeit*]" (ibid.). Similarly, it is the feeling soul as "object-free inner life" or "abstract subjectivity" that "alone is fitted for expression in music" (LA 891). It is also the feeling soul that is affected by music, the "inner life" that music stirs, where "what it claims as its own is the depth of a person's inner life [*Innerlichkeit*)" as such (ibid.). Recognizing the *Seele* in the context of the *Philosophy of Subjective Spirit*'s Feeling Soul as a pre-conscious, object-free instance allows us to comprehend its relation to the *Gemüt* (heart, soul) which is also presented there, and which is significant in the context of music.

The technical meaning of *Gemüt* becomes apparent with regard to the feeling soul (*fühlende Seele*) in the "Anthropology" section, where we see that *Gemüt* refers not to a faculty but to a state of mind. Indeed, if music is the art of the soul (*aus dem Gemüte ausprungen ist* [W15: 146]) and is directly addressed to the soul's "mental impressions [*Gemütseindrücke*]" (LA 900; W15: 146), it is because the *Gemüt* represents a mental state where the conscious attachment to outer objectivity has been suspended (W10: 124; ES 404 R). In the subsequent section of the PSS, Hegel refers explicitly to this condition as one of "*Herz oder Gemüt*" (W10: 127). My point is obviously not to claim that musical genius and appreciation is pathological but to show that it does involve a state where consciousness is suspended. Hegel makes a clear distinction between the inner, vibratory content and resonance of music and the aspects involved in everyday consciousness, with its aims, intentions, and objects (ibid.). In music, we are truly carried away, made "mad," to the extent that in making or being moved by music as *schöne Kunst*, we become "*gemütlicher Menschen*" (ibid.).

The distinction between music as the inner life of the soul (and the mental state that it involves) over against the conscious mind and its considered objectivity again gives rise to the essential ambiguity that we have observed throughout our discussion of music. Indeed, we have witnessed the ambiguous oscillation between the "riotous" temporal positing of the self and the subjective unity and ordering that I likened to Kant's synthetic unity of apperception, bringing about the production of sound, again in the interplay between the regularity of bars and the aleatory aspects of note lengths and accents, and further in the lively elasticity between strict, quantitative laws of harmony and the freedom of melody.

The content of music, which is what I am principally addressing in terms of meaningfulness, takes place within the *architectural* edifice of conscious musical theory and practice, a metaphor that Hegel uses at the beginning of his discussion of music, in the *Lectures*. While the relation between the inner state of *Gemüt* and the outer structures should best remain oscillating and dynamic, where "a specific sensuous material sacrifices its peaceful separatedness, turns to movement [and] vibrates in itself ... [producing] an oscillation vibration" (LA 890; W15: 134), the two aspects (inner and outer) sometimes occur at odds to one another. Whereas ideally, "what dominates in music is at once the soul and the profoundest feeling, and the most rigorous mathematical laws so that it unites in itself two extremes," these aspects can "very easily become independent of one another" (LA 894; W15: 139). In that case, music becomes too formal, acquiring a "particularly architectonic character," a soulless configuration that music "builds on its own account, with a wealth of invention, a musically regular construction of sound" (ibid.). Such music is meaningless, not because it eschews expression (and reception) of emotional content but because it forgoes the oscillation and vibration that is at the very heart of music itself, a lively ambiguity between the conscious, architectonic aspects of musical theory and the inner content of the soul, which is itself, as we have seen, essentially oscillatory. The "free movements of the heart [*des Gemüts*]" must "move and develop in a freedom made concrete only through that necessity [of musical architecture]" (LA 911; W15: 162).

Following Hegel's description in the "Anthropology" of *Gemüt* as a pathological condition, where consciousness has been suspended, we might say that the music made where outer (conscious) form and inner feeling are divorced is likewise "pathological." This is the "musical thinking" that I referred to above, which Hegel describes in the "Unhappy Consciousness" section of the *Phenomenology* as the "chaotic jingling of bells or a mist of warm incense" (W3: 168).

Vanishing, Ambiguity, and Meaning

The vibratory nature of music, at the heart of its generation and appreciation, is only possible because its notes are constantly disappearing, the essential "*Verschwinden*" that brings us closer to the question of music and meaning. Indeed, the "renewed vivication" of musical notes, their reiterated "rebirth" is only possible through their repeated disappearance (W15: 158). One might take exception to Knox's translation of "*das Innere*" or "*die Innerlichkeit*" (W15: 159) as "inner life" (LA 909) but Hegel does indeed insist upon the vitality involved in the production of musical notes, animating the musical forms of rhythm, harmony, and melody. Further, Hegel emphasizes that it is as a "living individual" that the musical artist conveys such innerness (ibid.). Of course, disappearance is an essential feature of being alive, a truth that is therefore at play in musical liveliness.

In Hegel, it is the disappearance of things, generally, that reveals their essential "having been," their *Wesen* as *gewesen*, and thus, their essential temporality. For us, it is the dying away of musical notes that best expresses the essence or meaning of their temporal existence. Consequently, in the reiterated disappearance of musical notes, their "significance [*Bedeutung*]" arises (LA 909; W15: 159). When we enjoy music and feel something meaningful in its performance, we are captivated by the finite temporality of its tones and the essential nature of their constant disappearance. Briefly, if notes did not end, they would not be notes at all. There would be no rhythm, no bars, no meter, no harmony, no melody ... no music. There would only be one tone, an endless indistinguishable monotone. If such a monotonous sound appears meaningless, it is because it does not vanish. To be a note and not simply the undifferentiated sound, the tone must pass away, for only in doing so might it be reborn as other notes, bringing forth the possibility of music within greater musicological structures (of bar, phrase, melody, song, aria, sonata, concerto, opera, symphony ...). Only in greater contexts do vanishing notes become *musically* meaningful.

Nonetheless, as I explained at the outset, the very production of pre-tonal sound involves a degree of vanishing, through the vibratory or oscillatory nature of sound itself, the fact that such subjectively generated sound involves temporal self-positing and self-annulling in an endless series of always vanishing "nows." Viewed this way, there is a grounding meaningfulness in sound itself, even before it is configured into the determinate figures of tones, notes, rhythms, harmonies, and so on. If we take the vibratory, ever-vanishing monotone of pure sound as a grounding meaningfulness per se, in all its universality, then more determinate meaning comes into play in the further vanishing by which sound becomes tones and notes. Crucially, while vanishing or disappearing allows us to grasp how meaning appears in music, it does not answer the question about what that meaning actually is or might be. In fact, the grounding indeterminacy of meaning qua sound ensures that whatever meaning we discover in music will remain indeterminate and hermeneutically open.

For Hegel, the "uniform stream [of] inherently undifferentiated duration" that we discover in sound itself (LA 913) presents indeterminate meaningfulness. We might say that the endless note, produced by the inner vibration of temporal self-positing and self-negating is pure *Sinn*, a kind of *Ur-tone* or "*Grundton*" [tonic note] (*Greater Logic*, W5: 421) on which the scale of musical determinacy is based.

The endless note of subjective ideality thus appears as the horizon of sound upon which all musical art must play. Consequently, we can just as easily say that the undifferentiated sound, the monotonous, endless "note" is a continual vanishing (the suppression of the temporal 'now') as we can say that, in its continuity, it eschews vanishing altogether. The essential ambiguity between meaning and meaninglessness remains a constant feature of musical art in spite of the most determined programmatic efforts (*the Pastoral Symphony, the Rite of Spring, Afternoon of the Faun, Summer, Spring, the 1812 Overture, Les Gymnopédies, the Military,* etc.). Indeed, beautiful music evokes an infinite palette of feelings, associations, and images in the mind of the listener. It is felt as deeply meaningful without telling us precisely what that meaning is, haunting us with the thought that it may, in fact, mean nothing.

Absolute Music and Revelation

We have seen how the purely temporal, pre-tonal Ur-tone of sound is associated with the "ideal," and it is perhaps this term that best enables me to make the transition back to the revelatory dimension of music, which I introduced above. My concluding hypothesis is that the Ur-tone of pure, indeterminate meaningfulness, as the ground for *any* possibility of determinate meaning, may be conceived as the agency of the Absolute, and thus as pure revelation, the breath of the ideal. Put differently, in musical art, the Absolute or the Idea's revelatory agency is first expressed as the "inaudible," even "silent" pre-tonal hum of pure sound, the background radiation upon which any human tonal conditioning configures itself, through reason, first as music, then in words.

When Hegel affirms that it is the temporality of music that so deeply affects the soul, as "subjective inner life itself" (LA 909; W15: 158), we may conclude that it is the tone of pure revelation that reverberates in the soul, and why our musical experience is so tinged with the ineffable and opens so readily onto feelings of the Absolute, even while those feelings remain necessarily ambiguous. For our experience of music, its enjoyment is neither monotonous nor inaudible. The rich, diverse scales of feeling that we experience in music are derived from the determinate forms that humans give to it. Our feet tap out its rhythms; we hum its notes, revel in its harmonies, are moved by its melodies. These determinate features are what makes music human, an art that is best performed and witnessed in settings that bring humans together in what may be described as a form of worship: where the Absolute and the human comingle in a celebration of ambiguous meaningfulness, a celebration that is experienced through the determinate vanishing of musical notes.

"Comingling" is a pleasant but rather vague term describing the aesthetic relationship between the agencies of the Absolute and the human. Whereas the former, in the realm of music, can be understood as the indeterminate background hum or Ur-tone, without measure nor beat, the vibratory ideality of *absolute* subjectivity itself, what punctuates, modulates and determines the revelatory hum as actual music is conscious human agency. This determinate activity "comingles" with the agency of the Absolute to produce the architectural features of rhythm, harmony, and melody, making music what it is *for us*: meaningful ambiguity, a lively, tonal oscillation between the human and the divine, between Reason and Revelation.

Notes

1. Reason and Revelation: The Limits of Worldly Actuality

1 Robert C. Solomon, *In the Spirit of Hegel* (Oxford: Oxford University Press, 1983), 582.

2 Emil Fackenheim, *The Religious Dimension of Hegel's Philosophy* (Bloomington: Indiana University Press, 1967).

3 H.S. Harris, *Hegel's Ladder. The Odyssey of Spirit,* vol. 2 (Indianapolis/ Cambridge: Hackett, 1997), 531.

4 John Russon, *Reading Hegel's Phenomenology* (Bloomington: Indiana University Press, 2004), 178. Russon's more recent book on the *Phenomenology* presents a highly nuanced account of religion in that work, one that acknowledges the existence of the "infinite" or the "absolute" as a supra-human dimension toward which religion points. John Russon, *Infinite Phenomenology: The Lessons of Hegel's Science of Experience* (Evanston: Northwestern University Press, 2016).

5 Tom Rockmore, *Cognition: An Introduction to Hegel's Phenomenology of Spirit* (Berkeley: University of California Press, 1997), 155–6.

6 Kenneth Westphal, *Hegel's Epistemological Realism* (Dordrecht: Kluwer, 1989), 185. When I capitalize "Science" or "Scientific" in this chapter, I am referring to Hegel's notion of speculative, systematic philosophy as *Wissenschaft.*

7 Two examples: Judith Shklar, *Freedom and Independence: A Study of the Political Ideas of Hegel's Phenomenology of Mind* (Cambridge: Cambridge University Press, 1976); Robert. Pippin, *The Satisfactions of Self-Consciousness* (Cambridge: Cambridge University Press, 1989).

8 Rockmore, *Cognition,* 155.

9 Ibid., 157. The question of Hegel's religiosity is debated, in an Anglo-American context, in the *Owl of Minerva* vol. 37, no. 1 (2005–6) where Cyril O'Regan, Robert Williams, and Stephen Crites stake out nuanced positions

in reaction to Peter Hodgson's book *Hegel and Christian Theology: A Reading of the Lectures on the Philosophy of Religion* (Oxford: Oxford University Press, 2005) and in Hodgson's *Auseinandersetzen* with William Desmond and his book *Hegel's God, a Counterfeit Double?* (Aldershot: Ashgate, 2003), in the last chapter of Hodgson's book. The question has defined interpretations of Hegel from the earliest Left (e.g., Bruno Bauer) versus Right (Hinrichs, Daub) Hegelian divide. More recently, volume 52, numbers 1–2 of *The Owl of Minerva* (2021) returns to the religion question in a discussion around Jon Stewart's *Hegel's Interpretation of the Religions of the World: The Logic of the Gods* (Oxford: Oxford University Press, 2018).

10 *Vorlesungen über die Religion,* in *Gesammelte Werke. Vorlesungen: Ausgewählte Nachschriften und Manuskripte,* vol. 3, ed. W. Jaeschke (Hamburg: Felix Meiner, 1983) [VR3] 96, translated into English by R.F. Brown, P.C. Hodgson, and J.M. Stewart, with assistance of H.S. Harris as *Lectures on the Philosophy of Religion* vol. 3, ed. Peter Hodgson (Berkeley: University of California Press, 1985) [LR3] 161–2.

11 See, for example, Kant's attempts to arbitrate between reason and faith in the *Pantheismusstreit* (i.e., the public epistolary debate between M. Mendelssohn and G. Jacobi) with his short essay "What Does It Mean to Orient Oneself in Thought" (1786) or in his later book, *Religion within the Bounds of Reason Alone* (1793), where Kant, unsuccessfully, attempts to reconcile religion with rational morality in order to stave off political threats to the Enlightenment project of reason-based freedom. See below, in chapter 5, where I discuss the "Orienting" text in detail.

12 H.F.W. Hinrichs, *Die Religion im inneren Verhältnisse zur Wissenschaft* (Heidelberg: 1822). The preface is found in W11: 42–67, translated by Eric von der Luft as *Hegel, Hinrichs and Schleiermacher on Feeling and Religion* (Lewiston/Queenston: Mellen Press, 1987).

13 See the chapter on Schleiermacher in Reid 2014. See also chapter 6 below.

14 Peter Hodgson, "*Hegel and Christian Theology*: Author's Summary," *Owl of Minerva* vol. 37, no. 1 (2005/6): 7.

15 W3: 70. Translated by A.V. Miller as *Hegel's Phenomenology of Spirit* (Oxford: Oxford University Press, 2007), section 75 [M 75].

16 W17: 382–3. My translation.

17 VR2 385.

18 *Jenaer Schriften 1801–1807,* W2: 553.

19 I remind the reader that Hegel's *Logics* end with reference to the Ideas of the True and the Good, followed by the Absolute Idea, in the place where we might expect the Idea of the Beautiful. When I refer to "Logics" in the plural, I mean both the *Greater Logic* [GL] (aka *Science of Logic)* and *Encyclopaedia Logic* [EL] *(Lesser Logic).* Of course, G.E. Lessing's influential *Letters on the Education of the Human Race* (1778) had already outlined, for

an entire intellectual generation, the project of reconciling reason and revelation, on a world historical level.

20 Fackenheim, *The Religious Dimension*, 79.

21 Ibid., 111.

22 "The problem of the Hegelian middle [on which the success of the system turns] thus turns into the problem of the relation between religious life [aka Revelation] and philosophical thought [aka Reason]" (ibid.).

23 Only the *Greater Logic* makes explicit the binary distinction between Objective and Subjective Logic.

24 In spite of Heidegger's Nazi failings, his philosophy is rarely, if ever, evaluated against contemporary actuality, other than in a positive light, as with his naturalist writings on technology.

25 See the introduction to Beiser's *After Hegel: German Philosophy Between 1840 and 1900* (Princeton: Princeton University Press, 2014) where he argues that the second half of the nineteenth century is more philosophically interesting than the first because its avowed materialistic secularism has gotten over questions of religious faith in its relation to reason.

26 *Enzyklopädie der philosophischen Wissenschaften im Grundrisse 1830. Erster Teil. Die Wissenschaft der Logik,* W8: 153, translated by T.F. Geraets, W.A. Suchting, and H.S. Harris as the *Encyclopaedia Logic, Part One of the Encyclopaedia of Philosophical Sciences, with the Zusätze* (Indianapolis: Hackett, 1991), hereafter referred to parenthetically in the text as EL followed by the section number. I will use "Add." to indicate the student-note based additions (*Zusätze*) to the sections.

27 In the EL 142 Add., Hegel remarks that Aristotle's view of "actuality" is the "principle of philosophy"; Aristotle's "actuality is that of the Idea itself and not ordinary actuality of what is immediately present."

28 Essentially, worldly things that are supposedly self-identical are undermined by self-differencing, which, in turn, is only possible within a pre-supposed identity.

29 While there is a tendency on the part of commentators, as I wrote above, to stress the moral community, at the end of the *Phenomenology*'s chapter 6, thus rendering questionable the importance of chapter 7 (Religion), the Morality section remains shot through with dialectical iterations of good and bad, confession and absolution. Whether we subscribe to the idea that the Morality section replays the contradictions of ironic Romanticism (evoking figures of Fr. Schlegel, Novalis, and Hölderlin) or the articulations of Kantian/Fichtean morality, there is no reason to establish a definitive ending in chapter 6 of the *Phenomenology*.

30 W3: 547/M 752.

31 It is significant that contemporary accounts often translate "*offenbare*" as "manifest," thereby accentuating the anthropological aspect of revelation

while deflating its metaphysical dimension. See, for example, Allen Speight, "Determinate Religion and the Philosophy of Art," *Owl of Minerva* vol. 52, no. 1–2 (2021): 15.

32 Hegel refers to the religious community celebrating "content in the form of picture-thinking [*Vorstellens*]." I believe such "representing" is essentially linguistic and different from the *Darstellen* [presenting] that characterizes art. The translation of *Vorstellung* as picture-thinking misses the crucial difference between it and the artistic instantiations of Revelation in singular sacred objections. The doctrinal language of Revelation is further spiritualized, further reflected upon and, thus, re-presented as a communal ritual. Hegel probably had in mind such doctrinal language as the Nicene Creed, which affirms the Trinity, as well as the divinity of Christ. See chapter 8 below.

33 W13: 117–19. My translation.

34 This is why Schleiermacher's religion of feeling represents such an existential threat for Hegel: For Schleiemacher, doctrine is no more than "a mausoleum of religion," as he writes in the second of his *Speeches on Religion*, a testimony to an absolute absence. Thus, the words in which Revelation takes place are desacralized, evacuated of their divine content.

35 In becoming historical, Revelation participates in human time, in the human narrative. The reconciliation between reason and revelation thus unifies the two apparently divergent temporal backgrounds: the Ancient, Aristotelian idea of truth as eternal is brought together with the modern, Christian, historical story of truth. See below, chapter 4.

36 As I mentioned above, Hegel generally refers to Church doctrine in terms of *Vorstellung* (representational language, rather than "picture-thinking").

37 VR2 383. In Hegel's words, philosophical Science must take us from knowledge "that God exists" to "*what* He is."

2. Absolute Selfhood and the Otherness of Nature

1 For simplicity, I refer to "Logics" in the plural, implying that the content discussed is common to both the *Encyclopaedia Logic* (EL) and the self-standing *Greater Logic* (GL). If not, I will specify the work referred to. It may be helpful to recall that in Hegel's *Encyclopaedia of Philosophical Sciences*, the most complete articulation of his system, the *Philosophy of Nature* follows the *Logic*. For an exploration of natural otherness in Hegel and a summary of different positions on the matter, see chapter 4 in Reid 2007, 40–54.

2 I believe Hegel's *Logics* share the ontological objective that Aristotle assigns to his *Metaphysics*: to be first philosophy or the science of Being as Being.

3 Charles Taylor, *Hegel* (Cambridge: Cambridge University Press, 1977), 225. See Simon Lumsden's "The Rise of the Non-Metaphysical Hegel," *Philosophy Compass*, 3, no. 1 (Jan. 2008): 51–65. Lumsden traces the rise of

the non-metaphysical Hegel to Klaus Hartmann and Robert Pippin (*Hegel's Idealism*) and sees Charles Taylor as the last important commentator in the metaphysical Hegelian tradition.

4 John Burbidge, *The Logic of Hegel's Logic* (Peterborough: Broadview Press, 2006). For Burbidge, Hegel's *Logics* should be understood as we understand logic generally: as dealing with the processes of thought as divorced from metaphysical investigations. Thus, Burbidge prefers the GL since in it we are better "able to examine how thought functions on its own" (25), whereas in the EL, "the dynamic movement by which thought develops is lost" (120). William Maker, *Philosophy Without Foundations: Rethinking Hegel* (Albany: State University of New York Press, 1994). For Maker, the *Logics*, like Hegel's systematic philosophy as a whole, is "self-grounding, self-determinative, presuppositionless or autonomous" (96).

5 EL 36 Add.

6 Stephen Houlgate, "Essence, Reflexion and Immediacy in Hegel's Science of Logic," in *A Companion to Hegel*, ed. S. Houlgate and Michael Baur (London: Blackwell Publishing, 2011): 139–58. There are exceptions to the general trend toward non-metaphysical readings of Hegel's *Logics*; for example, Karen Ng in her article, "Hegel's Logic of Actuality," *Review of Metaphysics* 63, no. 1 (2009):139–72. As she so eloquently writes, "The Concept does not need to be applied to intuitions because it is its own content and determinacy; it is the drive of Being as Being thought as much as it is the drive of thinking that thinks itself. The absoluteness of absolute idealism is due to its being both an idealism and a materialism, both a logic and an ontology."

7 Hegel writes, "The forms of thought are, in the first instance, displayed and maintained in language." *Wissenschaft der Logik, Die Lehre von Sein* (1832), edited by H.-J. Gawoll (Hamburg: Felix Meiner Verlag, 1984) [WL] Second Preface, 9–10. Or again: "It is in words that we think." *Encyclopaedia of Philosophical Sciences, Philosophy of Spirit* 462 Remark [ES 462 R]. See also the 462 Add.: "Words become an existence enlivened by thought. This existence is absolutely necessary to our thoughts."

8 Hegel distinguishes between "proposition" and "judgment" on the basis of the scientific destination of the latter, in contrast to the former's general, common language usage. (EL 167 Remark). This distinction is crucial in grasping how Hegel's "theory" of language is principally concerned with defining and refining its participation in scientific objectivity. Hegel distinguishes between everyday, common language and its scientific (*wissenschaftlich*) usage.

9 GL 72. Cf. EL 84: "[Undetermined] Being is the concept only in itself."

10 Since determination is to be thought of, in Hegelian terms, as negation, we can say that thought negates Being's nothingness and makes it a positive something. Further, since pure Being is nothingness, it is indistinguishable

from pure thought with nothing to think of. Thus, the EL "begins" with the last "position of thought" from the work's introductory *Vorbegriff*: Immediate Knowing as the unity of thought and Being.

11 Friedrich Hölderlin, *Sämtliche Werke*, ed. F. Beissner (Stuttgart: W. Kohlhammer, 1962) vol. 4, 226–7.

12 French translators Labarière and Jarczyk choose "*emplissement*." B. Bourgeois chooses the similar term, "*remplissement*." A.V. Miller, in his translation of the GL, chooses the surprising and tendentious "*impregnation*." Hegel's ontological take on judgment can perhaps be thought of as an elaboration on Spinoza's first definition of the Substance as *causa sui*, as well as involving the freedom of self-positing subjectivity and the cosmogonical (as pronounced at the beginning of John's Gospel) agency of the Word.

13 "Abstract," in Hegel, generally means one-sided or unilateral. Concreteness involves the interplay of contradictory positions, which are ultimately expressions of thought and Being. Thus, the ground of existing Being, as we will see, involves the fundamental interplay between identity (thought) and difference (Being).

14 The structural, organic nature of Hegel's use of the syllogism is far removed from its formal employ, which Hegel criticizes repeatedly: "Caius is a man; all men are mortal; therefore, he is mortal. Personally, I have never thought of anything so dull. It must be produced somewhere in our gut, without our being conscious of it." "Wastebook Fragments," W2: 541.

15 What is posited in the judgment form, one might say, is the "concept" in the Kantian sense of the word, i.e., an essential form of subjective mind but which is now, in Hegel, actually posited in reality through the agency of thought.

16 The ontological aspect of judgment, through the copula, is fundamental to Hegel in general and reflects his rehabilitation of the ontological argument for the existence of God, in his *Lectures on the Philosophy of Religion*, where he criticizes Kant for his refutation of the argument in the first *Critique*. For example, W17: 523–34. Indeed, Kant does specifically refuse the ontological acceptation of the copula.

17 W6 350–1. I have chosen to translate "*vorhanden*" here as "presented for us" rather than as simply "existing," which would better reflect the relatively neutral (impoverished) notion of "Dasein." I believe "*vorhanden*" implies "for us."

18 Hegel uses the example of acids and bases. Finite chemical entities are the result of the dynamic contradiction between the acidic and the basic, where one is inherently in the other. Similarly, the magnet only exists as such through the interplay between north and south poles. "Generally speaking, it is contradiction that moves the world." EL 119 Add. 2.

19 It may be instructive to refer again here to Spinoza, where the Substance is the immediate and total accomplishment of such grounded Being, and

so *is* absolutely. This is expressed immediately in the first Definition of the Substance as *causa sui*. Presenting the essence of substance in terms of cause already invites us, as reasoning beings, to contemplate and understand it. For Hegel, although this essential aspect is indeed immediately in Being (as nothingness) it must be scientifically demonstrated through the ful-filling of the copula. This mediation takes place in the *Logics*' Doctrine of Essence.

20 In the GL, *Sache* arises as grounded existence in the Doctrine of Essence, W6: 119. Later, in EL, *Sache* appears as grounded, conditioned existence, in the same Doctrine, although later, in the subchapter on Actuality (EL 147). In both cases, *Sache* is presented as grounded (meaningful) existence: existence that is "at stake," that is an issue for Science. Ultimately, the fullest expression of *Sache* is revealed, as we will see, in the desyllogizing of the copula as nature: Being that has every reason to be and is hence what is at stake *for us*.

21 Perhaps the best way to illustrate how identity and difference are involved in forming the determinate ground for *existence*, within a predicative proposition, is by referring to Leibniz's metaphysics of possibility and actuality (certainly the dominant metaphysics in the German pre-Critical/pre-Kantian world). In Leibniz, the principle of identity (where subject is equal to predicate) is guarantor of what is merely possible, while the statement of actuality must involve causal differentiation through the principle of sufficient reason.

22 It is again impossible to ignore Hegel's reference to the ideas in Hölderlin's foundational short text *Urteil und Sein*. Indeed, that text helps us see the ontological nature of judgment, i.e., how the move from identity to difference involves a move into Being. Friedrich Hölderlin, *Sämtliche Werke*, ed. F. Beissner (Stuttgart: W. Kohlhammer, 1962), vol. 4, 226–7. Hölderlin introduces the etymological device of writing the hyphenated "*Ur-theilung*" to express judgment as this original division, a device which clearly impressed Hegel who uses it himself (EL 166).

23 In EL 119, Hegel is probably referring to a little known, pre-Critical text by Kant, his 1763 essay on negative grandeur, according to which zero is presented not as null but as the existing middle or realized identity of + and – sums. In his essay, Kant applies this principle to ethical questions. Hegel refers, in EL 98, to Kant's application of the principle to cosmology: the *actual* orbits of the planetary bodies are the realized identities of opposing centrifugal and centripetal forces. Hegel extrapolates in EL 119 Add. An acid is at the same time, in-itself base, and the existing liquid is the positive identity of this opposition.

24 Significantly, the dialectic of finitude/infinity informs the determinations of Being in the *Logics*, both as Quality (being-there) and as Quantity (Quantum). See EL 92 Add.: "Thus we suppose, for instance, that the moon, which is something else than the sun, could quite well exist if the sun

did not. But, in fact, the moon (as something) has its other in itself, and this constitutes its finitude."

25 I believe "phenomenon" is a more satisfying translation for *Erscheinung* since the "appearance" that Hegel is discussing in EL 132–41 is one that is scientifically significant: a phenomenon.

26 Overall, the *Logics* can be said to articulate, in a completely different way, Schelling's definition of the Absolute as S = O. I am trying to show how, for Hegel, this absolute *Urteil* involves the emergence of knowable Being in the copula (=) through the dynamic interplay of identity and difference. Schelling tends to see the copula as an original unity that underlies all differentiation.

27 Which, once again, can be conceived in Spinozistic terms, as *natura naturata* and *natura naturans* or as the Substance's first definition as *causa sui.*

28 The "letting itself out" or "unbuckling" metaphor comes from Jean-François Marquet, who likened, in his lectures, the fulfilled Idea to a replete diner having to let out his belt after a particularly substantial and satisfying meal. There are too many interpretations of "*sich frei entlassen*" to mention. In chapter 11, I will read "*sich frei entlassen*" in terms of the Big Bang theory of cosmology.

29 The EL gives "*sich entschliesst*" EL 206 Add.; the GL: "*Entschluss.*" W6: 573. In the EL version, Hegel plays with the terms *schliessen, beschliessen, entschliessen* as signifying a decision to step forward out of one's inwardness.

30 The first moment of the *Philosophy of Nature,* the subsequent book in Hegel's *Encyclopaedia of Philosophical Sciences,* is "again" immediate Being, not in the element of thought, however, but rather in the element of external otherness (space) that characterizes nature in Hegel. At the end of the GL, W6: 573, Hegel anticipates how the immediate exteriority of Being, *as nature,* will be overcome, truly liberated, in the final book of the *Encyclopaedia, The Philosophy of Spirit.*

31 Perhaps this political dimension of the *Logics* (i.e., the possibility of realizing freedom in nature) is what lies behind Hegel's enigmatic, seemingly cautionary statement: "It is unsettling when a nation [*Volk*] loses its metaphysics." Preface to the first edition of the GL. *Wissenschaft der Logik, das Sein* (1812), ed. Hans Jürgen Gawoll [GL(1812)] (Hamburg: Felix Meiner Verlag, 1986), 3. Hegel's revision of the 1812 GL (published posthumously, in 1832) only got as far as the Doctrine of Being. The rest of the GL predates the EL by almost 20 years.

3. Comets, Moons, and the Voices of Nature

1 See Reid 2021.

2 The solar system is, thus, "the developed disjunction of the Concept." The EN quote is found in W9: 103–4. EN 78–80. Cf. the bilingual edition,

Philosophy of Nature, 3 vols., ed. and trans. M.J. Petry (London: Allen and Unwin, 1970).

3 See Alison Stone's work in this sense. *Petrified Intelligence: Nature in Hegel's Philosophy* (Albany: State University of New York, 2005).

4 Chapter 4 of Reid 2007 outlines a palette of positions on the relation between thought and nature, ranging from the "processional" view (Alison Stone and Stephen Houlgate) where nature is already shot through with logic, to the oppositional view (William Maker, me), which stress nature's otherness.

5 In my above-cited chapter of Reid 2007, I discuss how Hegel's *Philosophy of Nature* is a discourse reflecting speculatively on the discourses of the positive natural sciences.

6 For example, in the positive (empirical) sciences, singular cases form particular species that are generalized into laws. Conversely, the history of religion can be seen as beginning with God as universal Being, passing through the particular gods of Greece/Rome, arriving at the singularity of Spirit (Christ) in revealed religion.

7 Recall that the German "*Schluss*" means both syllogism and conclusion.

8 In EN 181, Hegel also presents the ultimate syllogism as "the Absolute," which is the U-P-S syllogism of the *Encyclopaedia*: Logic (Universal), Nature (Particular), and Spirit (Singular).

9 In Hegel, singularity and universality are unstable if not mediated by particularity. This is because that which is presented as the Universal can be seen as (absolutely) singular and so appears ontologically indistinguishable from other singular ones. Conversely, each singular one, taken (absolutely) on its own, tends collapse into universal oneness. It is this relative indifference, where qualitative particularity is absent, that characterizes the purely numerical "difference" that Hegel associates with strictly quantitative reality.

10 W9: 102–3. EN 78–80. Hegel seems to assume that all moons are like the earth's, turning only one face to its planet and thus not rotating freely on its axis.

11 W9: 128. EN 100. In the GL Doctrine of Being, being-for-itself is described as "an infinite return into self" and "the polemical, negative relating against the limiting Other." W5: 174–5. A more "spiritual" example of this might be observed in the *Phenomenology of Spirit*, where self-consciousness first appears as for-itself "against the limiting Other," before this hard recalcitrance is dissolved in the reciprocal relation where one self-consciousness becomes for-another. For an exhaustive look at Individuality versus singularity in Hegel, see Martin Donougho's *Hegel's Individuality: Beyond Category* (Cham, Switzerland: Springer, 2023).

12 W9: 102–3. On Hegel's reading, the comets' place within the syllogistic universe means they do not strike the earth. Regarding cometary fluidity, it

is interesting that the contemporary discovery of water on comets has led astronomers to theorize that water was first brought to earth through comet strikes.

13 Such recalcitrant difference can be seen as an entirely exclusive form of negativity: something is what it is because it is simply not anything else.

14 This is why, as Hegel writes in EN 275 Add., the true nature of light is only the "manifestation of itself, not for-itself but for-another" [W9: 113], and later, in EN 278 Add., "as visible, objects are for-another [*für andere*], and therefore are in relation to another" (W9: 124).

15 The ultimate carrying out of the process of fluidification for the crystal takes place through the other properties of the particular individual body and, specifically taste, where the salt crystal dissolves on the tongue, presaging the chemical process.

16 Hegel describes sound as "a kind of mechanical light" (W9: 172–5. PN 138–40).

17 In musical terms, Hegel's introduction of the cometary moment echoes the contemporaneous (e.g., Mozart, Beethoven) addition of the third, usually penultimate "Minuet" or "Scherzo" movement into the Baroque/Classical symphonic sonata form, preceding the finale movement, fluidifying, with its dancing, Walz-time, the strict tripartite structure (fast-slow-fast) that was the earlier rule. Indeed "Scherzo" means "joke" in Italian.

18 Perhaps the central question that the *Philosophy of Nature* seeks to address is this: Given the otherness of nature, why should we care about it at all?

19 Self-knowledge in otherness is the story behind Hegel's *Philosophy of Spirit* and further research might involve the possible interplay between lunar and cometary elements in that context.

4. History and the Absolute Now

1 In no way do I mean to diminish the importance of Löwith's great work. Indeed, one could argue that without such pivotal "misreadings," there would be no history of philosophy at all.

2 According to Heidegger's critique, Hegelian spirit (*Geist*) falls into time, as if the history of spirit were distinct from and less essential than a more fundamental temporality. Heidegger conceives Hegelian time as a limitless representation of present instants, each one a self-negating negation, according to a levelling, banal logic. Thus, the only "eternity" involved is in the unlimited series of present and evanescent moments, conceived (erroneously) as an essential substance (*ousia*). My colleague Francisco Gonzales, who has worked on the archives from Heidegger's seminars, has told me that Löwith attended the seminar of 1925–26 (with the student Gadamer). The theme was time. In the seminar, there was constant reference to Hegel and Aristotle. The Hegel texts that Heidegger refers

to in *Being and Time*, and probably in his seminar, are the same ones that Löwith quotes in his book.

3 Löwith 209.

4 Löwith 174.

5 *Jenaer Systementwürfe II, Logik, Metaphysik, Naturphilosophie*, 206–10.

6 That is, the EL. As with the EL lengthy *Vorbegriff* (Preconception), the GL's introduction also presents the historical aspect of pre-Scientific philosophical positions (empiricism, pre-critical metaphysics, intuition or intellectual faith), all of which are dissolved in the initial moment of indeterminate Being-nothingness where the Logics begin.

7 The *Phenomenology*'s text on time is discussed by Heidegger, which seems to show that Löwith, through the above-mentioned Heidegger seminary, was aware of it.

8 Hegel refers regularly to the genius of the German language and its sense of the *Perfekt*, e.g., in the ES 450 Add. The same sense of the present perfect exists in English.

9 The ambiguity of the "now," equally sensuous and sublime, will allow Kierkegaard to conceive of the ecstatic commonality between the aesthetic and the religious stages.

10 Löwith 385.

11 Löwith 69.

12 Löwith 63. Translation modified.

13 Löwith 33.

14 Löwith 33.

15 Of course, the first edition of the *Encyclopaedia* had the same mission, at the University of Heidelberg, where Hegel taught before moving to Berlin in 1818.

16 See Reid 2007, chapter 6 on Hegel and the State University.

17 Löwith 64.

18 While he does briefly discuss Hegel's pedagogical theory and its humanist and political mission, citing his graduation speeches from his time as a gymnasium principal, Löwith does not refer to Hegel's reflections on the university institution, as found in the letter-report to his friend Raumer. In fact, the letter was only published in 1938 and would have probably been unavailable to Löwith, cf. W4: 418–25.

19 W4: 422.

20 Löwith 66. Translation modified.

5. Knowledge of God and the Perils of Insight

1 In the *Phenomenology*'s preceding sections of Culture, Hegel has shown how bipolar contradictions within forms of the *ancien régime*, namely between noble and ignoble, good and bad, sovereign and vassal have collapsed

under the weight of their own nullity. The truth of these fixed oppositions is the truth of the French Enlightenment itself: the vanity of everything substantial, leaving, on one hand, the eviscerated world of material utilitarianism and, on the other, the vacuous divinity of Deism; essence has taken the form of a *deus absconditus.* It is the evacuation of all substantial reality that is conclusively expressed in the subsequent section on "Absolute Freedom and the Terror."

2 Terry Pinkard, in his book *Hegel's Phenomenology, the Sociality of Reason,* takes pure insight as synonymous with the "unbiased scrutiny" of the French *philosophes* against "established Christian religion." However, for Pinkard, this latter takes on two forms: either as orthodoxy or as emotionally immediate faith (aka Jansenism, pietism, feeling). In this context, "pure insight" is "the detached, unbiased observation of things or the exercise of the faculty of reason itself" (Cambridge: Cambridge University Press, 1994), 167–8. H.S. Harris's commentary, in *Hegel's Ladder* vol. 2, "The Odyssey of Spirit," refers to a large palette of French inspirations: Pascal, Diderot, Descartes, Rousseau, Voltaire, but also Bacon and Lessing. D'Holbach, "the most outspoken atheist among the philosophes [is] the voice of Pure Insight" (Indianapolis/Cambridge: Hacket, 1997).

3 This is of course the theme of one of Hegel's earliest published writings, the essay *Glauben und Wissen* (1802, *Faith and Knowing*). Examining Hegel's use of *Einsicht,* as the present chapter does, shows how the theme is not confined to Hegel's early interests but rather should be seen as present throughout his philosophical career (W2: 283–433).

4 Particularly, Mendelssohn's *Morning Hours* and his *To Lessing's Friends.* See *Mendelssohn: Philosophical Writings.*

5 Kant's intervention in the debate was much anticipated and, given the prominence of the journal in which it appeared, we can safely assume that Hegel read it.

6 "What It Means to Orient Oneself in Thinking?' [OT] in I. Kant, *Religion and Rational Theology,* ed. and trans. A.W. Wood and G. di Giovanni (Cambridge: Cambridge University Press, 2001), followed by page reference to *Kants Werke, Akademie Textausgabe* (1902), vol. 8 (Berlin: de Gruyter, 1968). For the "Orienting" essay, see OT: 3–18.

7 The transition from faith to superstition in the "Orienting" essay seems to anticipate the same movement in the subsections of chapter 6 of the *Phenomenology*: "Faith and Pure Insight" to "The Struggle of the Enlightenment with Superstition."

8 Allan Arkush, *Moses Mendelssohn and the Enlightenment* (Albany: SUNY, 1994), 85.

9 Moses Mendelssohn, *Morning Hours: Lectures on God's Existence,* ed. and trans. D.O. Dahlstrom and C. Dykk, *Studies in German Idealism* 12 (Dordrecht: Springer, 2011).

10 Indeed "common sense" sometimes takes the form, in Mendelssohn's *Morning Hours*, of "*Menschenverstand*."
11 "Concerning the Doctrine of Spinoza (1785)," ed. and trans. G. di Giovanni, *Friedrich Heinrich Jacobi, The Main Philosophical Writings and the Novel Allwill* (Montreal, Kingston: McGill-Queen's University Press, 1994) [CS], 190.
12 CS: 190. In his informative introduction, di Giovanni writes: "So far as Spinoza is concerned, the only way to deal with the surd is to move beyond the process of ratiocination through a process of intellectual ascesis that allows the mind to escape from the determination of space, time, and logic and see things all at once *sub specie aeternitatis*. Accordingly, insight, not conceptualization, was for Spinoza 'the best part of all finite natures'" (CS: 20).
13 Johann Lavater publicly challenged Mendelssohn to refute the faith-based arguments of the theologian Charles Bonnet or convert to Christianity, a challenge that Mendelssohn compellingly refused in the name of tolerance and the philosophical vocation of the Jewish religion.
14 Such oppositional exclusivity stems from the fact that both faith and pure insight per se are anchored in the faculty of understanding (*das Verstand*), which presides over all the fixed, mutually exclusive dualities of the Culture chapter.
15 The "Allegorical Dream" chapter in Mendelssohn's *Morning Hours* also involves an illustration of how the exclusivity of speculative insight, divorced of common sense, can be seen as dangerous to holistic reason, as is fanatical faith. The rude awakening that ends the allegory comes in the form of "an awful clamour" made by "a fanatical swarm of locals [who] rallied around the lady, contemplation, and resolved to drive away both common sense and reason."
16 Recall that, regarding insight, "it is obviously religion we are talking about" (W3: 392/M 528). In OT, Kant pleads: "Men of intellectual ability and broadminded disposition! I honour your talents and love your feeling for humanity. But have you thought about what you are doing and where your attacks on reason will lead?" Without rational faith, both dogmatic tendencies (insight and faith) lead to superstition and arbitrary lawlessness, where "the authorities get mixed up in the game," taking away freedom, even the "freedom to think." Consequently, "freedom in thinking finally destroys itself if it tries to proceed in independence of the laws of reason" (OT 17–18).
17 Immediate knowing thus appears as the ultimate position of thought *prior* to Hegel's scientific demonstration, whereby the formal emptiness of insight is carried over into the first position: the determination of being as the abstract nothingness of pure thought.

18 Jacobi: "Through faith we know that we have a body, and that there are other bodies and other thinking beings outside us" (CS: 231). The text from EL 74 reads: "… the insight that the content … is *mediated through an other* reduces the content to its finitude and untruth. [Nonetheless], such insight is a knowing which contains mediation, since content brings mediation with it. The same understanding [i.e., Jacobi] which thinks it has emancipated itself from finite knowing and from the understanding's [reflective] identity, from metaphysics and the Enlightenment, immediately again makes this immediacy, i.e., the abstract self-relation or the abstract identity, into the principle and criterion of truth. Abstract thinking (the form of reflective metaphysics) and abstract intuiting (the form of immediate knowing) are one and the same."

19 While I cannot here develop the hypothesis further, it is possible that, in the *Vorbegriff*, written some three decades after the French Revolution, the attendant danger posed by the unreconciled (anti-Scientific) positions of the understanding takes the form of modern irony, which Hegel characterizes elsewhere in similar terms to those he uses in the *Vorbegriff*: "savage arbitrariness," "arrogance of feeling," opposition to philosophy, and above all, the universal presuppositions of the age: we can only "know what is finite and contains no Truth" along with the attendant belief that such Truth may only be attained through "wholly abstract faith (EL 77). See (Reid 2014b 109–13).

6. Overcoming Understanding: The Language of Representation

1 Johannes Hoffmeister, *Briefe von und an Hegel* [*Briefe*] (Hamburg: Felix Meiner, 1953), letter 6, Christmas Eve, 1794.

2 *Briefe*, letter 8.

3 *Briefe*, letter 10.

4 For an extensive treatment of the relationship between Reinhold, Schelling and, above all, Hegel, see Martin Bondeli's essential article "Hegel und Reinhold," *Hegel-Studien* vol. 30 (1995): 45–87. See also Rolf Ahlers, "Reinhold and Hegel on the Principle and Systematicity of Philosophy," *Idealistic Studies* vol. 35, Issues 2–3 (Summer-Fall 2005): 215–53, and Pierluigi Valenza, *Reinhold e Hegel: ragione storica e inizio assoluto della philosofia* (Padova, Cedam, 1994).

5 Hegel, *Briefe*, letter 31, September 26, 1801.

6 *Glauben und Wissen, oder die Reflexionsphilosophie der Subjectivität, in der Vollständigkeit ihrer Formen, als Kantische, Jacobische, und Fichtesche Philosophie.*

7 For the critical edition of the psychology manuscript, see *Gesammelte Werke*, ed. Rheinische-Westphalischen Akademie der Wissenschaften (Hamburg: Meiner, 1968-) [GW] vol. 1: 167–92, as well as the *Anhang* and the *Anmerkungen*. See also Johannes Hoffmeister, ed., *Dokumente zu Hegels*

Entwicklung (Stuttgart: Frommann-Holzboog, 1974 [1936]): 195–217 for the manuscript, with Hoffmeister's commentaries: 448–53.

8 For the relation between these thinkers and the first Kantian *Critique*, and for background on Reinhold and the period immediately following its publication, see George di Giovanni, *Freedom and Religion in Kant and His Immediate Successors – The Vocation of Humankind, 1774–1800* (Cambridge: Cambridge University Press, 2005).

9 For the relation between the 1794 manuscript and the ES, see Reid 2013.

10 Reinhold's theory of representation or "Philosophy of Elements" is expounded in three of his works: *Versuch einer neuen Theorie des menschlichen Vorstellungsvermögens* (1789); *Beyträge zur Berichtigung bisheriger Missverständnisse der Philosophen, Erster Band* (1790); and *Über das Fundament des philosophischen Wissens* (1791). However, the content of these works on representation had already been popularized by Reinhold through earlier lectures and publications in learned and literary journals. Consequently, Flatt could already have a passing knowledge of the theory when he was preparing in 1789 course at Tübingen, which Hegel attended.

11 Recall that *Seele* refers to the natural, anthropological dimension of soul, while *Gemüt* refers to its more creative, sensitive, spiritual side.

12 For example, Hegel uses the term "*Barbarei*" to describe the ratiocinating thought of the Middle Ages (W19: 544) and the intuitive representations of Jakob Böhme (W20: 94). Schiller uses the terms *Wilder* and *Barbar* in Letter 4 of his *Letters on the Esthetic Education of Mankind.* Friedrich Schiller *Lettres sur l'éducation esthétique de l'homme – Briefe über die äesthetische Erwziehung des Menschen*, ed. and trans. into French by Robert Leroux (Paris: Aubier, 1992 [1942]), 106.

7. The Death of God and the Beautiful Finitude of Art

1 The question of art's finitude necessarily raises the issue of its "end," in Hegel. I deal with this question extensively, in relation to important readings by other scholars, in the article from which research for the present chapter is drawn: Reid 2020.

2 The artforms presented in the *Phenomenology*'s "Natural Religion" section correspond to the pre-Classical, "Symbolic" category presented in the *Lectures on Aesthetics.*

3 I am translating *offenbare* as "revelatory" rather than "revealed" or "manifest."

4 Cf. Robert R. Williams, *Tragedy, Recognition, and the Death of God: Studies in Hegel and Nietzsche* (Oxford: Oxford UP, 2012). Williams, like most others who discuss the theme in Hegel, mistakenly takes the death of God as that of the father, not the son.

5 Conceiving artistic beauty as the unity of freedom and necessity replays Kant's ideas of both aesthetic judgment, where the categories (necessity) play with the imagination (freedom), and artistic production, where genius is both natural (necessity) and feely creative.

6 For Hegel, "Romantic" or "modern" art is that which follows the culmination of Classical art, i.e., after the death of Christ. In other words, Romantic, modern art is that of the Christian era.

7 For example, in the *Lectures on Aesthetics* we find, "Among the various artforms, sculpture is best suited to present (*darstellen*) the Classical in its simple repose ..." (W14: 87). In his own lecture notes on the *Philosophy of Religion*, distinguishing between the art, religion, and philosophy, Hegel writes that the first comes to consciousness in "the form of immediate intuition [*Anschauung*]," the second (religion), in the form of "representation [*Vorstellung*]," and the third, in the form of "thinking *[Denkens]*" VR3 143.

8 One of the most remarkable passages of the *Phenomenology*: "The statues are now only stones from which the living soul has flown ..." (W3: 547/M753).

9 Again, I refer curious readers to Reid 2020 for references.

10 In EL 142 Add., Hegel refers to systems of taxation. In section 344 of *the Principles of the Philosophy of Right* [PR 344], Hegel describes the "determinate principle" of each people or state, within the narrative of "world history," as "having its actuality in their constitutions" (W7: 505). Against Kant's idea of perpetual peace, Hegel states that international accords between nations can never get beyond the "ought-to-be" since they are always infected by contingency – i.e., world history, as objective spirit, is a feature of actuality, and thus a never-ending approximation of peace. PR 333 (W7: 499–500).

11 EL 145 Add. (W8: 286).

12 This ending might correspond to what Desmond celebrates, above as an "open wholeness" of art's "infinite inexhaustibility."

13 William Desmond, *Art and the Absolute* (Albany N.Y.: SUNY, 1986), 75.

14 In the words of Fr. Schlegel, "Since today philosophy criticizes everything it finds, a critique of philosophy could only be a just revenge," or: "One can never be too critical." P. Firchow, trans. and introduction, *Friedrich Schlegel's Lucinde and the Frangments* (Minneapolis: University of Minnesota Press 1971), *Athenäum* Fragments 56 and 281. Art's ending in ironic Romanticism is the subject of Carl Rapp's "Hegel's Concept of the Dissolution of Art," in William Maker, *Hegel and Aesthetics* (Albany: State U of New York P, 2000), 13–30. Rapp, like me in Reid 2014, sees Hegel's characterization of Romantic irony as prescient of certain currents in post-modern thought.

15 See Reid 2014b 47–8. *Vereitelung* might also be translated as "rendering vain" or "emptying out." It also expresses the narcissistic, self-reflective

quality that Hegel attaches to the Romantic ironist and to Fr. Schlegel particularly (W11: 233). The reference is from Hegel's review of K.W.F. Solger's writings. For Hegel's (tendentious) take on Romantic irony, see also W13: 96, from the introduction to his *Lectures on Aesthetics.*

16 "[I]n his games and festivals, man no longer recovers the joyful consciousness of his unity with the divine"; works of ancient art are "beautiful fruit, already plucked from the tree" (W3: 547/M 753).

17 See Reid 2003.

18 The first reference is found at W13: 92, the second, polemical reference to Friedrich Schlegel is found on W13: 93–5.

19 Hegel was certainly inspired, as were many of his generation, by G.E. Lessing's influential essay *Education of the Human Race* (1780).

20 The text has been assigned together and separately to Hegel, Schelling, and Hölderlin, from their time together at the Tübingen Seminary. For the text: W1: 234–6.

21 In Kant, the judgment of beauty in the Third *Critique* can be seen to reconcile the First *Critique,* on theoretical knowing (necessity in the form of natural determinacy) and the Second *Critique,* on morality (the science of freedom).

22 "[O]nly Spirit that is object to itself as absolute spirit is conscious of itself as a free actuality to the extent that it remains conscious of itself therein" (W3: 497/M678). Absolute spirit is the truth that human or actual spirit and the spiritual agency of the Absolute are one, through reciprocal self-knowledge: "The distinction which was made between actual Spirit and Spirit that knows itself as Spirit ... is superseded in the Spirit that knows itself in its truth" (W3: 500/M681).

8. The Hermeneutics of Worship

1 For an English translation, see Eric Von der Luft, *Hegel, Hinrichs and Schleiermacher on Feeling and Religion.* (Lewiston/Queenston: Mellen Press, 1987), 245–68.

2 Schleiermacher, Friedrich. *Kritische Gesamtausgabe,* vol. 2, ed. by Günter Meckenstock (Berlin: De Gruyter, 1984): 242.

3 Of course, as we saw in chapter 3, on cometary negativity, and again in chapter 7, on art, the critical moment may also be harnessed, outside the culture of *Verstand* and within the system of Science, as the motor for dialectical progression.

4 Peter Hodgson, "*Hegel and Christian Theology*: Author's Summary," *Owl of Minerva,* vol. 37, no. 1 (2005/6): 7.

5 Liberation, in general, for Hegel, means making mine that which immediately presents itself to me as foreign and thus enslaves me, and

coming to see myself in it, to be at home in it. For example, the slave liberates himself from the master by making the immediacy of natural life his own through work.

9. Philosophy and Its Scientific Conclusion (*Schluss*)

1 Hegel's introductory lectures on the history of philosophy can be found in a convenient English publication: G.W.F. Hegel, *On Art, Religion and History of Philosophy: Introductory Lectures,* trans. E.S. Haldane, ed. J. Glenn Gray, introduction by Tom Rockmore (Indianapolis: Hackett, 1997 [1970]), pp. 207–317). These lectures are translated from Johannes Hoffmeister's and Karl Ludwig Michelet's early editions, which synthesized Hegel's notes along with the available student notebook sources, from both his Heidelberg and Berlin lectures, to provide a coherent narrative. I will relate the (sometimes modified) English translation to W18. Any quotations will cite the page number of the Haldane translation (H), followed by the Suhrkamp volume (W18) and page reference. More recent philological and critical efforts have consisted in separating out these notes, allowing scholars to distinguish between Hegel's own manuscript and sources drawn from his students' lecture notes. See *Vorlesungen über die Geschichte der Philosophie,* ed Pierre Garniron and Walter Jaeschke (Hamburg: Felix Meiner, 1994 –) [VG]. Readers wanting to approach the secondary literature on the subject might begin with David A. Duquette, ed., *Hegel's History of Philosophy: New Interpretations* (Albany: State University of New York Press, 2002).

2 A contemporary expression of this view can be found in Jonathan Rée's *Witchcraft: The Invention of Philosophy in English* (New Haven: Yale University Press, 2019).

3 "The absolute alone is true, or the Truth alone is absolute" (W3: 70).

4 Cf. Jere Surber's foundational article "Hegel's Speculative Sentence," *Hegel-Studien* 10 (1975): 210–30

10. Organic Systematicity and Its Excremental Challenge

1 Karen Ng, *Hegel's Concept of Life* (Oxford: Oxford University Press, 2020), 3. See also Emmanuel Chaput, *Vie et Système chez G.W.F. Hegel* (PhD diss., University of Ottawa, 2021).

2 For the record, Hegel himself describes society as "an organism" in the *Philosophy of Right* [PR] section 269, and its Addition.

3 *Hegel Bulletin,* 41.3 (2020)

4 The "Functions of the Organism" consist of "sensibility," "irritability," and "reproduction" (EN 353), the same elements that enliven the "Life" of the absolute Idea in EL 218.

5 *Gramma, Journal of Theory and Criticism*, https://doi.org/10.26262/gramma.v14i0.6510, 24.

6 A friend doing her medical residency in the urology department of a prominent Parisian hospital told me that the inspirational mantra of those in that particular service was quite simply, "Pisser ou mourir!" More anachronistically, one might liken the proposed examination to the important work carried out by the Groom of the Stool, in monarchical times, diagnosing the health of the kingly organism. When I refer to "excrement," it is feces that I have in mind, and which Hegel is concerned with.

7 Jane O'Hara-May, "Measuring Man's Needs." *Journal of the History of Biology* 4:2 (1971): 249–73. Accessed May 27, 2021. www.jstor.org/stable/4330561.

8 Hegel recognizes that animal excrement also contains "fibrous residue of the ingested food" (ibid.). However, this material, as we will see, is only philosophically significant in that it represents the "non-organic" Other.

9 I share the view of Simon Richter, "Hegel and the Dialectics of Digestion."

10 "*Zwecktätigkeit*." The notion of life as purposive activity obviously brings Kant to mind, a reference discussed by Hegel in EN 360 R, along with a reference to Aristotle.

11 With reference to the digestive agency of the Idea, Hegel states, "The result of this process is not, as in the case of the chemical process, a neutral product [...] instead, the living being proves itself to be what overgrasps its other, which cannot resist its power" (EL 219 Add.).

12 Chemically, what is excreted can be analyzed as "the same ingredients of which the animal organs consist" (EN 365 Add.), for example, besides bile and albumen, "sodium carbonate, sodium chloride, and sodium phosphate, phosphate of magnesia, and phosphate of lime ..." (ibid).

13 Douglas Finn writes "that excretion is the animal's repulsion of the animal's own process of digestion from itself and a return of the animal into itself as a nascent subject." Or again, "the animal transcends that process and 'knows' itself as a universal power greater than its externally oriented activity, as subject, being-for-self." I would simply add "individual" before "subject" in these sentences. *The Owl of Minerva* 47:1–2 (2015–16): 130.

14 Regarding the genesis of specifically human subjectivity, we have to refer to the "Anthropology" section of the *Philosophy of Subjective Spirit* in the ES, and to a discussion of human reproduction. See ES 405: "Initially, feeling individuality is certainly a monadic individual, but it is so immediately, not yet as it is itself as an inner reflected subject ..." And in the Remark: "In its immediate existence this is the relationship of the child in its mother's womb." Perhaps we might say that the subjectivity of the animal individual persists in the human animal as a form of unconscious mind.

15 “Das abstrakte Abstossen seiner von sich selbst ... ist die Exkeretion” (W9: 492).

16 Hegel, W2: 541. The same link between the judgments of the understanding and excrement is made in the *Phenomenology*: “The consciousness of the infinite judgment that remains at the level of representation (*Vorstellung*) behaves as pissing” (W3: 262/M 346).

17 Recall that “The organism in thus separating itself from itself is disgusted with itself [*erkelt er sich selbst an*]” (EN 365 Add.,/W9: 492).

18 In the preface to the *Phenomenology*, Hegel refers to such entanglement as a “Vermischung der speculativen und der räsonierenden Weise” (W3: 60/M 64).

19 Are we parasites? Perhaps. More likely, zookeepers, veterinarians, practitioners of animal husbandry?

20 Monstrous: as that which is hybrid, both animal and something else, and shows or reveals itself (*montrare*). In the recent film *Life*, astronauts inadvertently “hatch” an alien lifeform on their spaceship. Fascinated by this instance of extra-terrestrial life, the humans seek to nurture it. However, as an animal lifeform, the “monster” is monstrously hungry, growing in size and appetite until it gobbles up all the astronauts and, one supposes, the world from which they come. In conceiving their animal organism, however, the screenwriters neglected to consider the fundamental element of excretion, as is the case with Hegel specialists who apply the organic trope to their philosopher’s system.

21 This claim is supported by the fact that at least four decades of contemporary Hegel studies have been devoted to rehabilitating Hegel against the critiques of contemporary “excremental” (analytic/materialistic) philosophies, often by discovering covert analytic elements in his thought.

11. Reason, Revelation, and the Big Bang

1 Fortunately, I am not alone in this juxtaposition. See Errol E. Harris, *Cosmos and Theos: Ethical and Theological Implications of the Anthropic Principle* (Amherst: Humanity Books, 1992), and his *Cosmos and Anthropos: A Philosophical Interpretation of the Anthropic Cosmological Principle* (Amherst: Humanity Press, 1993).

2 This is already implicit in the fact that the Big Bang theory takes the singularity as an axiom; as such it is both a reason and a thing.

3 A helpful physicist reader of this chapter commented that most cosmologists are “pinning their hopes on something non-anthropic, such as string theory.” Again, I am exercising my Hegelian prerogative in choosing the scientific accounts I want to speculate on.

12. Absolute Music and Meaningfulness

1 *Lectures on the Philosophy of Art: The Hotho Transcript of the 1823 Lectures,* ed. and trans. Robert F. Brown, with an introduction by Annemarie Gethmann-Siefert (Oxford: Oxford University Press, 2014) [AT]

2 It's important to recall that at Hegel's time, composition and performance were often conjoined, i.e., it was the composer who was the performer: Beethoven, Schubert, Paganini, Mozart, Mendelssohn, etc. Similarly, the non-composing, expert performer-soloist was generally chosen by and worked with the composer. His "genius" consisted, in part, in "channelling" that of the composer.

3 Making this crucial distinction, I am assisted by John McCumber's remarkable chapter in Jere Surber's book, *Hegel and Language* (McCumber: 111–25). While McCumber's aim is to show how subjective thinking comes to express itself in words, as the real but transient embodiments of spirit, the homonymous nature of "Ton" leads him to consider the question of music. On the relationship between vanishing and meaning in Hegel, see Reid 2021.

4 A striking illustration of this is John Cage's *Organ ASLSP*, calling for a note played every few years. Following Hegel, each single note, as performed on the Halberstadt organ, is only meaningful within the completed work, over a 639-year period, concluding in 2640! The concept of the piece is its framework of meaning.

5 For the pathology of *Gemüt* in Novalis, see Reid 2024a.

6 Within harmony itself, we find the same oscillation ambiguity played out between the different vibratory characteristics of individual instruments and voices, over against the rigorous laws of harmony (LA 919–229).

7 A recent experiment in AI involved having a computer generate Beethoven's "10th Symphony," having been programmed to compose likely Beethoven-like outcomes from massive data inputs from his nine symphonies. The result, as reviewed by both musicologists and music lovers, could only be described as meaningless and therefore as deeply boring.

8 Between the 1827 and 1830 editions of the *Encyclopaedia,* Hegel changes the section heading at §403 from "The Dreaming Soul (*Die traümende Seele*)" to "The Feeling Soul (*Die fühlende Seele*)." See Reid 2013.

Bibliography

Works by Hegel

Briefe von und an Hegel. Edited by Johannes Hoffmeister. Hamburg: Felix Meiner, 1953.

Dokumente zu Hegels Entwicklung. Edited by Johannes Hoffmeister. Stuttgart: Frommann-Holzboog, 1974 [1936].

Encyclopedia of Philosophical Sciences (including the *Encyclopedia Logic* [EL], *the Philosophy of Nature* [EN] *and the Philosophy of Spirit* [ES], followed by section number, Addition [Add.] and Remark [R] if applicable).

Gesammelte Werke. Edited by Rheinische-Westphalischen Akademie der Wissenschaften (Hamburg: Meiner, 1968-) GW, followed by volume and page numbers.

Hegel's Aesthetics: Lectures on Fine Art, volume II. Translated by T.M. Knox. Oxford: Oxford University Press, 1975. [LA followed by page number].

Hegel's Philosophy of Mind [Subjective Spirit]: Part Three of the Encyclopedia of the Philosophical Sciences (1830). Translated by William Wallace, together with the Zusätze in Boumann's text (1845); translated by A.V. Miller, with foreword by J.N. Findlay. Oxford: Oxford University Press, 2003 [1971]. PS followed by the page numbers.

Hegel's Philosophy of Subjective Spirit, vol. 2. Edited, translated, and notes by M.J. Petry. Dordricht: D. Reidel, 1979.

Jenaer Systementwürfe II, Logik, Metaphysik, Naturphilosophie. Edited by Rolf-Peter Horstmann. Hamburg: Felix Meiner, 1982.

Lectures on the Philosophy of Art: The Hotho Transcript of the 1823 Lectures. Edited and translated by Robert F. Brown, with an introduction by Annemarie Gethmann-Siefert *(Oxford: Oxford University Press, 2014).* [AT, followed by the page number].

Lectures on the Philosophy of Religion vol. 3. Translated by R.F. Brown, P.C. Hodgson, and J.M. Stewart, with assistance of H.S. Harris. Edited by Peter Hodgson. Berkeley: University of California Press, 1985. [LR3].

On Art, Religion and History of Philosophy: Introductory Lectures Translated by E.S. Haldane. Edited by J. Glenn Gray. Introduction by Tom Rockmore. Indianapolis: Hackett, 1997 [1970] [H].

The Phenomenology of Spirit. Translated by A.V. Miller. Oxford: Oxford University Press, 1977. [W3 followed by page number/M followed by Miller's section number].

Philosophy of Nature, Part II of the Encyclopedia of Philosophical Sciences (1830). Translated by A.V. Miller from Nicolin and Pöggeler's edition (1959) and from the *Zusätze* in Michelet's text (1847. Oxford: Oxford University Press, 1970. [EN followed by section number.]

Philosophy of Nature (German/English) 3 vols. Edited and translated by M.J. Petry London: Allen and Unwin, 1970.

The Science of Logic Translated by A.V. Miller. New York: Humanities Press, 1976. [GL followed by the page number.]

The Science of Logic. Translated by George di Giovanni. Cambridge: Cambridge University Press, 2010. [SL 2010, followed by the page number.]

Vorlesungen über die Geschichte der Philosophie. Edited by Pierre Garniron and Walter Jaeschke. Hamburg: Felix Meiner, 1994 –. [VG].

Vorlesungen über die Religion, in *Gesammelte Werke. Vorlesungen: Ausgewählte Nachscriften und Manuskripte*, vol. 3. Edited by W. Jaeschke. Hamburg: Felix Meiner, 1983. [VR3].

Werke in 20 Bänden. Edited by Eva Moldenhauer and Karl Markus Michel. Frankfurt am Main: Suhrkamp, 1970 –. [W, followed by the volume number and page number.*]*

Wissenschaft der Logik, Das Sein (1812). Edited by Hans Jürgen Gawoll. [GL(1812)] Hamburg: Felix Meiner Verlag, 1986.

Wissenschaft der Logik, Die Lehre von Sein (1832). Edited by Hans Jürgen Gawoll. Hamburg: Felix Meiner Verlag, 1984.

Other Works Cited

Ahlers, Rolf. "Reinhold and Hegel on the Principle and Systematicity of Philosophy." *Idealistic Studies* vol. 35, Issues 2–3 (Summer–Fall 2005): 215–53.

Arkush, Allan. *Moses Mendelssohn and the Enlightenment.* Albany: SUNY, 1994.

Beiser, Frederick. *After Hegel: German Philosophy Between 1840 and 1900.* Princeton: Princeton University Press, 2014.

Billeter, Bernard. "Die Musik in Hegels Aesthetik." *Die Musikforschung* 26 (1973): 295–310.

Bondeli, Martin. "Hegel und Reinhold." *Hegel-Studien* vol. 30 (1995): 45–87.

Bowie, Andrew. *Music, Philosophy, and Modernity.* Cambridge: Cambridge University Press, 2007. *See* "Hegel, Philosophy and Music." 105–37.

Burbidge, John. *The Logic of Hegel's Logic.* Peterborough: Broadview Press, 2006.

Chaput, Emmanuel. *Vie et Système chez G.W.F. Hegel.* PhD diss., University of Ottawa, 2021.

Crites, Stephen. *Owl of Minerva* vol. 37, no. 1 (2005–06).

Dahlhaus, Carl. "Hegel und die Musik seiner Zeit." *Hegel-Studien* 22 (1983): 337–42.

Desmond, William. *Art and the Absolute.* Albany, N.Y.: SUNY, 1986.

–. *Hegel's God, a Counterfeit Double?* Aldershot: Ashgate, 2003.

Di Giovanni, George. *Freedom and Religion in Kant and His Immediate Successors: The Vocation of Humankind, 1774–1800.* Cambridge: Cambridge University Press, 2005.

Donougho, Martin. *Hegel's Individuality: Beyond Category.* Cham, Switzerland: Springer, 2023.

Duquette, David A., ed. *Hegel's History of Philosophy: New Interpretations.* Albany: State University of New York Press, 2002.

Eldridge, Richard. "Hegel on Music." In *Hegel and the Arts,* edited by Stephen Houlgate. Indiana: Northwestern University Press, 2007. 119–44.

Fackenheim, Emil. *The Religious Dimension of Hegel's Philosophy.* Bloomington: Indiana University Press, 1967.

Finn, Douglas. "Spiritual Consumption: Eating and the Christian Eucharist in Hegel." *The Owl of Minerva* 47:1–2 (2015–16): 130. DOI: 10.5840/owl2016121418.

Gethmann-Siefert, Annemarie. "The Shape and Influence of Hegel's Aesthetics." Introduction to *Hegel: Lectures on the Philosophy of Art: The Hotho Transcript of the 1823 Berlin Lectures.* Edited by Robert F. Brown. Oxford: Oxford University Press, 2014.

Harris, Errol E. *Cosmos and Theos: Ethical and Theological Implications of the Anthropic Principle.* Amherst: Humanity Press, 1992.

–. *Cosmos and Anthropos: A Philosophical Interpretation of the Anthropic Cosmological Principle.* Amherst: Humanity Press, 1993.

Harris, H.S. *Hegel's Development,* 2 vols. Oxford: Oxford University Press, 1972.

–. *Hegel's Ladder. The Odyssey of Spirit,* vol. 2. Indianapolis/Cambridge: Hackett, 1997.

Hinrichs, H.F.W. *Die Religion im inneren Verhältnisse zur Wissenschaft.* Heidelberg: 1822.

Hodgson, Peter. *Hegel and Christian Theology: A Reading of the Lectures on the Philosophy of Religion.* Oxford: Oxford University Press, 2005.

–. "Hegel and Christian Theology: Author's Summary." *Owl of Minerva* vol. 37, no. 1 (2006):1–7.

Hölderlin, Friederich. *Sämtliche Werke.* Edited by F. Beissner. Stuttgart: W. Kohlhammer, 1962.

Houlgate, Stephen. "Essence, Reflexion, and Immediacy in Hegel's Science of Logic." In *A Companion to Hegel*, edited by S. Houlgate and Michael Baur. London: Blackwell Publishing, 2011.

Jacobi, Friedrich Heinrich. *Friedrich Heinrich Jacobi, The Main Philosophical Writings and the Novel Allwill*. Edited and translated by G. di Giovanni. Montreal, Kingston: McGill-Queen's University Press, 1994.

Jarvis, Simon. "Musical Thinking: Hegel and the Phenomenology of Prosody." *Paragraph* Vol. 28, no. 2 (July 2005): 57–71.

Johnson, Julian. "Music in Hegel's Aesthetics: A Re-evaluation." *British Journal of Aesthetics* vol. 31, no. 2 (April 1991). Presented as Johnson followed by the page number.

Kant, Immanuel. *Kants Werke, Akademie Textausgabe* (1902), vol. 8. Berlin: de Gruyter, 1968.

–. *Religion and Rational Theology*. Edited and translated by A.W. Wood and G. di Giovanni. Cambridge: Cambridge University Press, 2001.

Krell, David Farrell. "Genitality/Excrementality from Hegel to Crazy Jane." *Boundary 2*, 12:2 (1984): issue "On Feminine Writing," 113–41.

Lessing, G.E. "The Education of the Human Race (1777–80)." In *Lessing: Philosophical and Theological Writings*, edited and translated by H.B. Nisbet. Cambridge: Cambridge University Press, 2005. DOI: https://doi.org/10.1017/CBO9780511810138.022

Löwith, Karl. *From Hegel to Nietzsche*. Translated by David E. Green. New York: Anchor Books, 1967.

Lumsden, Simon. "The Rise of the Non-Metaphysical Hegel." *Philosophy Compass* 3, no. 1 January 2008: 51–65.

Maker, William. *Philosophy Without Foundations: Rethinking Hegel*. Albany: State University of New York Press, 1994.

Maraguat, Edgar. "Hegel's Organizational Account of Biological Functions." *Hegel Bulletin* 41, no. 3 (2020): 407–25. doi:10.1017/hgl.2020.17.

McCumber, John. "Sound – Tone – Word: Toward an Hegelian Philosophy of Language." In *Hegel and Language*, edited by Jere Surber. SUNY, 2006. Presented as McCumber followed by the page number.

Mendelssohn, Moses. *Philosophical Writings*. Edited and translated by D.O. Dahlstrom. Cambridge: Cambridge University Press, 1997.

–. *Morning Hours: Lectures on God's Existence*. Edited and translated by D.O. Dahlstrom and C. Dykk. *Studies in German Idealism* 12. Dordrecht: Springer, 2011.

Ng, Karen. "Hegel's Logic of Actuality." *Review of Metaphysics* 63, no.1 (2009): 139–72.

–. *Hegel's Concept of Life*. Oxford: Oxford University Press, 2020.

O'Hara-May, Jane. "Measuring Man's Needs." *Journal of the History of Biology* 4, no. 2 (1971): 249–73. Accessed May 27, 2021. www.jstor.org/stable/4330561

O'Regan, Cyril. *Owl of Minerva* vol. 37, no. 1 (2005–6).

Peterson, Mark C.E. "Animals Eating Empiricists: Assimilation and Subjectivity in Hegel's Philosophy of Nature." *The Owl of Minerva* 23, no. 1 (1991).

Pinkard, Terry. *Hegel's Phenomenology, the Sociality of Reason.* Cambridge: Cambridge University Press, 1994.

Pippin, Robert. *The Satisfactions of Self-Consciousness.* Cambridge: Cambridge University Press, 1989.

Rapp, Carl. "Hegel's Concept of the Dissolution of Art." In *Hegel and Aesthetics,* edited by William Maker. Albany: State U. of New York Press, 2000): 13–30.

Rée, Jonathan. *Witchcraft: The Invention of Philosophy in English.* New Haven: Yale University Press, 2019.

Reid, Jeffrey. "Hegel on Schleiermacher and Postmodernity." *Clio* 32, no. 4 (Summer 2003): 457–72. Presented as Reid 2003, followed by the page number.

–. "Hegel's Ontological Grasp of Judgment and the Original Dividing of Identity into Difference." *Dialogue* 45, no. 1 (Winter 2006): 29–43. Presented as Reid 2006.

–. "How the Dreaming Soul Became the Feeling Soul Between the 1827 and 1830 Editions of the Philosophy of Subjective Spirit." In *Essays on Hegel's Philosophy of Subjective Spirit,* edited by David S. Stern. Albany: SUNY Press, 2013. Presented as Reid 2013, followed by the page number.

–. "Comets and Moons: The For-another in Hegel's Philosophy of Nature." *The Owl of Minerva* vol. 45, no. 1/2 (2013/2014). Presented as Reid 2014b, followed by the page number.

–. *The Anti-Romantic: Hegel Against Ironic Romanticism.* London: Bloomsbury, 2014. Presented as Reid 2014, followed by the page number.

–. "Ful-filling the Copula, Determining Nature: The Grammatical Ontology of Hegel's Metaphysics." *Journal of Speculative Philosophy* vol. 31, no. 4 (Penn State University, United States, 2017): 575–93. Presented as Reid 2017.

–. "Reason, Revelation: Absolute Agency and the Limits of Actuality in Hegel." *Symposium* vol. 21, no. 1 (2017). Presented as Reid 2017b.

–. "Hegel's End-of-Art Revisited: The Death of God and the Essential Finitude of Artistic Beauty." *Clio, a Journal of Literature, History, and the Philosophy of History* vol. 48, no. 1 (Fall 2020): 77–101. Presented as Reid 2020, followed by the page number.

–. *Hegel's Grammatical Ontology: Vanishing Words and Hermeneutical Openness.* London: Bloomsbury, 2021. Presented as Reid 2021, followed by the page number.

–. "Hegel's Dialectics of Digestion, Excretion, and Animal Subjectivity." *The Owl of Minerva (Journal of the Hegel Society of America)* vol. 53, no. 1–2 (2022): 71–97.

–. "Mental Illness as Irony: Hegel's Diagnosis of Novalis." *Studia Hegeliana Hegel y la Psiquiatria* (06/2024). Presented as Reid 2024.

–. "The Meaning of Music in Hegel." *Journal of Philosophical Research* 49 (2024). Presented as Reid 2024b.

Rockmore, Tom. *Cognition, An Introduction to Hegel's Phenomenology of Spirit.* Berkeley: University of California Press, 1997.

Russon, John. *Reading Hegel's Phenomenology.* Bloomington: Indiana University Press, 2004.

–. *Infinite Phenomenology: The Lessons of Hegel's Science of Experience.* Evanston: Northwestern University Press, 2016.

Sallis, John. "Soundings: Hegel on Music." In *Blackwell Companion to Hegel,* edited by Stephen Houlgate and Michael Baur. Chichester: Wiley-Blackwell, 2011. 369–84. Presented as Sallis, followed by the page number.

Schiller, Friedrich. *Lettres sur l'éducation esthétique de l'homme – Briefe über die äesthetische Erwziehung des Menschen.* Edited and translated into French by Robert Leroux. Paris: Aubier, 1992 [1942] 106.

Schlegel, Friedrich. *Schlegel's Lucinde and the Fragments.* Translated and introduced by P. Firchow. Minneapolis: University of Minnesota Press, 1971.

Schleiermacher, Friedrich. *Kritische Gesamtausgabe*, vol. 2. Edited by Günter Meckenstock (Berlin: De Gruyter, 1984).

Schleiemacher, Friedrich. *Speeches on Religion to Its Cultured Despisers.* Edited by Richard Crouter. Cambridge: Cambridge University Press. 1996

Shklar, Judith. *Freedom and Independence: A Study of the Political Ideas of Hegel's Phenomenology of Mind.* Cambridge: Cambridge University Press, 1976.

Solomon, Robert C. *In the Spirit of Hegel.* Oxford: Oxford University Press, 1983.

Sorgner, Stefan Lorenz, and Oliver Fürbeth, eds. *Music in German Philosophy: An Introduction.* Translated by Susan H. Gillespie, with preface by H. James Birx and introduction to the English-language edition by Michael Spitzer. Chicago: University of Chicago Press, 2010.

Speight, Allen. "Determinate Religion and the Philosophy of Art." *Owl of Minerva* vol. 52, no. 1–2 (2021).

Stewart, Jon. *Hegel's Interpretation of the Religions of the World: The Logic of the Gods.* Oxford: Oxford University Press, 2018.

Stone, Alison. *Petrified Intelligence: Nature in Hegel's Philosophy.* Albany: State University of New York, 2005.

Surber, Jere. "Hegel's Speculative Sentence." *Hegel-Studien* 10 (1975): 210–30.

Taylor, Charles. *Hegel.* Cambridge: Cambridge University Press, 1977.

Valenza, Pierluigi. *Reinhold e Hegel: Ragione storica e inizio assoluto della philosofia.* Padova, Cedam, 1994.

Von der Luft, Eric. *Hegel, Hinrichs, and Schleiermacher on Feeling and Religion.* Lewiston/Queenston: Mellen Press, 1987.

Westphal, Kenneth. *Hegel's Epistemological Realism*. Dordrecht: Kluwer, 1989.

Williams, Robert R. *Tragedy, Recognition, and the Death of God: Studies in Hegel and Nietzsche*. Oxford: Oxford University Press 2012.

Žižek, Slavoj. "Hegel and the Object, Or, the Idea's Constipation." *Gramma, Journal of Theory and Criticism* vol. 14 (2006). https://doi.org/10.26262/gramma.v14i0.6510)

Index